Pedro Reyes

Sanatorium
Operations Manual

Published by Ridinghouse and
Geneva University of Art and Design [Head — Genève]

SANATORIUM
OPERATIONS MANUAL

First published in 2013; this edition published in 2015 by

Geneva University of Art and Design
[Head — Genève]
15 Boulevard James-Fazy
1201 Geneva
Switzerland
hesge.ch

and
Ridinghouse
46 Lexington Street
London W1F 0LP
United Kingdom
ridinghouse.co.uk

ISBN 978 1 909932 11 1

This book was published thanks to the generous support of Geneva University of Art and Design

Printed in Germany
DZA Druckerei zu Altenburg

Distributed in the UK and Europe by
Cornerhouse Publications
c/o Home
2 Tony Wilson Place
Manchester M15 4FN
United Kingdom
cornerhousepublications.org

Distributed in the US by
RAM Publications +
Distribution, Inc.
2525 Michigan Avenue
Building A2
Santa Monica, CA 90404
United States
rampub.com

British Library Cataloguing-in-Publication Data
A full catalogue record of this book is available from the British Library

sanatorium.org

Table of Contents

Introduction

In 1992, a book titled *The Nervous System* was published by Michael Taussig, a former doctor from Australia. In it he compiled various anthropological essays on terror and fetishism of the State, healing, and the place of the subject in postcolonial condition, luminously retracing a series of medical experiences confronting both the biological and social body in order to shed light on the crucial issues of our times. Using stunning examples taken from his career in the medical field, Taussig demonstrates that one of the main problems facing our society (must we recall that the text was written almost exactly twenty years ago?) is what he calls, after Georg Lukács, the "reification and the consciousness of the patient." In other words, Taussig analyzes the way medical practice lies in between a "cultural construction of clinical reality and the clinical construction of culture," and considers its patients' bodies as pure mechanics, which suffer from various dysfunctions that define them as "sick" or "ill" objects to be repaired through contemporary technologies of healing. Following his point of view, patients are not considered individuals who can express a form of reaction — one might say of critique — to social situations through physical symptoms; they are simply reified as most of the goods the Capital puts at the center of global exchange.

In my mind, Pedro Reyes's *Sanatorium* poses similar questions to today's society: a society that is, even more so than twenty years ago, based on a clinical construction of its reality, relying on the massive use of pharmaceutical drugs, the symbolic power of its scientific institutions, and the various alternative medicines developed in the shadow of medical enlightenment, as well as on countercultural systems of belief. But this project is relevant for today's education not only for its pertinent thematic questioning; its field of research is approached through the form of a laboratory — based on a collective, cooperative, and decentered organization — leading to a kind of educational laboratory itself. I am glad that our students were able to experience the forming of the theoretical bases of the Sanatorium through open interactions, readings, and exchange of ideas. I am happy that they had the chance to activate, incarnate, and interpret it — even sometimes to create and invent therapeutic activities of their own. I am very proud that they can participate in this publication today, that this work is a common project, a brick that completes a yearlong collaboration.

This project echoes a specific history of artistic creation of alternative social constructions in Switzerland. A history of utopia finds one of its keystones in Monte Verità, an anarchist, vegetarian, artistic community that was founded on top of a hill near Ascona, in front of Lake Maggiore, in the very early twentieth century. Soon after a period of free experiments, the colony built a sanatorium, which became successful amongst left-wing thinkers, European eccentrics, avant-garde artists such as painter Paul Klee, writer Hermann Hesse, and choreographer Mary Wigman, among many others, all of whom were at the core of Harald Szeemann's seminal exhibition *The Breasts of Truth* from 1978, which retraced this visionary experience. So, with our willingness to continuously re-articulate the history of these interactions in between artistic practice, social visionary projects, and alternative sciences, it makes a lot of sense for Head — Geneve to be associated with Reyes's proposal.

After one long century of fights, oppositions, and contradictions, the Sanatorium symbolically becomes a temporary community again, one that is formed of artists. And our school has the unique opportunity to transform itself, at least for a while, into a laboratory that is not only aesthetic, but also political: an educational laboratory where another social reality can be modeled, tested, and transmitted. This book is a testimony of it.

Yann Chateigné
Dean of the Visual Arts Department
Geneva University of Art and Design
(Head — Genève)

TO HEAL YOURSELF, START HEALING OTHERS
A Conversation between Pedro Reyes and Laurent Schmid

<u>Laurent Schmid:</u> At the first workshop with the volunteers there was a good energy in the air. In Kassel at Documenta it was contagious; it went from the therapists to the visitors. So Pedro, is the Sanatorium an optimistic project?

<u>Pedro Reyes:</u> I believe so. It may be optimistic in the sense that the environment allows for a plethora of insights, which happen in an almost effortless way. Many small miracles happen. It is optimistic in the sense that we are always surprised by the fact that helping each other is easier than what we had thought. So after you test the experience you gain confidence. There is a general assumption that when you help someone you somehow lose energy, but often the opposite happens. There is a spark of excitement that you get from helping others.

<u>LS:</u> You said that it is important to you that the therapies can be conducted by anyone and everyone, and you reference Jacob Levy Moreno's "sociatry." Moreno wrote in *Who Shall Survive?* that "…a truly therapeutic procedure should have as its objective nothing less than the whole of mankind." You also mentioned the aim to open the Sanatorium to a wider public and to share this project, to let it develop in a broader terrain.

<u>PR:</u> These days therapy is a luxury for a lot of people, and every day there are more people in the world who need it but can't afford it. There is also a stigma attached to it that makes many people think that those who go to therapy must be crazy. Yet today, especially in cities, there is a vast population who could benefit from it: unattended victims of depression, loneliness, neurosis, family violence, suicide, etc. That's why I'm so interested in alternative structures, like Moreno's sociatry, in which human connection is paramount. You won't find it in prescription drugs or hospitals, but it's crucial to generate healthier communal life.

I am also very interested in deprofessionalization, which Iván Illich wrote extensively about in the 1970s in Mexico.[1] In Illich's terms, our obsession with growth and productivity discourages people from satisfying their needs and forces them to consume the treatment and services of specialists who do not care for the poor. In many different fields, like education, social work, and transportation, he finds a vicious cycle in which new knowledge is applied and progress is measured and then used to exploit society as a whole to the benefit of the professional elite. In opposition to that capitalist model, he defines convivial society as the result of social arrangements that guarantee everyone free and ample access to the tools of the community, limited only to ensure the equal access of others. In other words, individuals relate to society in the way they use its tools.

In the case of Moreno, when he developed psychodrama and the notions of "encounter" and group therapy, he was basically creating a toolbox that reveals the resourcefulness of the group. The beauty of these approaches is that their procedures are equally effective regardless of the credentials of those who use them.

LS: So these ideas have to do with acknowledging that you could not wait for solutions to come from the top in order to achieve greater social justice?

PR: Yes. Paulo Freire articulated this in his *Pedagogy of the Oppressed*, and his ideas had enormous penetration in Latin America from the 1960s into the 70s and 80s. In his own words, the school system "teaches the need to be taught," when true learning has to be driven by the curiosity and desire of every person.[2] Likewise, in the sphere of hygiene and mental health, Iván Illich offers an example to illustrate this:

I know a North American girl, a sixteen-year-old that was jailed for treating 130 cases of first-stage syphilis. A technical detail pointed out by an expert earned her pardon: the results she obtained were statistically better than those of public health services. Six weeks after the treatment she performed satisfactory control tests on all of her patients, without exception. This is about knowing whether progress should mean progressive independence or progressive dependence.[3]

I like this quote because it clarifies that the desire for these alternative approaches is to move towards progressive independence. Today we cannot expect to reach good results out of pure spontaneity nor pure planning. The Sanatorium is not conceived as a substitute for existing therapies and social services, but as a space for encounter, since so many of our everyday pathologies result from this lack of connection.

LS: Illich often mentioned the need to rethink the very idea of learning, rather than the methods used in its enforcement. What could this mean if we apply it to therapy? Could this also mean that it is necessary for everyone?

PR: Illich introduces the idea of *iatrogenesis*, which means diseases that stem from previous treatments, prescribed by physicians, that have a negative impact on health. These begin, in many cases, at the moment of birth, the main example being excessive reliance on Cesarean deliveries, as well as doctors who encourage mothers to feed their children with formula instead of breast milk.

We're waging a "war on drugs" right now for the reason that drugs are considered a threat to public health. But if you compare the number of deaths each year from legal and illegal drugs, you see that in the United States the number of prescription drug-related deaths rose from 6,000 in 1990 to 27,658 in 2007.[4] Each year at least 106,000 people die from the drugs they are prescribed and administered,[5] while illegal drugs result in around 10% as many deaths.[6] This shows how much we need to readjust our priorities.

There is another concept that is the opposite of *iatrogenesis*: *salutogenesis*, which Dr. Gabriel Stux lectured us about at the Sanatorium in Kassel. The term describes an approach focusing on factors that support human health and well-being, rather than on factors that cause disease. Aaron Antonovsky developed this theory in rejection of the "traditional medical-model dichotomy separating health and illness." He described the relationship as a continuous variable, what he called the "*health*-ease versus *dis*-ease continuum."[7] Antonovsky says that we have to understand health not as the absence of disease, but as the way people maintain their "sense of coherence," by which he means the belief that life is manageable and meaningful. It's how we retain our ability to keep going when facing changes internally and externally. Here the key is to be prepared to make changes in your life.

LS: How can the Sanatorium help prepare you for these changes?

PR: This is an amazing question, because that's why play is so important in the Sanatorium. One of the main aims of the Sanatorium is to be a rehearsal space. In the Museum of Life you can do a kind of draft for your future developments. In the Philosophical Casino you can reflect on a decision that you have to make in the same way that people in ancient times consulted with oracles. In Goodoo you prepare for reconciliation with another person. This has to do with the idea of "surplus reality" that Moreno talks about. In Moreno's psychodrama you stage a confrontation that you plan to have, and this helps you foresee all the interactions that can happen in that future conversation. This provides the patient with a new and more extensive experience of reality, a "surplus" reality.

At the Sanatorium Moreno founded along the Hudson River in Beacon, New York, part of it was a psychodrama stage, which I find remarkable. It's like the equivalent of an operating room in a hospital, with the difference that on the psychodrama stage you can rehearse the changes needed in your life.

I realize that it may be too much to ask for a work of art to have such an impact. But here I see art, and particularly play, as a warm-up phase that prepares us for change. What is most important to achieve is a mental state where we have the confidence to produce changes, but it is very difficult to arrive at this state. That's why the warm-up of the light-hearted spirit of play is so critical.

<u>LS:</u> So you are talking about discoveries that are the result of a collective process. It seems that in all these processes the "other" is very important, as if these kinds of breakthroughs were hard to reach on your own. How important is it that the Sanatorium's activities are done in groups?

<u>PR:</u> Moreno defines encounter as an exchange between two people where each of them sees themselves from the other person's perspective. This stuff doesn't happen every day, where people get to really talk to each other and forget about their roles or whatever other ways they define themselves. What we're looking for at the Sanatorium is for people talk to each other without the client-specialist relationship. Actually, there is an advantage that these encounters happen among strangers, which is that you may never see this guy again. It's not your family or friend or coworker; these are people you usually just make small talk with, but here it's the inversion of small talk. You talk about what's most important and share deeply personal experiences.

There is a famous quote from a poem by Moreno, which is super trippy:

A meeting of two: eye to eye,
*   face to face,*
And when you are near
*   I will tear your eyes out*

And place them instead of mine,
And you will tear my eyes out
And place them instead of yours,
Then I will look at you with
*   your eyes…*
And you will look at me with mine.[8]

It's interesting that some visitors to the Sanatorium requested to conduct therapies in addition to receiving treatment. On occasion the students have become their coaches and taught them how to conduct the sessions. This is an example of how the protagonist is the process, and how important it is to have a companion with whom you can do a role-reversal and warm up your spontaneity. It's important to have horizontal structures where everyone can take the lead as well as follow.

LS: Were the students always ready to take the lead?

PR: I remember that when we were doing the training in Geneva prior to Documenta, we had a session of questions and answers. I knew the expectation was for me to be the resource for all answers, but what I did instead was to ask the person on my left if he had a question. Then, instead of answering, I deferred the question to the second person on my left. Once that person had come up with an answer, she asked a question that was answered by the person on her left, and so on until everyone in the group had both asked and answered a question. This is one quick activity that takes less than fifteen minutes and shows the group its own resourcefulness and independence from a leader.

However, it was equally important for me to be available as a resource when questions came up, especially because it's necessary to know where the therapies come from.

LS: Now to reverse roles on you, what have you learned from the volunteers?

PR: Well actually, if I've done each therapy a dozen times, an average volunteer may have done it fifty times by the end of Documenta. So you could say they have more mileage. That is why I felt it was so important for this book to include testimonials on the encounters they had. In every case there were discoveries that I had not foreseen.

LS: All therapists had a shared common background as art students/artists. Did this change the parameters? In what ways?

PR: It was a very privileged situation where people were ready to be surprised with progressive ideas. When one person is more creative, his inquisitive skills become more sophisticated. So there was a constant inquiry about the meaning of the project.

LS: Have the therapies ever changed from the input of the volunteers?

PR: Sure, there have been suggestions that have been incorporated. For instance, with the Goodoo doll, one therapist from the Sanatorium in New York suggested that the patient should press each of the five points in order to "switch on" their intentions. This is a sort of symbolic acupressure. In the Museum of Hypothetical Lifetimes, Sylvain, one of the therapists in Kassel, pointed out a missing space for friendships between the work axis and the love axis. This is something I'm still trying to fit into the blueprint. At first, in the Compatibility Test for Couples each couple could only choose two fruits; each person only picked one for themselves. But then a therapist suggested that each person pick a fruit for herself and one for her partner. When the partner does the same, you have four fruits total. You can make one juice per person, which is the couple according to A or B, or mix them all together. There are many possible combinations.

LS: Your project is participatory and also questions the hierarchic structure of common therapies. It was interesting to see the problems this led to. I remember that we discussed with the students/therapists the power relationship they found themselves involved in without actually wanting it. The aesthetic you used, from lab coats to the architecture, relies on a well-known system and instantly transformed visitors to patients. I see a certain contradiction here, and I never really understood to what extent you play with irony here — for me it was intriguing and disturbing not to be sure. At the same time I liked to feel this resistance of the piece.

PR: Role play is fundamental to free oneself from the one-dimensional labels that society assigns to each of us. While white coats are used by doctors, they're also used in schools when you go to the lab or in other work environments. So the white coats actually have more than one connotation, and there is room to play here. Friedrich Schiller says that someone is only fully a person when she plays, and she has to play in order to fully become a person.

LS: But you are clearly empowering the volunteers with the white lab coat…

PR: In hospitals, doctors who don't wear a white coat usually carry a stethoscope when attending patients, whether they need to use it or not. The white lab coat is in itself part of the placebo effect. The placebo effect doesn't only refer to sugar pills but to the entire aura surrounding medical practice, which encompasses the clinical aspect of hospitals, medical jargon, etc. The whole idea of bedside manner is actually something close to what a shaman or medicine man would do: to use the expectation of the patient to activate the healing process. One of the Sanatorium's advisers, neurologist and writer Alice Flaherty, had extensively studied this. She gives as an example that if an overweight doctor asks a patient to lose weight, the patient is less motivated to comply than if that doctor were a healthy weight.

LS: So once a volunteer is "in character," thanks to the lab coat, what specifically happens next?

PR: Every therapy is like a small ritual. Rituals are procedures that help you reconcile your desires and change your mindset. The problem is that you often access rituals in a religious or esoteric context, so you have to subscribe to those systems of beliefs. So what the Sanatorium attempts is to reproduce the same psychodynamics by conducting rituals without any ethnic specificity, without their aura of authenticity. It's not only about creating an alternative space from the health system; it's also an attempt to create alternative spaces to those provided by magic, religion, etc. Because these places are also industries in which a few gurus concentrate huge followings.

So in that sense it's very important that in the Sanatorium there is not one dogma or fundamental text and that volunteers have the opportunity to develop therapies, which after a phase of trial and research can become part of the inventory of services the Sanatorium provides. I'm interested in the democratization process here. In a way what I'm doing is a sort of reverse engineering of medical environments, borrowing their clinical packaging as a neutral space in which you can benefit from these rituals that are often beyond our reach.

LS: The notion of ritual makes me think of Félix Guattari. He understood ritual as a "machine" that determines the fluctuations of real and virtual forces, producing subjectivity in a process-driven concept not limited by subject-object division and reloading the real with possibilities ("possibles"). This seems to me quite near to your project. I suppose that Guattari's thinking, as well as the way he got to practice his theories in the context of the experimental La Borde clinic, has influenced you?

PR: Yes, indeed. La Borde is one of the most inspiring anti-psychiatric experiments, since it blurred the division between patients and psychotherapists. The interns took on duties, including in management and administration of the clinic. It is a Marxist-Leninist idea that members of a community must engage in both manual labor and intellectual labor.

But this idea can be traced back to Plato's ideal community. Just as Guattari wanted the asylum to embody a shelter, a place of refuge, and a sanctuary, in Mexico, Vasco de Quiroga also created "hospitals" were also places where the peasants learned trades such as music, sculpture, iron work, etc. But I'm interested in Guattari because, at a time when deconstruction was so hyped, he was also interested in reconstruction. Reconstruction has a specific aim, it's therapeutic in itself. When it's made through ritual, as you said, the subject and the object are integrated. That's why it works.

LS: Often you are doing a recontextualization of existing techniques, which were intended for a different context than the ones you use here.

PR: Actually, most of the therapies are combinations or mashups of existing traditions. What we are going for is spiritual promiscuity, not exclusivity! We are trying to borrow whatever works, anything, from anywhere, getting rid of tunnel vision. The Sanatorium is "dogmatically anti-dogmatic."

LS: Artists are often afraid of being copied and thus to lose control over their work, but you chose to open your project, to think it as a medium of circulation.

PR: You mention circulation, which is indeed appropriate. Moreno proposes that creativity is like a "sleeping beauty" that has to be woken up by the catalyzer, spontaneity. He says spontaneity is something that operates in the present, in the here and now, that propels people to find a good response to a new situation or a new response to an old situation. He describes the relationship as an arch: spontaneity awakens creativity, which then produces "cultural conserves," the name he gives to works of art and inventions —books, music, theories, technology, etc. In turn these cultural conserves inspire more spontaneity when they are experienced, like when you whistle or hum along with a song. Doing this, a musician may come up with a melody that can become a song or a score. So when this song is played again, it triggers more spontaneity and people dance and sing and may interpret the song, incorporating new elements.[9]

In the Sanatorium, the therapies are crystalized as cultural conserves, but it is in their nature to inspire the spontaneity of those who take part either as therapists or participants. In that way the participant is incorporated into the system as an artist, which is very close to the notion of the "spect-actor" articulated by Augusto Boal, where the spectator becomes an actor.

LS: You have called the Sanatorium a prototype and have mentioned plans to multiply it, to transfer it from the space of art into a wider cultural field. How will this be done?

PR: I feel very fortunate to be working in the field of contemporary art because it's a cultural environment that welcomes uncommon ideas. However, it would be a sad prognosis to expect these inventions to remain under the umbrella of art institutions. The nature of the project itself asks to be tested in different environments, to try itself in the wider arena of culture. My plan for the Santorium's future would be to tour around Mexico. It could travel to different cities, but I would prefer to avoid local museums and instead place it in street festivals and traditional fairs that have combined commerce and culture for centuries. The Sanatorium mobile unit would be composed of several geodesic tents and remain in one place for two weeks at a time. In these contexts it is local governments that can sponsor each installment out of the budget they would otherwise dedicate to music, theater, and traveling amusement parks. So the Sanatorium is "marketed" not much differently from a roadside attraction. What I find interesting about this is the creation of new audiences that otherwise would not go to a museum.

In a way, treating the Sanatorium as entertainment is also a tactical device, because in certain social sectors there is a stigma for those who go to therapy: they may be seen as weak or disturbed. It is the pretense of being a Sanatorium that helps people drop their defenses. Also, it is important that as a space of encounter you can visit it in different groups: with friends, classmates, coworkers, family, on a date, etc.

LS: The Sanatorium—like other projects of yours—has notions of utopian thinking. Do you refer directly or indirectly to utopian communities?

PR: In the early 1990s Harald Szeemann came to Mexico. I attended a week-long seminar where he presented some of his groundbreaking exhibitions in detail, such as *Gesamtkunstwerk*, *When Attitudes Become Form*, etc. But what left the biggest impression on me was his exhibition about Monte Verità, which was established in 1900 in Ascona, Switzerland, as a cooperative colony based on the principles of primitive socialism. It later became the Monte Verità Sanatorium. The members detested private property and practiced a strict standard of conduct based on vegetarianism and nudism. They rejected marriage, dress, party politics, and dogmas. One remarkable aspect of Monte Verità is how many artists spent time there, such as Isadora Duncan, Paul Klee, Hugo Ball, Mary Wigman, as well as intellectuals such as Carl Jung and Rudolph Steiner, among many others. So it was not only noteworthy for its utopian ideals but for the imagination it took to come up with it and what it inspired in these people.

LS: Which other utopic projects do you feel connected to?

PR: Charles Fourier has been another important inspiration for me. His invention of the *phalanstery* is one of the most fun things to read, and "fun" is no small adjective; for me, it is a combination of imagination and intelligence. Obviously, Fourier is far out there, and it's good to read visions that far exceed that which could happen in reality. There are many parts of his vision of the phalanstery and all the activities that happen inside that make a lot of sense, such as the mix of urban and rural environments, as well as the fact that jobs would rotate so people could do different jobs, which were compensated in such a way that everyone could make a decent living. Also, a big part of leisure time at the phalanstery was spent in grandiose parties that were carefully choreographed.

LS: What about contemporary references?

PR: One to mention is the Flux Clinic, which was originally started in the 1960s as a kind of happening in New York. It was then adapted into van, a "mobile clinic" that drove around Seattle in the 1970s, visiting only streets that began with the letters V, T, R, and E. I don't know why, there is not much information about it. And of course there are many important places such as Esalen in Big Sur and Patch Adams's Gesundheit Institute.

In the case of Patch Adams, I'm very interested in his sense of humor, yet I don't like how it translates into a visual form. Clowning is very canonical. There is this attachment to red noses and big shoes. It's curious that the same often happen to alternative healing places; they look like hobbit dungeons, which really creep me out. I'm interested in a wide range of esoteric subjects but I dread all the packaging. I can't stand incense, Celtic diagrams, mandalas, etc.

<u>LS</u>: So it seems that in the Sanatorium itself there is a role reversal between reason and magic, between science and art…

<u>PR</u>: I believe that one of the most important parts of life is to pay attention. When we get used to things, we cease to pay attention and things become grey. So how do we bring color back? What is needed is a sense of estrangement, of wonder, of surprise. What art can do is to make the normal look strange, as well as the opposite process, to make the strange normal. Let's look closer at these effects. If you suddenly look at normality with estrangement, you may realize how much of the status quo is arbitrary, even ridiculous. In the reverse operation, art may also be useful to introduce something strange but somehow necessary in life and to welcome this change.

1 Iván Illich, *Némesis médica. Obras Reunidas*, eds. Valentina Borremans, Javier Sicilia (Mexico City: Fondo de Cultura Económica, 2006).
2 Paolo Freire, *Pedagogy of the Oppressed*, Trans. Myra Bergman Ramos (New York: Continuum, 2006).
3 Ivan Illich, *La Convivencialidad* (Mexico City: Editorial Posada, 1978).
4 Jeffery Kluger, "The New Drug Crisis: Addiction by prescription," *Time Magazine*, September 2010.
5 J. Lazarou, B.H. Pomeranz, P.N. Corey, "Incident of adverse drug reactions in hospitalized patients," *JAMA* 280, no. 20 (1998).
6 *Morbidity and Mortality Weekly Report* 56, no. 5 (2007).
7 Aaron Antonovsky, *Health, Stress and Coping* (San Francisco: Jossey-Bass Publishers, 1979).
8 J.L. Moreno, *The Essential Moreno: Writings on Psychodrama, Group Method and Spontaneity*, ed. Jonathan Fox (New York: Springer, 1987).
9 Ibid.

Nine Tenets of the Sanatorium

VOLUNTEER-RUN
Most Sanatorium therapies wouldn't necessarily yield best results if conducted by a professional. Our intention is not to put down existing methods, but to create an alternative space where everyone can help each other, regardless of their credentials. By being volunteer-run, we aim to access society's untapped human capital.

INTIMATE STRANGERS
Encounter is a face-to-face exchange between two people, both willing to understand and adopt the perspective of the other person's reality to shed new light on their own experience. When the right procedure is offered, you can have the most insightful conversation even with (or perhaps, thanks to) a complete stranger.

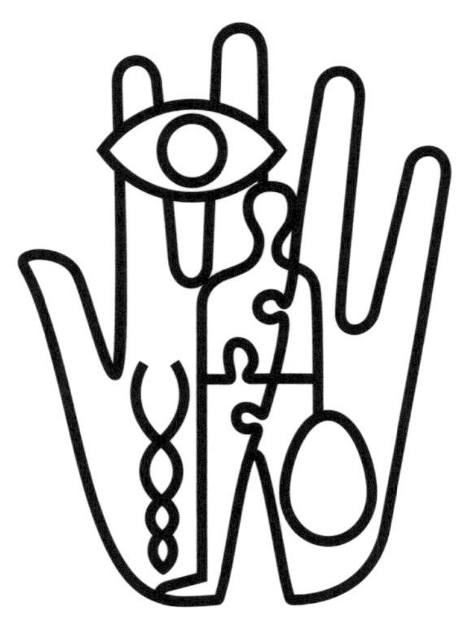

SALUTOGENESIS
Health is not the absence of disease. It's a state in which we know that life is manageable and meaningful; it's how we retain our ability to keep going when facing changes internally and externally. These therapies are an extensional device to enhance your present state, to help you find your sweet spot.

ROLE PLAY
Even though the Sanatorium is a horizontal organization where the public's status is as important as that of the therapists, we play roles, using props such as lab coats to free us from the one-dimensional labels society assigns to us.

SECULAR MAGIC
When we say that the Sanatorium is a delivery system of placebos, it's important to explain that medical environments have an aura that helps us believe that we as patients will be cured. We use this clinical "packaging" to stage small rituals, which are often only accessible to those who subscribe to a system of beliefs. The Sanatorium takes these rituals out of their ethnographic specificity and makes them available to everyone.

PLAY DRIVE
To achieve a mental state where we have the confidence to produce changes, we need a warm-up process. That's why the light-hearted spirit of play is so useful. To tap into our creativity, we need to train our spontaneity, which is a way of meeting the moment, of responding as the present situation requires.

ALL ARE WELCOME
The Sanatorium is not intended for
one specific audience. It's a place
you can visit in different groups:
with friends, classmates, coworkers,
family, on a date, etc. Inspired by
the notion of sociatry, its ultimate
goal is to leave the sphere of art
to provide a cost-effective service
to restore sanity in stressed
communities.

STRANGE/FAMILIAR
The Sanatorium is primarily a work
of art. The pretense of being a
Sanatorium allows people to play
with the idea of sharing their problems, while its status as a work
of art lets us test innovative techniques. This ambiguous nature also
helps us get a fresh perspective
on our world. Art can make the normal look strange (challenging the
arbitrariness of the status quo), as
well as the opposite process, to
make the strange normal (paving
the way for the acceptance of
new ideas).

SPECT-ACTOR
The most important work at the
Sanatorium is that done by the
patient. They are spectators that
become actors. In that sense,
the therapist is not *doing* the therapy. He is allowing it to happen.
Although it may appear that the
therapist is doing something *to* or
on someone, this is not the case.
The therapist is doing something
with the other person.

Sanatorium Manifesto

SANATORIUM	takes out of and into	PSYCHOSOMATICS BIOLOGICAL INTERPRETATION A DELIVERY SYSTEM OF PLACEBOS
SANATORIUM	takes out of and into	SHAMANISM ETHNOGRAPHIC SPECIFICITY INSTRUCTION BASED ACTIVITIES
SANATORIUM (The Museum of Hypothetical Lifetimes)	takes out of and into	CURATORIAL PRACTICE THE SYSTEM OF ART OBJECTS NARRATIVES OF THE SELF
SANATORIUM (Vaccine against Violence)	takes out of and into	ANGER MANAGEMENT 12-STEP PROGRAMS SOCIAL CATHARSIS
SANATORIUM (Ex-Voto)	takes out of and into	WORSHIP RELIGION SECULAR MEANINGFULNESS
SANATORIUM (Goodoo)	takes out of and into	SORCERY THE GLOOM RATIONAL INTENTIONALITY
SANATORIUM (The Great Game of Power)	takes out of and into	PROXEMICS ANTHROPOLOGY WARM-UP ROUTINES
SANATORIUM	takes out of and into	SOCIAL PSYCHOLOGY DIAGNOSTICS TACTICAL IMPLEMENTATION
SANATORIUM (Ontological Algebra)	takes out of and into	ONTOLOGY PHILOSOPHY THE OCCAM'S RAZOR OF ALGEBRA

SANATORIUM | takes | CONFESSION
(Citileaks) | out of | THE ECONOMY OF GUILT
| and into | INNOCUOUS HEARSAY

SANATORIUM | takes | SYNESTHESIA
(Synesthetic Test) | out of | POETICS
| and into | EXPERIMENTAL METHOD

SANATORIUM | takes | ORACLES
(Philosophical Casino) | out of | ESOTERISM
| and into | MAIEUTICS

SANATORIUM | takes | BODY LANGUAGE
(Mudras) | out of | LOCAL CULTURAL SYNTAX
| and into | A GRAMMAR OF MINDSETS

SANATORIUM | takes | VISUAL MNEMONICS
(Heraldry Mint) | out of | ICONOGRAPHY
| and into | SELF-MADE MANDALAS

SANATORIUM | takes | WORD GAMES
(Anagrams) | out of | LANGUAGE POETRY
| and into | A SELF PORTRAIT

SANATORIUM | takes | MEDITATION
| out of | SPIRITUALITY
| and into | AN AESTHETIC PURSUIT

SANATORIUM | takes | COUPLES THERAPY
(Compatability Test for Couples) | out of | COUNSELING
| and into | PRACTICAL JOKES

SANATORIUM | | AIMS TO BE A TOOL
| | IN THE ADVANCEMENT
| | OF SOCIATRY

Sanatorium Chronology

DECEMBER 1, 2010
David van der Leer, Associate Curator of Architecture and Urban Studies at the Guggenheim in New York City, approaches Pedro Reyes to invite him to create a public art project for the upcoming series *stillspotting nyc*, in which five artists do five interventions for the five boroughs of New York City. Reyes is to launch the series with an intervention in Brooklyn.

FEBRUARY 2011
Reyes visits New York and together with Van der Leer scouts spaces. They discuss ideas; Van der Leer wants to create spaces of stillness within the city, and Reyes introduces him to the concept of "sociatry," which he has used in previous workshops. During this conversation they discuss a therapy-based intervention with a structure similar to speed dating, in which visitors could test different therapies in one visit. The working title at that time is *Urban Speed Therapy*.

MARCH 2011
Interviews to recruit volunteers begin. Reyes starts to design therapies, consulting with experts in different fields such as neurologist Alice Flaherty, hypnosis specialist Mel Bucholtz, and artist Rafael Montañez Ortiz. In Mexico City Reyes conducts experiments with high school students, which leads to the development of Museum of Hypothetical Lifetimes, Goodoo, Epitaphs, and Citileaks. He tests Antanas Mockus' Vaccine against Violence and further develops previous projects such as Philosophical Casino and Compatibility Test for Couples.

MAY 2011
After evaluating several locations, project coordinator Sarah Malaika secures a former hardware store in downtown Brooklyn in the Metrotech Building.

JUNE 2011
Sanatorium at *stillspotting nyc* opens. Seventy volunteers work in two shifts each day when operations begin. Fifteen therapies are offered: Museum of Hypothetical Lifetimes; Vaccine against Violence; Citileaks; Goodoo; Ex-voto; Compatibility Test for Couples; Mudras; Philosophical Casino; Epitaphs; Transmigration Express; Anagrams, Aliases, and Acronyms; Synesthetic Test; Heraldry Mint; The Great Game of Power; and Ontological Algebra. Mel Bucholtz leads Tuning Effect sessions with visitors.

During eight weeks of operation the Sanatorium is visited by 2,000 people, all of whom participate in two-hour sessions involving two individual sessions and one group.

OCTOBER 13, 2010
Reyes is invited by Documenta artistic director Carolyn Christov-Bakargiev to participate in the 13th edition in Kassel, Germany. Raimundas Malasauskas, one of the Documenta agents, visits the Sanatorium in New York and suggests that this should be the project Reyes brings to Kassel.

JANUARY 23, 2011
On a side visit to Kassel, Reyes confers with Christov-Bakargiev about the Sanatorium's presence, and they walk through Aue Park to choose a location.

JANUARY 26, 2011
Documenta agent Chus Martinez meets with Yann Chateigné, dean of the Visual Arts Department at

Geneva University of Art and Design (Head — Genève), to recruit art students as volunteer therapists.

MAY 7—9, 2011
Reyes visits Geneva to conduct a training session with the students from Head — Genève who will make up the Sanatorium staff at Documenta.

OCTOBER 2011
Reyes introduces Philippe Von Stauffenberg, board chairman of the Green Building Group specializing in sustainable constructions in Germany, to Christov-Bakargiev. The Green Building Group agrees to sponsor the construction of the Sanatorium Building at Aue Park.

JUNE 9, 2012
Documenta 13 opens and eight therapies are presented: Museum of Hypothetical Lifetimes; Vaccine against Violence; Citileaks; Goodoo; Ex-voto; Compatibility Test for Couples; Mudras; and Philosophical Casino. A total of forty students from Head — Genève are appointed as therapists. One group of twenty begins working on the opening day, and the other twenty students will arrive to work the second half of the 100-day show beginning on Day 51. Reyes conducts initial sessions together with the students and encourages them to develop some of their own therapies. In conjunction with Laurent Schmid and Yann Chateigné, Reyes plans to have two kinds of parallel activities: the clinics and the check-ups. Clinics will consist of guests who will visit the Sanatorium to talk about issues related to psychology, etc, and check-ups will be internal meetings for the students to discuss any issues that arise related to the Sanatorium. One of the students, Elorri Harriet, is appointed manager of the group and follows up on needs from the students upon Reyes's departure.

JUNE/JULY 2012
The Sanatorium continues to function. Several clinics are conducted. Dr. Ludwig Möller, professor at Kassel University, visits the Sanatorium and does weekly coaching sessions with some of the volunteers.

JULY 11, 2012
Whitechapel Gallery director Iwona Blazwick, who had visited the project in Kassel, invites Reyes to present Sanatorium in London in the context of the exhibition *The Spirit of Utopia*.

JULY 29, 2012
As the first group of therapists is about to leave, a new group of students arrives. Two students, Caroline Tripet and Leo Sexer, stay for the relay of duties and hold a second training for the new students, based on their experiences during the first fifty days.

AUGUST/SEPTEMBER 2012
On Day 70, the second group of students is experiencing burnout. Public attendance is high, and the intensity of their interactions with the public creates strain. Christov-Bakargiev visits the Sanatorium, and the students ask if the Sanatorium can close for a couple of days. She suggests "Strike!" The staff decides to continue to function while doing "Strike Therapy," which is followed by a weekend seminar organized by therapist Mathilde Fernandez. There they watch and discuss a documentary about Antanas Mockus and are visited by Chus Martinez. Fellow Documenta artist Stuart Ringholt conducts his *Laugher Workshop*, which consists of all participants getting naked, doing breathing exercises,

and running in the forests
of Aue Park.

SEPTEMBER 4, 2012
With renewed energies, the students
make improvements to the Sanatorium's operations and management to
better attend to the demands created by the high public attendance.

SEPTEMBER 2012
When Documenta 13 ends, the
building that housed the Sanatorium
is offered to a worthwhile institution
to be reused. Klassic Radio, a German radio station, hosts a contest
for listeners to vote for the best
recipient of the donation. An organization devoted to the youth of the
town of Sachsen wins the contest
after collecting ten thousand votes.

JANUARY 2013
The materials and testimonials
collected in New York and Kassel
are developed into this *Operations
Manual*.

MARCH 2013
During a visit to London, Reyes
meets several times with curator
Kirsty Ogg to prepare for the
Whitechapel gallery installment
of the Sanatorium.

JULY 4, 2013
The Sanatorium opens in London
and the *Operations Manual* is
presented. At the time of publication, future editions of the project
are in development for Canada
and Mexico.

General Management

GENERAL MANAGEMENT
The most important part of the
Sanatorium is its human resources.
Working here is a lot of fun, serious
fun. For this machine to constantly
produce pleasure and consciousness, it is important to consider the
technical and administrative elements that allow the magic to happen.

This section explains how the team
works. To keep the project functioning properly, it is important to
have proper training, adequate
spaces, and clearly assigned responsibilities.

In this section you'll find information about things we have learned at
past editions of the Sanatorium.
But keep in mind that this is meant
to be adaptable. It is easy to foresee
that in the future many new improvements will happen. That is to
say, this is a work in progress…
and that progress depends on you.

Sanatorium Sociogram

The following is a basic outline of the responsibilities of those involved in the Sanatorium:

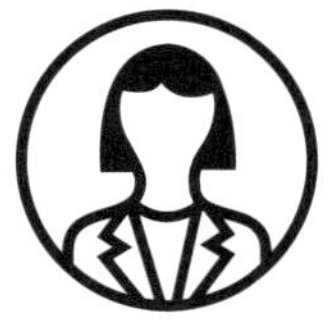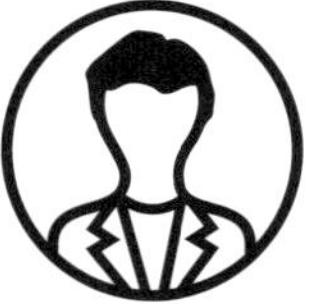

THE VOLUNTEERS
operate the Sanatorium, running reception, processing visitors, leading therapies, and evaluating how things are running.

THE STAFF MANAGER
is chosen from among the Volunteers to hold administrative responsibilities. She will report to the Assistant Curator when supplies are low, when repairs or maintenance are needed, or when an operational issue arises that the Volunteers need assistance in resolving.

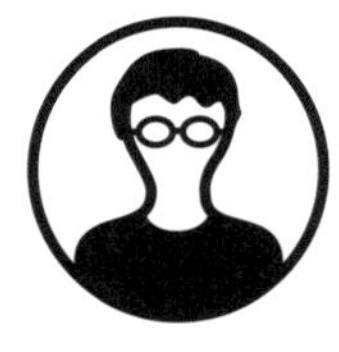

THE ASSISTANT CURATOR
supervises the operations of the Sanatorium, purchasing supplies when they run low, organizing repair or maintenance to the space as needed, and answering operational questions. If an operational issue arises that the curatorial assistant cannot resolve, he will speak to the Curator. If a content-related issue arises, the Assistant Curator will contact Pedro Reyes.

THE CURATOR
oversees the conceptual integrity of the project and works with the Artist to make decisions about both operational and content-related questions.

THE ARTIST
Pedro Reyes oversees the project's content and the training of the Volunteers. While Volunteers should direct operational issues to the Assistant Curator via the Staff Manager, any volunteer is welcome to contact the Artist directly with questions regarding content. Reyes in turn will oversee therapist training and respond to issues related to the Volunteers' adoption of their roles as therapists.

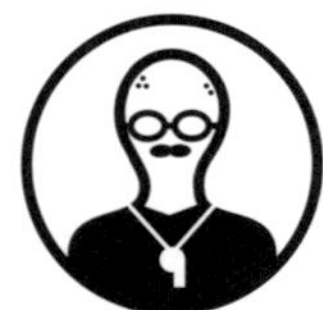

THE COACH

A Coach will visit the Volunteers
on a weekly basis to meet with them
and discuss the experiences and
dilemmas of the week. His contact
is direct and individual with each
Volunteer, and they should be able
to contact him with questions related
to the therapist-patient relationship.
The Coach must have experience
in psychotherapy; he should be a
trained psychologist or social worker.

An additional figure of a Trainer
may be helpful. This person, ideally
someone who has volunteered as
a therapist in the past, will provide
additional training supervision.

THE GUEST LECTURER

Guest Lecturers will visit the
Sanatorium on a one-time basis to
deliver clinics on a range of topics.

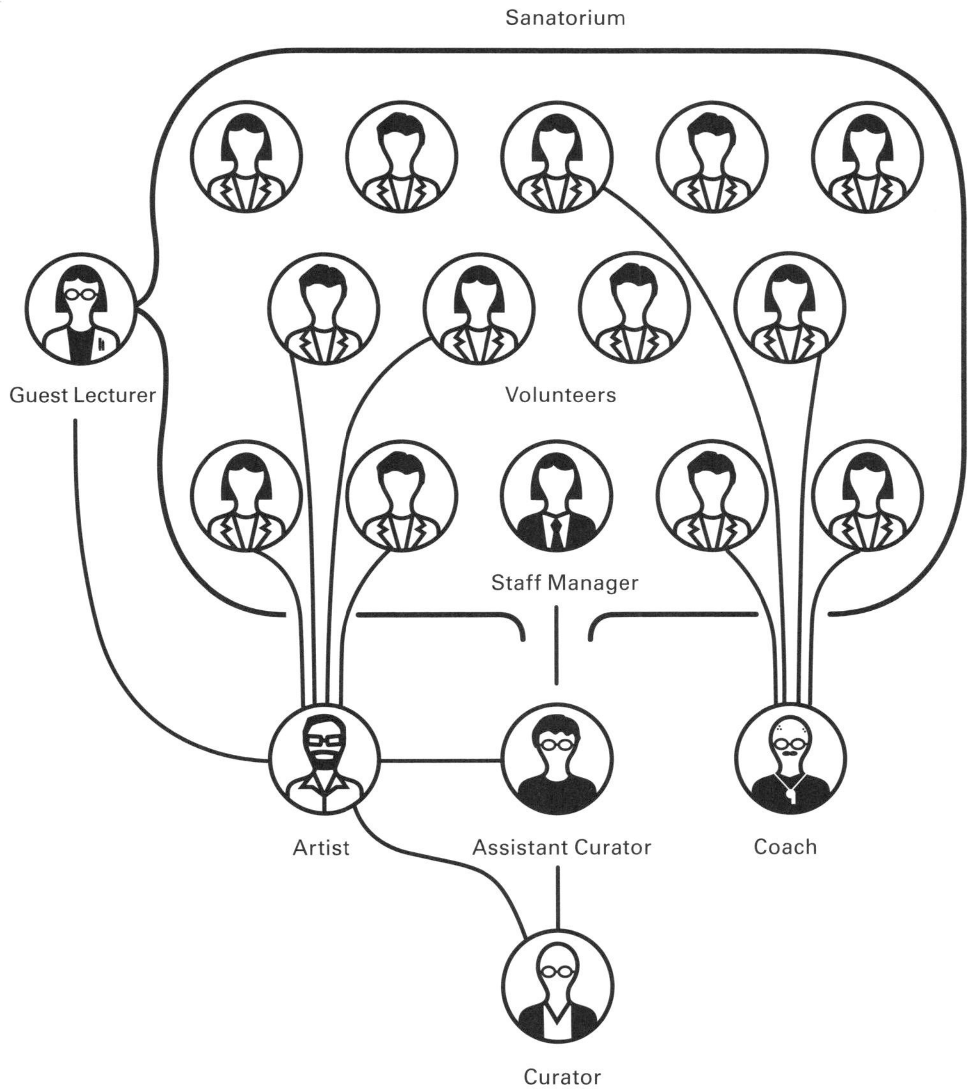

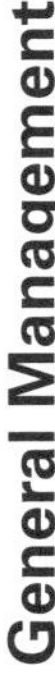

Sanatorium
Guest Lecturer
Volunteers
Staff Manager
Artist
Assistant Curator
Coach
Curator

Kassel Sanatorium was to combine enclosed spaces (for therapies that require more intimacy, such as the Museum of Hypothetical Lifetimes and Goodoo) with open spaces where you could do therapy while enjoying the majesty of Aue Park. One of the things we learned was that as much as the open spaces were very enjoyable on warm days, they were unpleasantly cold on rainy days. Another problem we experienced was related to the proximity of the therapy spaces. Some quiet therapies such as Mudras happened in spaces adjacent to louder therapies like Vaccine against Violence, so the noise created by yelling at and beating up the dummy interrupted the meditative aspect of Mudras. But the most important lesson learned from this custom-made building was that some therapies require absolute privacy, so any window or door must have the potential to be closed or shielded with curtains or shutters.

3. LONDON, EXISTING INDOOR VENUE

The Sanatorium installment in London, to take place at the Whitechapel Gallery, is also an existing venue, yet the project happens under the umbrella of group exhibition *The Spirit of Utopia*. Due to space restrictions, this will be a compact edition of the Sanatorium offering mostly individual sessions. Similar in size to the location at Documenta/Kassel, it will have one main difference, which is that while sessions are taking place, shutters or curtains will allow therapists to control the intimacy of each room, limiting the public's ability to observe the therapies in progress.

4. MOBILE UNIT

The mobile unit is designed to allow the Sanatorium to travel to different cities, operating for certain periods of time (for instance, two weeks) before moving to the next station. The therapy rooms are semi-geodesic tents, which can be connected in order to form larger spaces. They are linked with tunnels that work as corridors, permitting many different configurations. The fabric of the tent walls is supported by an exoskeleton of aluminum tubing, which makes the unit very lightweight. The floor is made of pallets that are raised from the ground to keep the inner surface dry and flat, regardless of the weather and topography of the location.

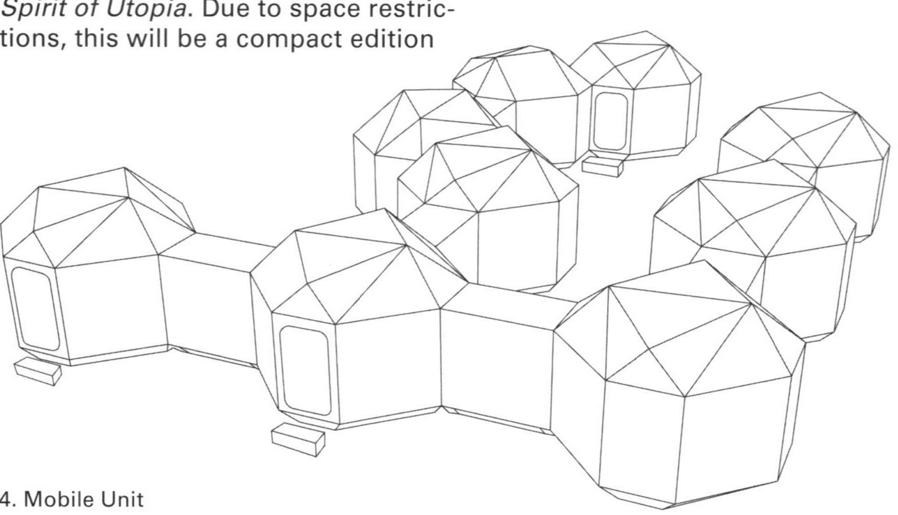

4. Mobile Unit

Sanatorium Spatial Layout

The Sanatorium is flexible and can adapt itself to different sizes of spaces. It can occupy existing indoor venues or a custom-made building, or it may exist as a mobile unit. The general footprint of the project depends on the number of therapies and projected attendance. At the beginning of each therapy description the minimum size of the room is stated. In addition to the spaces for each therapy, one has to consider reception, the waiting room, the break room (which may or may not be the same as the storage room), and hallways. It's important that the venue be accessible for persons with limited mobility and have adequate emergency exits. If the space is a custom-made building, it must be nearby restrooms that can be easily accessed by volunteers and visitors.

Very few elements are needed to "trick" the public into believing they are in a hospital. A combination of blue painted walls and fluorescent light creates a clinical, cold feel that people associate with hospitals and sanatoriums. The Sanatorium staff wears white lab coats with nametags, and a red cross and/or the Sanatorium logo should be displayed in the reception area — not on the exterior of the Sanatorium to prevent passers-by from mistaking it for a place to seek first aid or medical treatment.

Here are four case studies for spatial layouts of various editions of the Sanatorium.

1. NEW YORK CITY, EXISTING INDOOR VENUE

In New York the Sanatorium was housed in a former hardware shop, which provided expansive spaces for each room. For this reason, the rooms were separated by generous empty space, so there was no need for walls to divide the different sections of the Sanatorium. Also, everyone present at the Sanatorium was a ticketed participant. There was no one milling around either inside or outside, trying to observe the activities. So even though there were no divisions, the Sanatorium was still able to offer intimacy in the therapy experience, as each participant was able to concentrate on his activity without distraction and without distracting others. The space available at this location determined the number of therapies the Sanatorium could offer: sixteen total. A carpeted area in the basement allowed us to do group sessions, which were always conducted with dim light and isolated from exterior noises. This Sanatorium location was highly accessible for the public, just steps away from a subway station and in busy downtown Brooklyn.

2. KASSEL, CUSTOM-MADE BUILDING

The prospect of doing a custom-made building first inspired designs that were more daring than the one that was eventually built. The structure that was built had function as its top priority due to the desire to create the maximum space possible to achieve with existing resources. The layout alternated square, enclosed rooms with open-air patios of the same size, similar to a chessboard, with a space for circulation in the middle. This floor plan is inspired by the section of the Sarah Kubitschek Brasilia Hospital for Diseases of the Motor Organs designed by João Filgueiras Lima Lelé. In this structure, every even floor of the building is displaced from the center, creating a terrace. Hospital beds on wheels can be moved back and forth from inside spaces to the balcony. In the same sense, the intention of the

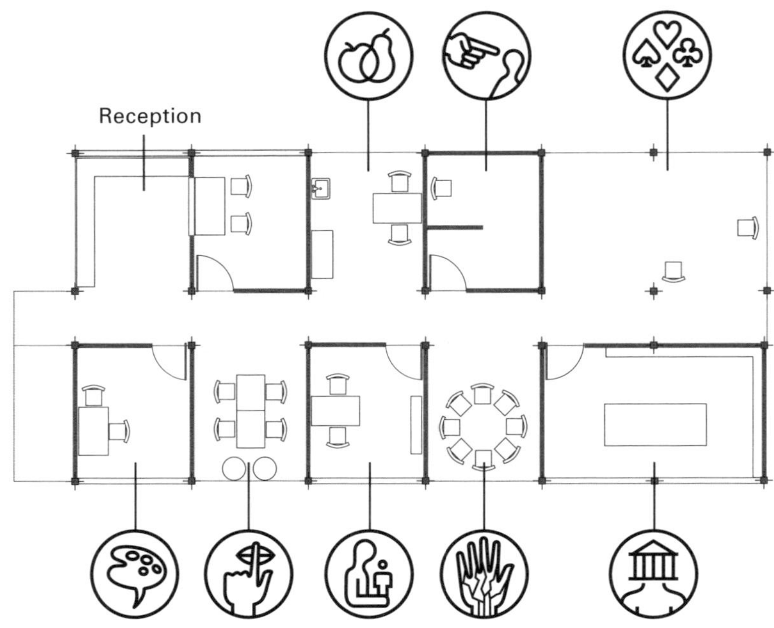

Reception

2. Kassel

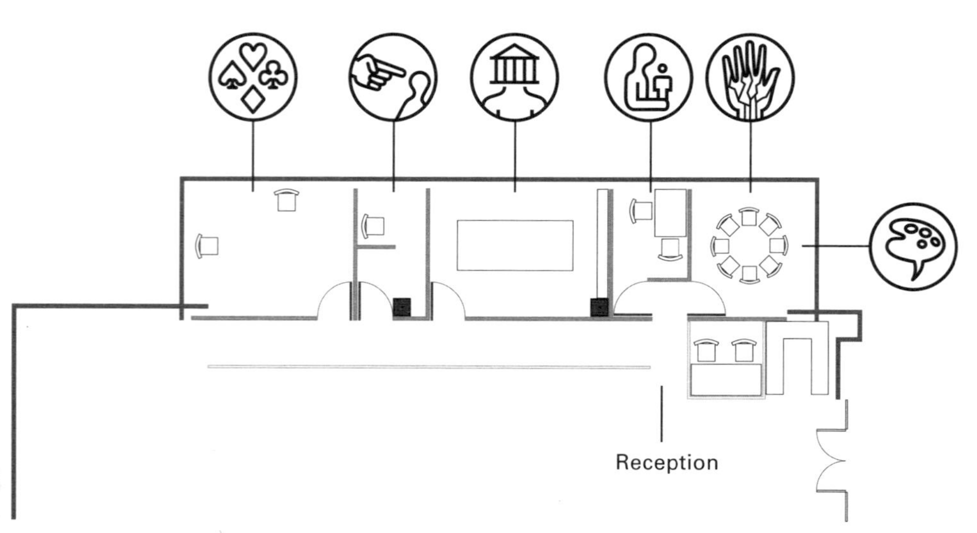

Reception

3. London

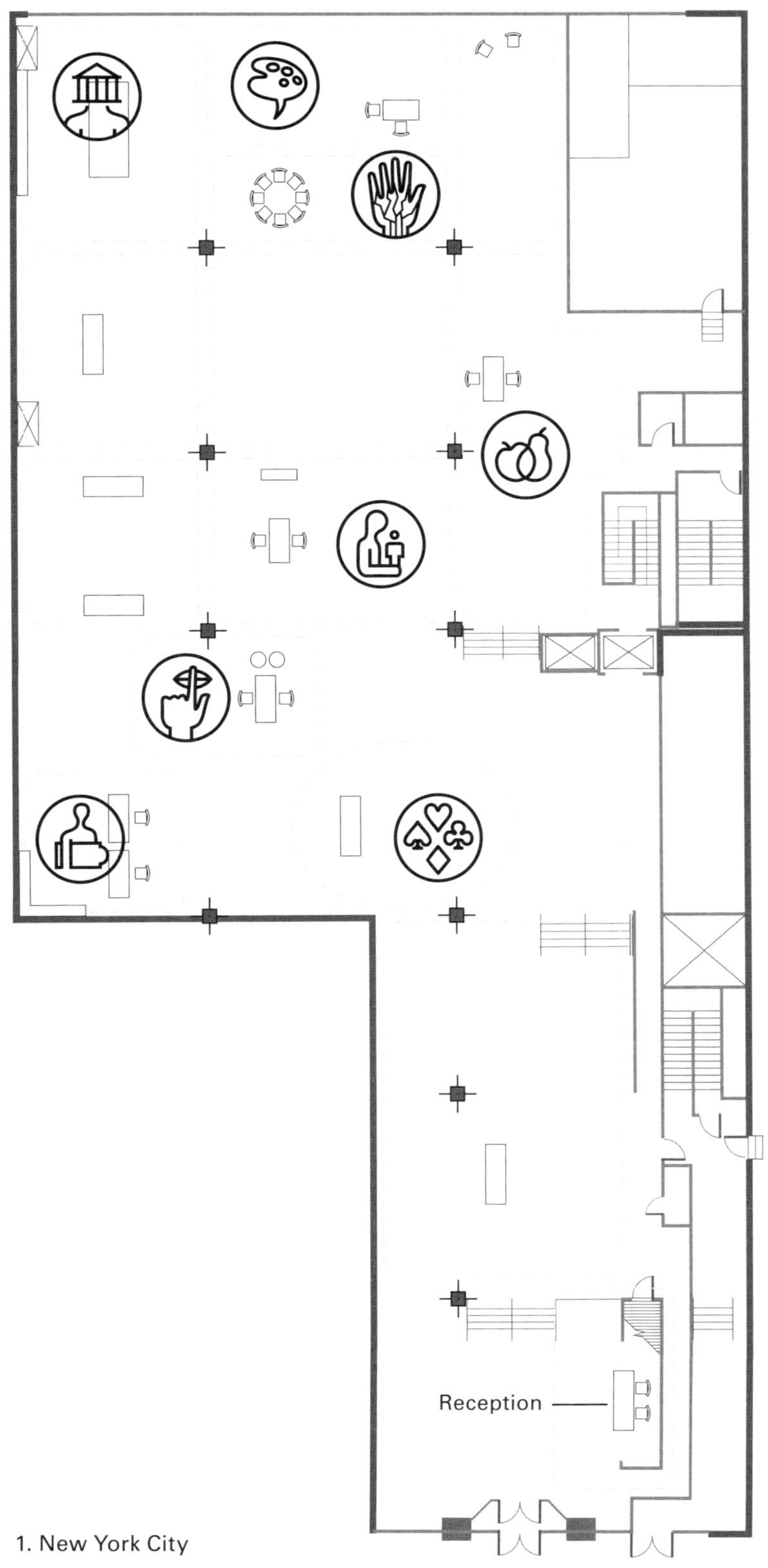

1. New York City

Reception and
the Break Room

RECEPTION
It is recommended that at least two people are stationed in the reception area at all times. If the Sanatorium is installed at a ticketed event, the ticketing services should be located at a different spot. Working at reception is a task that is shared among the therapists; every volunteer will work there according to a rotating schedule. The role of a receptionist is very important because this is the first impression the visitors will have of the Sanatorium.

> *"I had fun prowling around outside the reception, showing off my white jacket and letting my picture get taken. When too many people were attacking the front desk, I climbed onto a bench and explained all the therapies in a loud voice, like a carnival hawker."*
>
> *Kassel Therapist Gloria Maso*

People will enter with many expectations about what kind of place this is. It's appropriate to have a sign at reception stating brief descriptions of the therapies offered. Before any visitor begins therapy, he or she must sign a release form.

WHAT IS THE PURPOSE
OF THE RELEASE FORM?
There is always plenty of confusion about whether the Sanatorium is serious or not, whether it is art or therapy. We welcome that ambiguity because it is necessary for art to work its magic. The Sanatorium is self-described as a "delivery system of placebos." The mind works in a curious way, so even if we are told that this is a fictional space, often that does not prevent us from believing or "buying into" the process. However, it is important that this fiction is clearly stated from the beginning. This is why all participants have to read and sign the release form, acknowledging:

A that this is a work of art and a place for encounter. It is not a substitute for therapy and does not pretend to be a real sanatorium.
B that the volunteers are not real therapists.
C that the materials produced during their sessions will become part of the Sanatorium files and may be used in future trainings or publications, always protected by anonymity. No names, personal details, or places will be disclosed.

BREAK ROOM
In Sanatorium locations where space is very limited, it is possible to combine the break room with the reception area, but ideally the break room is a separate space. The break room must contain the following:

1 Lab coats
2 Name tags
3 Water cooler and electric kettle
4 Board for internal announcements
5 Volunteer schedule
6 Emergency contact list including phone numbers for project managers

If possible add the following:

1 Refrigerator
2 A bed for naps
3 Games for breaks (cards, checkers, chess, etc)

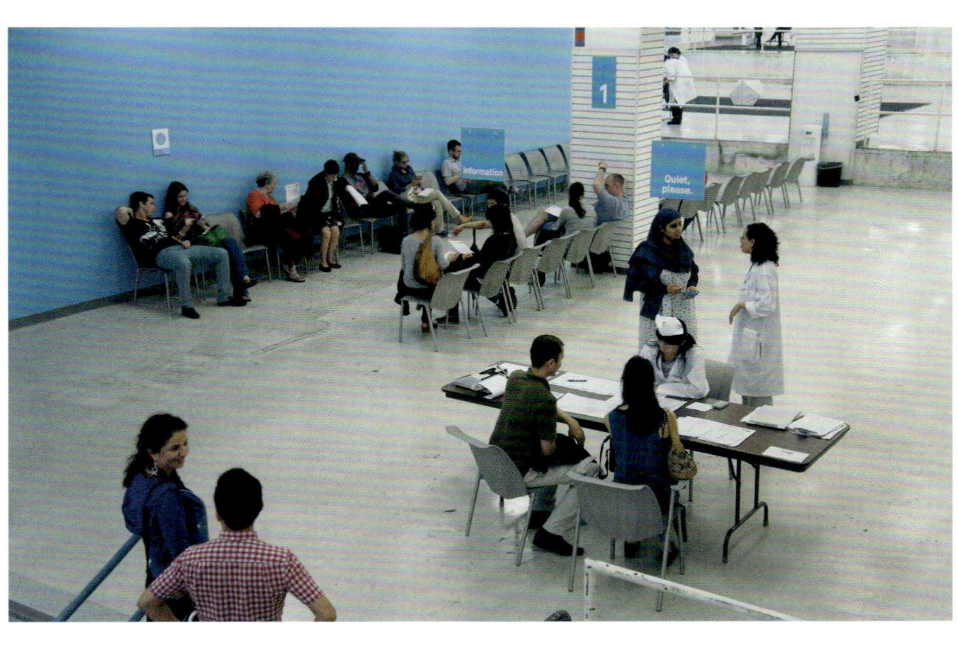

Simi
Information
Quiet,
please.
1

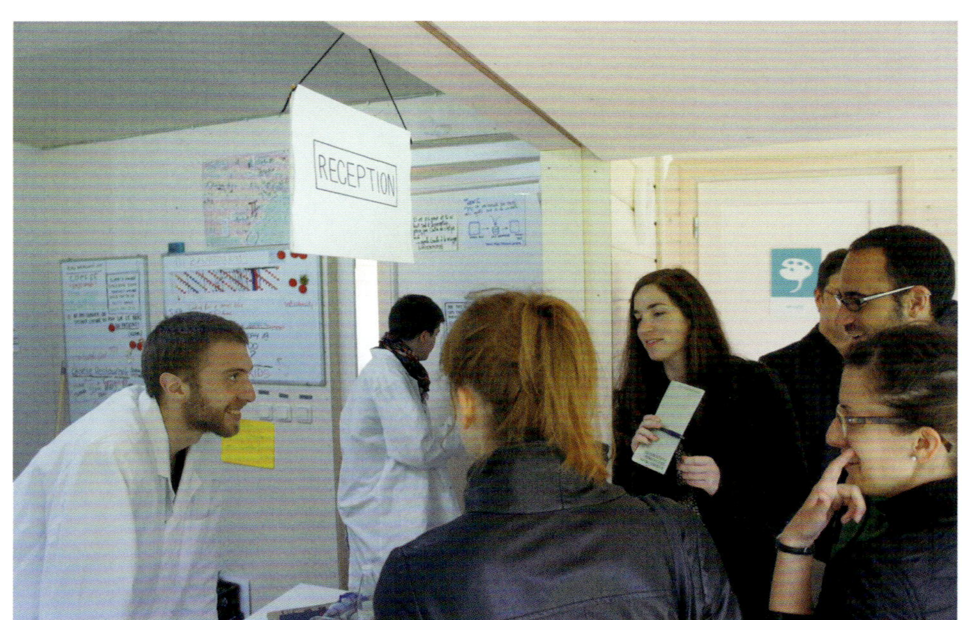
RECEPTION

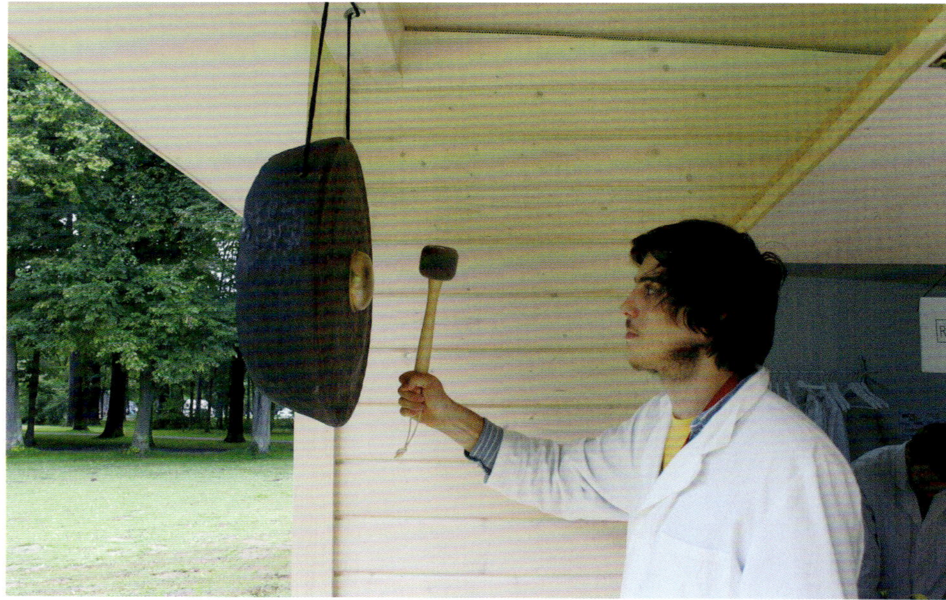

How to Assign Therapies

There are three ways
of assigning therapies:

THE NEW YORK EXPERIENCE
In New York City, the Sanatorium
was a ticketed event, and with your
ticket you were invited to experience
a two-hour-long visit that included
two individual therapy sessions and
one group session. Tickets were
available to be purchased for specific times throughout the day, so just
as when one goes to the theater or
movies, people tended to arrive a
few minutes early. As people came
in, the receptionist had visitors sign
release forms recognizing that the
therapies offered were not real.
On the back side of the release form,
a survey gave them the chance to
provide an assessment of their mood
before and after their two-hour
session.

The receptionist then assigned
therapies to each visitor before they
passed to a waiting room. Every
person had an intake form with the
three appointments to be assigned.
The receptionist asked each visitor
general questions, such as "How are
you feeling? Is there anything you
would like to work on today?" in order to assign the most appropriate
therapy. For example, couples could
be given the Compatibility Test.
Some people who confessed to feeling stressed would go to Vaccine
against Violence. People feeling over-
whelmed by decisions to be made
would be sent to the Philosophical
Casino, and so on.

When the scheduled time of each
appointment arrived, participants
were called by the sound of a bell or
a gong to find the space for the
therapy they were assigned. Some
would discover that they would have
individual therapies, while others
found they would be participating in
a group. At the sound of the second
gong, participants would move to
their second appointment, and later
to the third.

*"Once or twice I hit my head
very hard on the gong, getting up
too suddenly from a break."*

Kassel Therapist Gloria Maso

The first two sessions were small
group or individual therapies, and
they took up the first of the two
hours. Then everyone would go to
a group therapy. This allowed therapists to have a break for nearly an
hour before taking on new patients.

THE KASSEL EXPERIENCE
At Documenta the exhibition opened
at 10 a.m., but from 10 a.m. to 12 p.m.
only reception was open to take appointments. Therapies began at noon.
At the beginning everyone who came
to reception was given a pamphlet,
but quickly we realized we were at
risk of running out of pamphlets, so
we made a sign with descriptions
of the therapies. Visitors could choose
which therapies they wanted to try,
and the nearest available time slot for
that therapy was offered to them.
If the patient did not show up for the
session, it was offered to someone
visiting the Sanatorium at that
moment. In general we provided up
to only two appointments per person in Kassel, which worked well
since most attendants wanted to see
the rest of the works at Documenta,
although there were persons who
could afford more time and came for
therapies on multiple occasions.

THE KASSEL VARIATION
Towards the end of the exhibition
in Kassel, the volunteers decided to
try a new dynamic and decided to
invite all the participants at once into

a Mudras session. In Mudras,
everyone discloses a particular issue they want to improve or work
on, and the therapists attempted to
then choose with which participant
they wanted to work and with which
therapy. The rest were referred
to group sessions such as the Philosophical Casino.

The examples described above
should be used as general guidelines
for planning how to assign therapies.
They may be combined or adapted
into new systems to suit the characteristics of future Sanatoriums.

Volunteer Checklist:

o   Report and sign in for your
    shift half an hour before
    the scheduled time.

o   Pick up your lab coat.

o   Pick up your nametag.

o   Make sure not to have any
    valuables with you.

o   Make sure all materials are at
    hand at your station.

o   Let the Staff Manager know
    if there are any materials
    missing from your station.

o   Check your break schedule for
    that day.

o   If you have any questions
    please refer them to the Staff
    Manager before the beginning
    of your shift.

During the shift:

o   After you are finished with a
    session make sure to rearrage,
    clean up, and prepare your
    station for the next group of
    guests.

o   Be sure you know who to
    contact if you have any
    health or safety issues.

After the shift:

o   Check your work station and
    let the Staff Manager know
    if there are any materials
    missing from your station.

o   Leave your lab coat and
    nametag in the volunteer
    break room.

o   Sign out before you leave
    the Sanatorium.

The Therapy Session

Co-authored by Dr. Ludwig Möller and Pedro Reyes

The aim of counselling and therapy — and the Sanatorium — is to offer a safe place where people are welcomed as they are and where they can enter a space of friendliness and security. Such places are rare for quite a number of people, especially if they are in a vulnerable state or if their feelings, thinking, or lifestyle differ from mainstream society. Offering such a space has a healing potential.

OPENING THE THERAPY SESSION
The attention of the therapist begins in the moment when the person enters the room. Those first few seconds of communication can decide the success of the session. It is important to meet the guest in a friendly manner. The best is a firm handshake. However, this is not permitted in certain cultures, so it is important to clarify if needed.

Introduce yourself by name and offer some detail about yourself to create a personal atmosphere. All therapists should wear nametags so that the patient is able to recall and use their names. Think how to make a friendly and humorous start. It should include sentences like:

> *"I am an volunteer and not a therapist."*

> *"There is nothing to fear! If there is anything you don't feel good about, please tell me right away."*

Show interest in your client and ask her to introduce herself to you.

HELPFUL THERAPIST BEHAVIOUR
The required behaviour of the therapist can be trained. Examples include body posture and the tone of the therapist. Therapists should sit with the upper body inclined towards the client, arms open, hands loose in the lap (at least not entangled). Nod once in a while, listening to the client. What you say should be emphasized with lively gestures. The legs should be open rather than crossed. The tone of a therapist should be independent of the content of what is said. Be warm, professional, competent, and fearless.

REFLECTING FIRST CONTACT
Your first contact with a client in the Sanatorium will often be also the last contact you have with him or her. First contacts are very important in psychotherapy for various reasons. Responsible facilitators of the Sanatorium must know that even short contact with the client can be very powerful and significant. You can open people up to their interest in therapy or close it down. This is especially important if they are in a situation where they need to seek crisis intervention immediately or begin a longer therapy to solve a problem.

It is equally important to neither interpret nor judge. Don't laugh unless you are laughing with the person, never at him.

The role of the therapist is to listen but not interpret. If the patient demands an interpretation, therapists should comment that symbols are not universal and that what something may mean for the patient will have a different meaning for the therapist. The therapist is interested in the meaning the patient is attributing to the symbol.

ENDING THE THERAPY
Ending a therapy session means saying farewell to a personal encounter. It's the time to round things up if possible and depart from each other with respect and gratefulness, asking a question such as "How did you like it?" or "What kind of feelings do you take from here?".

This moment gives the opportunity to collect the client's resonance: what affected him. Is he or she in a good state right now? If you want personal feedback you can ask: "How was it for you working with me today?". Talking and reflecting together about the therapy is coming back from a journey, having an exchange about ups and downs, preparing to go out of the Sanatorium into the real world again. It's the opportunity to clarify misunderstandings or bad feelings and to prepare a next healthy step in life. In the rare case that there is a crisis intervention needed because a therapy has triggered something overpowering, you can take care of the client: "Are you with friends here?" or "Where do you go from here?".

Wherever the Sanatorium is stationed, Sanatorium management will locate support groups, hotlines, and anger management programs, etc., and print their contact information and service hours on cards or flyers to give to those who are identified as in need of help.

To say goodbye after talking, therapists can acknowledge the person's trust, saying, "Thank you for your trust. I wish you all the best on your way to explore life."

DOS AND DON'TS
FOR THERAPY SESSIONS
This list of Dos and Don'ts was developed by the Guggenheim Museum for the New York City Sanatorium. This is only an example of suggested guidelines; the Dos and Don'ts of other editions of the Sanatorium will depend on local customs and cultural boundaries. This list may be adapted to fit each Sanatorium location.

Dos:

- Have fun and enjoy the Sanatorium.
- Point using your open hand or two fingers.
- Be descriptive when describing activities and provide instructions before giving participants the tools; don't force people into anything.
- Model activities for participants as you explain.
- Walk over to get someone's attention.
- Stand up when you are waiting so you can welcome the new group.
- Be gracious at the end of every session; tell visitors that you enjoyed their visits and hope they enjoyed their therapies as well.
- Be relaxed.
- Don't rush, make connections with each individual visitor. Create a unique experience for each of them.
- Be pleasant.

Don'ts:

- Make comments about participants' appearances or abilities.
- Touch participants.
- Try to diagnose participants.
- Be upset with anyone who is late.
- Point or yell to get someone's attention.

Volunteer Training

Co-authored by Dr. Ludwig Möller and Pedro Reyes

WHO AM I IN THE SANATORIUM? "I am an art student, not a therapist! What if someone who wants to commit suicide comes to me? I don't want to be responsible!" This was an angry comment I got from a student in one of my coaching sessions for the Sanatorium crew. Despite the fact that every visitor to the Sanatorium signed a release form and was warned that this is not a substitute for therapy and that the volunteers were not real therapists, they were unsure of how to deal with the trust that people placed in them. I tried to address the volunteers' confusion about roles and their responsibility to the people who booked therapies.

People's roles shimmer when they enter the artwork of Pedro Reyes. Visitors would start a therapy as interested participants of the Documenta 13 art exhibition and came out as clients having had a personal experience. Art students began their assignment to facilitate the Sanatorium as co-workers of the artist and found themselves in the middle of a personal encounter with foreigners. This is inherent to the Sanatorium because it mixes art and psychology.

I strongly believe in the aim of the Sanatorium to create a space of encounter where people can meet on a horizontal level, where they can be helped and be useful to others. We desperately need more and more of these spaces in our societies to provide balance. Although the students felt uneasy acting as "therapists," it was a learning experience for most of them that they are useful to others just by being there,

offering a personal meeting in a structured way, having listened to somebody's story. Student Leo Sexer tried to encourage his fellow students, saying, "It's not much different from your daily life when you are trying to help a friend." For many of the art students, this was the experience: to be able to do this human service for strangers and receive in return a smile and gratitude. In that sense, the Sanatorium was a training center for young art students learning to be concerned about others, which in their own perspective is often lacking in art school. The fifty days each group exercised this concern in Kassel gave room for experience and developing skills in empathy and communication.

To answer the question of "Who owns counseling?", Colin Feltham says:

> *Counseling at its simplest is about two people sitting down in privacy with one of them listening intently and responding helpfully to the other expressing his or her concern about problems … Original counseling was a grassroots movement, linked with voluntary organizations and resistant to medical models of psychological help and intervention. It would not be true to say it was "owned by the people," rather, the issue of ownership hardly arose. Passion and faith were the engines.*

The alternative is not between professionalization and de-professionalization! We need trained therapists, and we need a lot more people who are hospitable and listen to people in need of other human beings sharing life and its challenges and difficulties. This is the important

impulse the Sanatorium gives.
The experience and conceptual work
involved could bring this impulse
out of the art world into society.
In Kassel things moved in this direction a great deal because the
Sanatorium was located in a public
park and no ticket was required at
the entrance. This made the service
accessible for everyone.

Whenever I brought people to the
Sanatorium, they were curious
about the therapies in the environment of an exhibition. In public
perception, therapy is bound up with
heavy thoughts and has a high
barrier to approach. Nevertheless,
I was concerned about people enter-
ing a therapy room in an unsteady
state of mind or even with a trauma.
You never know what the setting
of a so-called Sanatorium, with its
white coats, enclosed small rooms
and therapies, would trigger in the
"clients." The students told me about
dense personal experiences with
visitors in their therapies, and fortu-
nately they did not encounter situations they could not handle. Sure, the
short but sometimes intense meetings left their impressions on them.
One day a young art student was
leaning against the wall of the reception area, exhausted after a therapy.
A young woman had followed him
to the Goodoo therapy. Her bare arms
were covered in cuts, and while she
applied the charms to the Goodoo
doll she was in tears, blaming herself
as a weird and bad person. Doing
the exercise she calmed down, but
she left the art student quite moved
with this experience.

The Sanatorium wants to bring
"mild remedy to mild affliction, like
a psychological first aid kit," but
not only people with mild affliction
enter it. People with deep wounds
from life and psychic illnesses come,

too. They come with their desperate
need to be listened to and with a
desire to be supported and healed.
They, along with others, will forget
about the artsy part of the Sanatorium and will long for the psychological part. The use of the Sanatorium by visitors and facilitators
shows that this division of art and
psychology cannot be made.
They are inseparably intertwined
— art is psychology and psychology
is art. From a phenomenological
standpoint both belong to the sphere
of creativity. Human beings are
constantly creating. Creating in a
positive way means bringing whole-
ness and healing into existence.

In order to deliver a good perfor-
mance in this creative act that aims
at "best practice," or "good enough
practice," some kind of training is
needed. Especially for those who
don't have the "gift" of counseling,
those who haven't had the chance
to develop empathy and listening
ears within their own family lives or
through working in youth groups.
The therapies are designed so that
anyone can give them. But due
to the sustained effort required by
doing this with the public for an
extended period of time, it is recommended that therapists receive an
introductory talk to prepare them
for their roles and the wide range of
experiences they may encounter.

For those who want and need more
than a 15 or 30-minute first aid
counseling, the aim of the Sanatorium should not be just clearing mild
afflictions but becoming a starting
point. We recognize that this is beyond both the capacity and responsibility of the Sanatorium, but we can
do our best to refer people to services, hotlines, and support groups
in the surrounding area.

The training of the Sanatorium facilitators should take away the bias of their personal roles. It should give them confidence in their abilities and limitations. It should help to develop soundness in dealing with clients who want or need further assistance. Every facilitator of the Sanatorium needs to be open and ready to behave as a human being, listening to other people's desires and needs, ready to support them on the spot.

TRAINING FOR
SANATORIUM FACILITATORS
The quality of the input obviously influences the quality of the work in the Sanatorium.

Volunteers will participate in a two-day introductory workshop that includes a series of training activities plus the chance for all volunteers to become patients and test the therapies for themselves. Workshops should be done as a mixture of exercises and mini-lectures.

GROUP WARM-UP
During the introductory workshop, getting to know the other members of the group is an important starting point for the training.

THE THERAPIES
Volunteers must be familiar with the processes and intentions of each of the therapies to be offered. In order to learn and understand them, the volunteers should test the therapies on themselves at the introductory workshop, taking turns as therapists and participants and practicing each role until they are comfortably familiar with them.

ONGOING TRAINING
During the Sanatorium's course of operations, volunteers should receive supervision and attend weekly group meetings where they can share their experiences with each other. To prepare the group sessions each member should write personal reflections in a daily journal about experiences at the Sanatorium; a kind of diary in notebooks provided to each volunteer by management. The journals from previous Sanatorium exhibitions were instrumental in developing the manual you have in your hands.

The learning journal starts the self-experiencing process of one's own learning journey and preserves important information and questions for the group discussion in supervision.

About writing a learning journal:

– Find a form of journal that suits you: a notebook, single sheets that can be put in a folder, a folder in the computer, etc.
– Keep it in a safe place for privacy.
– Put a date and title to your daily writing. It helps to see connections and development.
– Write in a flow, without thinking too much about spelling and grammar. It helps not to censor your thoughts.
– Try out different forms of entries: lists, single words, full sentences, drawings, graphs, different colors of pens, etc.
– Some people like to set a special time a day for journal writing. Others find it helpful to take the journal wherever they are to write when a thought comes to their mind.

PROJECTION TEST
This form is not a test but an opportunity for the unconscious
to speak. There are no right or wrong responses. The statement
completions are based on more conscious attitudes, but can
be strongly influenced by the unconscious, especially if a word
touches upon a sensitive area in your psyche. The form allows
someone to express his own uniqueness in a situation where he
might otherwise be inarticulate.

I like ____
I want ____
My family ____
I must ____
Art is ____
I hope ____
I love ____
I feel ____
People think of me ____________________________________
I often ____
I hate ____
Someday I ____
My father ____
I cannot ____
I fear ____
I wish ____
I failed ____
My greatest success ___________________________________
My mother ____
I need ____
I believe ____
My worst fault ____
Drugs are ____
Women ____
Love ____
Sisters are ____
I regret ____
I was happiest when __________________________________
People ____
Therapy is ____
Men ____
Sex ____
At home ____
I miss ____
I think ____
Marriage ____
Brothers ____
A spouse ____
I think of myself as ___________________________________
My dreams ____

Therapies

INTRODUCTION
The therapies are the main activity
at the Sanatorium. The following
section contains detailed instructions and information on ten different therapies. There have been more
therapies offered at past Sanatoriums than those described here, and
it should be expected that other
therapies will be added in future editions of this manual, but those
selected here are meant to show the
diverse range of activities that
have become part of the Sanatorium's standard offerings.

At the moment of facilitating a
therapy, it's important to keep in
mind some of these tips:

1. In a therapeutic procedure, there
will be a channeling of energy and
consciousness. You are not *doing* the
channeling. You are *allowing* it to
happen.

2. Although it may appear that the
therapist is doing something *to* or
on someone, this is not the case.
The therapist is doing something
with the other person. This may
seem like a subtle different, but it is
essential to remember.

3. Judgment has no place in a therapy session. There is no right way to
do it, and there are no right answers.
Refrain from interpreting. Let the
patient find his or her own meaning.

4. Be kind, caring, and professional.

The Museum of Hypothetical Lifetimes

Number of participants: Individuals (On certain occasions couples have asked to do this therapy together. This is possible, although the intention of the therapy is to provide a space for autobiographical reflection.)
Time: Minimum 45 minutes, maximum 2 hours
Space size: 3.5×6m
Space requirements: Well-lit, silent, intimate
Furniture: Shelves, table, two chairs
Props: Architecture model, assorted small figures
Therapist qualifications: Basic

DESCRIPTION

This activity is centered on a scale model of a hypothetical museum, where each room or gallery represents a different part of your life. You are about to see your entire life as an exhibition, from the cradle to the grave, looking both prospectively and retrospectively at your past, present, and future.

On the shelves you will find a large collection of small objects and figures. They represent the widest selection possible of objects, people, animals, and symbols that we find in the world around us, or sometimes within our own imaginations.

Select objects from the shelves to illustrate each area of your life. Arrange the figures in the same way sculptures and paintings are arranged in a gallery. Your therapist plays the role of the museum's curator. If you wish, you can explain what you are doing as you go, or you may wait until the end. Therapists can explain how some galleries are supposed to be used, but remember that the rules are simple and you are the artist. Your vision is what counts.

THERAPIST INSTRUCTIONS

1. Greet and welcome the participant.
2. Explain the therapy and provide the participant with the laminated key.
3. Allow the participant to select objects.
4. If needed, explain the ways the galleries can be used.
5. Encourage the participant to share the stories of the museum he creates.
6. This therapy is appropriate for children as participants.
7. This therapy is not appropriate for blind visitors.
8. This therapy is appropriate for deaf visitors if accompanied by an interpreter to facilitate discussion with the therapist.

PARTICIPANT INSTRUCTIONS

1. Using the key provided, review the significance of the museum's galleries.
2. Select objects from the shelves that you feel represent your world. Place them in each of the galleries in the model museum.
3. You may explain your choices as you work or you may wait until the end to do so. When you have finished, the therapist will help you present your exhibition.

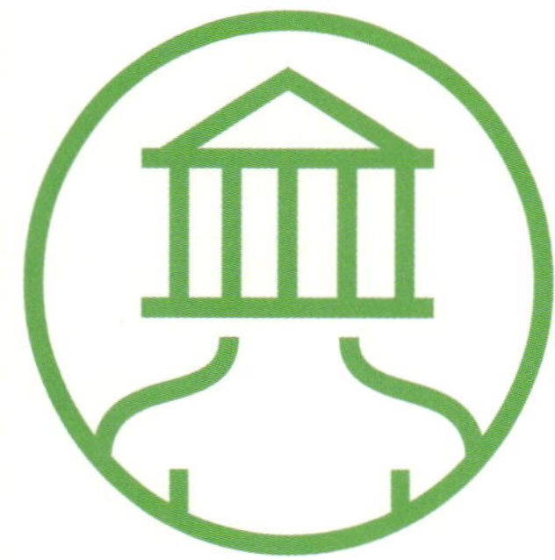

What is the Intention of this Therapy?

Artists, curators, and architects use models not only as an aid for design but also in a narrative way. When planning an exhibition it is very useful to have a model and small reproductions of artworks in order to plan what the experience of the visitor will be. We use models from a very early age. When children arrange their toys on the floor it helps them build a map of the world they live in. This is something that Dora Kalff pays special attention to. An accomplished professional pianist, she was also a neighbor of Carl Jung. Her children and Jung's grandchildren used to play together, and Jung encouraged her to explore her interest in children's psychological development. Noticing a correlation between the way children play arranging external objects in the sand and their own internal processes of the psyche led Kalff to the creation of sand tray therapy, also known as sandplay.[1]

Sandplay is a therapy that can be used with both adults and children, in which the patient plays in a sandbox with a wide range of small figures to which the subconscious attaches symbolic meaning. As the patient plays and organizes these objects and shapes, it creates a bridge between the conscious and the subconscious. Kalff says, "It becomes possible to break through the narrowing perspective of our bogged-down conception and fears and to find in play a new relationship to our own depth. Immersed in play, the person succeeds in making an inner picture visible. Thus a link is established between internal and external."[2]

While the sandbox is a *tabula rasa* where paths and topographies can be created at will, the Museum of Hypothetical Lifetimes has clearly defined spaces. These spaces are designed to tell a story and create feelings in ways similar to the proposals of Mexican architect Mathias Goertiz, co-founder with Luis Barragán of the emotional architecture movement. While the principle of "form follows function" is a hallmark of modern architecture, Goeritz declared a counter-manifesto: "form follows emotion." The emotional architecture movement places the person, rather than the design of an object or a building, at the center; it is the design of an experience. Goeritz and Barragan shared a key procedure: to resist the temptation to draw and to instead create a story, a narration to guide the design.

Goeritz, while building the Museo Experimental El Eco in Mexico City, used these principles and describes the space thus:

> The lot for the Eco is small, but the walls are seven to eleven meters tall, with a long hallway that narrows at the end (while the floor rises and the ceiling lowers) in attempt to cause the impression of greater depth. The wooden planks in the floor follow the same tendency, growing more and more narrow, finally ending in almost one point. At this endpoint of the hallway, visible from the entrance, a sculpture is planned to be placed: a shout, which will have its Echo in a grisaille mural of about 100 square meters, possibly derived from the very shadow of the sculpture, which should be created on the main wall of the great salon.[3]

The shrinking hallway ends in a great hall with a towering wall. These physical aspects were derived from a sequence of emotions; the narrowing corridor is the angst felt with the closing of one's throat, which leads to the monumental hall, a shout of catharsis so strong it was followed by an echo, the wall. Form follows emotion, emotion follows sensation. Here, architectural design is seen less as a diagram or a blueprint and more like the script of a film. The architect is the writer and the inhabitants are the moviegoers. A sort of storyboard can be made following the script, and from the storyboard comes the floor plan.

Following these ideas, I wanted to condition the meaning of spaces in the model of the Museum of Hypothetical Lifetimes, as I think most lives share a group of universal experiences. The model is roughly divided into four axes: Genealogy, Work, Education, and Love. This is an arbitrary arrangement and arguably an oversimplified vision of life, but simplifying this diagram helps the participant to avoid getting lost in the overwhelming task of doing an autobiographical sketch in forty-five minutes.

The first section, Genealogy, uses squares and circles, which are a convention in genograms and sociograms: circles for female relatives and squares for male relatives. Our lives begin before our birth, so grandparents and parents serve as an introduction to the "departure lobby" shaped like a pill, which we call the cradle. This interplay of lines and curves continues in the world of work (straight lines) and the world of love (curved lines).

Education is represented by a group of square spaces representing classrooms that grow in size as information and responsibility increase with time. As responsibility increases, the play space (or garden) starts to shrink, but on the right, perhaps caused by the shrinking of the play space, a space with sharp corners and irregular shapes starts to grow. It represents truancy, rock and roll, drugs, parties, and all the experiences of youth.

As we exit the years of education and move into the Work axis, we find a maze that represents the series of odd jobs that we do in an effort to discover which field of activity we want to concentrate on. A square follows that represents how we come to define ourselves. Some of us may want to fill this space with more than one object if we participate in more than one field of activity. Next is a smaller square for the activity that pays the bills, which may or may not have to do with our self-definition. Directly opposite, an open triangle stands for our legacy, what we will be remembered for, and following that is a space that widens in a stairstep pattern representing the steps we must take to advance our career and plans.

The last axis is Love, which begins with several incomplete circles in which to place exes and past relationships. This moves into a series of three large, connected ovals. The first is for the partner we choose to commit to, the second the process of settling down with that partner (moving in together, having children, getting married, buying a house, etc.), and the third represents the process of growing and aging with that person. As the first oval moves into the second, the narrow conjuncture is a crisis that usually occurs as we begin to settle down and fulfill our commitments to our partners.

Alongside the crisis, we see a pill-
shaped space to the side that is the
dilemma we face when trying to
balance our career with our family
— some of us decide to invest more
energy in work and postpone or
neglect family life, while others make
professional sacrifices in order to
care for our families.

In the third oval, a small opening
on the side stands for death, and a
larger opening, shaped like an in-
verted funnel, is what part of us will
live on through our descendents.
The last space, in between the Work
and Love axes and composed of a
combination of straight and curved
lines, is the key, where we can place
whatever might be the solution to
the dilemma or any other points of
conflict present in the museum.
It may be something that is missing
from our lives or something we
are striving for that will help us find
resolution.

1   Lois Carey, *Sandplay Therapy with Children and Families*
    (Lanham: Rowman & Littlefield, 1999).
2   Dora Kalff, "Introduction to Sandplay Therapy,"
    Journal of Sandplay Therapy 1, no.1 (1991).
3   Mathias Goeritz, *Manifiesto de la arquitectura emocional*, trans. Lacey Pipkin,
    1954, http://www.eleco.unam.mx/sitio/index.php/el-eco-contenido/manifesto

THERAPIST REPORT
Mathilde Fernandez, October 2012

I have very good memories of this therapy, as it is a very
intimate moment with the participant.

Some objects are chosen frequently: the image of
the mother, for example, or the transparent ball for
the offspring. The snail for death so that it arrives slowly.
The partner is generally difficult to define. An eighteen-
year-old girl chooses the pattern of the hand for acupuncture
for the partner, and when I ask why she replies that the
hand is easier to catch than the heart.

Grandmothers are angels or cakes for cooking.
The grandfathers are seashells or important characters.
Fathers are cars, motorcycles and minerals. Mothers are
pretty ceramic statues or an ostrich. The play-space is usually the tree, nature, and friends. The classroom is books
and pens. Personal experience, travel, alcohol, women,
death ... Broken hearts are aggressive animals, fish tails, or
representations of macho men. "Finding My Way" is
often the boat, the car accelerating, or again the snail.
"I am" is always different. "The Dilemma" is the hourglass.
The "Money Maker" varies; this is a strange subject.
Partner, labour, family, table, chairs, sofa, or something related to the community. Aging also relates to the community. The Key is meditation or writing a book. Death is
difficult. I've done the therapy myself, and I do not remember what I put for death. Maybe nothing at all, but as
time passed I asked myself over the last few days of the
Sanatorium what I could put to represent death. I chose the
Jamaican wristlet.

I remember the museum of Kim. Her mother was
an ostrich: very protective, very strong. She took Kim
everywhere during her childhood. Her father was absent:
a motorbike driving off. Her maternal grandmother was
cooking. The paternal grandmother was a diva aging badly;
she was unkind. The paternal grandfather was a small
stone; he did not matter so much. The cradle was nature.
Her playground was nature and her mother. School was
philosophy and books. She told stories of the heart: a
figurine of a man that looks like Michael Jackson, with a

red jacket and long hair, looking like he was walking outside the lines.

She couldn't see herself with children or with any particular partner. She replaced the Family with the community; she would like a castle in the center of France, lost in nature, a castle with her friends. With her Career, everything went very fast. She was hired as a lawyer just before she graduated from her studies in law and philosophy. Now, her boss wanted her to try to work less. First she chose time for her Dilemma, but later she replaced it with a mini plastic nuclear station, explaining that she defends a business related to pollution that has interests in the nuclear field.

She felt responsibility, thinking of her values and her cradle close to nature. She said that she was studying philosophy and analyzed everything. She put a book in the Legacy box and also in the Key: she wanted to write book about what she sees and what disturbs her.

THERAPIST REPORT
Gloria Maso, August 2012

I was always eager to give the Museum therapy, even though people often chose the same objects to signify the same things: the mermaid of Copenhagen for the Mother, the heavy brain for Education, the most unidentified objects for the Dilemma. I preferred when people went a little further, making combinations: the green Frankenstein in the empty cube for old age. But what I enjoyed most was being invited into people's lives and listening to their stories.

At the beginning of the therapy I left participants alone to choose the objects comfortably. I thought that my presence might keep them from taking their time to choose. I would come back after fifteen minutes and have them guide me through their exhibit. Some asked for my interpretation (I hated doing that, feeling phony). Some didn't want to give any explanation, truly satisfied with their private reflection, keeping the reasons for their choices to themselves.

I quickly found that the most efficient and interesting way to proceed in the museum therapy was to start by going through the meanings of the rooms on the model while the participant followed with the booklet. Then, with a large gesture indicating the three shelves along the walls, I introduced the objects:

"All these objects are at your disposal to signify people, events and memories from your life. They can give shape to any person or gesture, or even thoughts yet to occur. I suggest you inspect the collection [I would walk the participant closer to the shelves] without looking for anything special. Just grab the objects that catch your eye and we'll figure out what to do with them together."

When a person left a room empty, I always wondered if it was for lack of inspiration, bashfulness, or perplexity. I didn't ask them to fill the whole museum. I even encouraged them to leave blanks if they couldn't find a suitable object for their idea.

Some participants told me there were objects the museum was missing and needed: a plastic lobster, a small camera, a miniature book, a pen or pencil, a living plant in a pot, and a mountain. They also asked, "How did you collect these objects? Where do you get them? Are they part of the artist's personal collection or did he choose them all for this piece? Do the objects vary depending on where you are showing the piece?"

One man asked me about the corridors, the non-spaces that have no assigned meaning. We decided they were storage rooms or emergency exits. He filled them up, too, as alternatives to the objects in the officially significant rooms, with the shepherd (tall enough to look over the wall of Legacy) and the sailboat (just in case, on the way to the Key).

The stone penis disappeared from the shelves one day. I missed it, as it was a strong object with a certain weight in your hand. People who chose it often held it for a while before placing it in the model.

A sixty-year-old woman made it the Key of her life, along with the acupuncture hand and the Buddha. She told me masturbation made her serene and powerful. She had had lung cancer (plastic lungs jammed into the Dilemma room, upside down), a husband she had married only to have children (a lonely pint of beer), suicidal grandparents (doll chairs) and a rigorous education (filled with musical instruments). She now owns several houses and is wealthy enough to care for her handicapped child on her own, living a reclusive life in the mountains with a pack of dogs.

Another memorable museum belonged to a young man with a charming face, blue eyes, and light cotton pants. He interested me at first glance. But his way of going through therapy was also captivating. Spontaneous and excited by all the possibilities, he gathered dozens of objects for each room, creating carefully balanced compositions. He gave me his permission to take pictures and video while he continued his constructions. I taped his entire explanation. As he told me his tale, he added depth and precision with a new object, or repositioning the object in the room itself. His grandfather (a standing wooden figure with no arms) died of too much drinking (he knocked him down with the bottle).

At some point he gathered all the remaining objects in reach and poured them into the last stage of Education: "That's what studying art looks like," he said, pointing at the jumble of stuff.

THERAPIST REPORT
Sylvain Bourdoux, July 2012

During the Museum of Hypothetical Lifetimes therapy, participants see their lives as exhibitions. They have a multitude of small objects at their disposal. I noticed that many objects symbolized the European, Asian, and American continents, but none conveyed images directly connected with Sub-Saharan Africa. I bought a bracelet made of the colors of Africa from the stand of a Kenyan woman in Kassel. This new object has taken its place among the others at the Museum of Hypothetical Lifetimes.[1]

1   NOTE FROM PEDRO REYES: After Documenta 13 this therapist suggested a new guideline for the Museum of Hypothetical Lifetimes. Any donated object is welcome and should be placed on the shelves with the rest of the items.

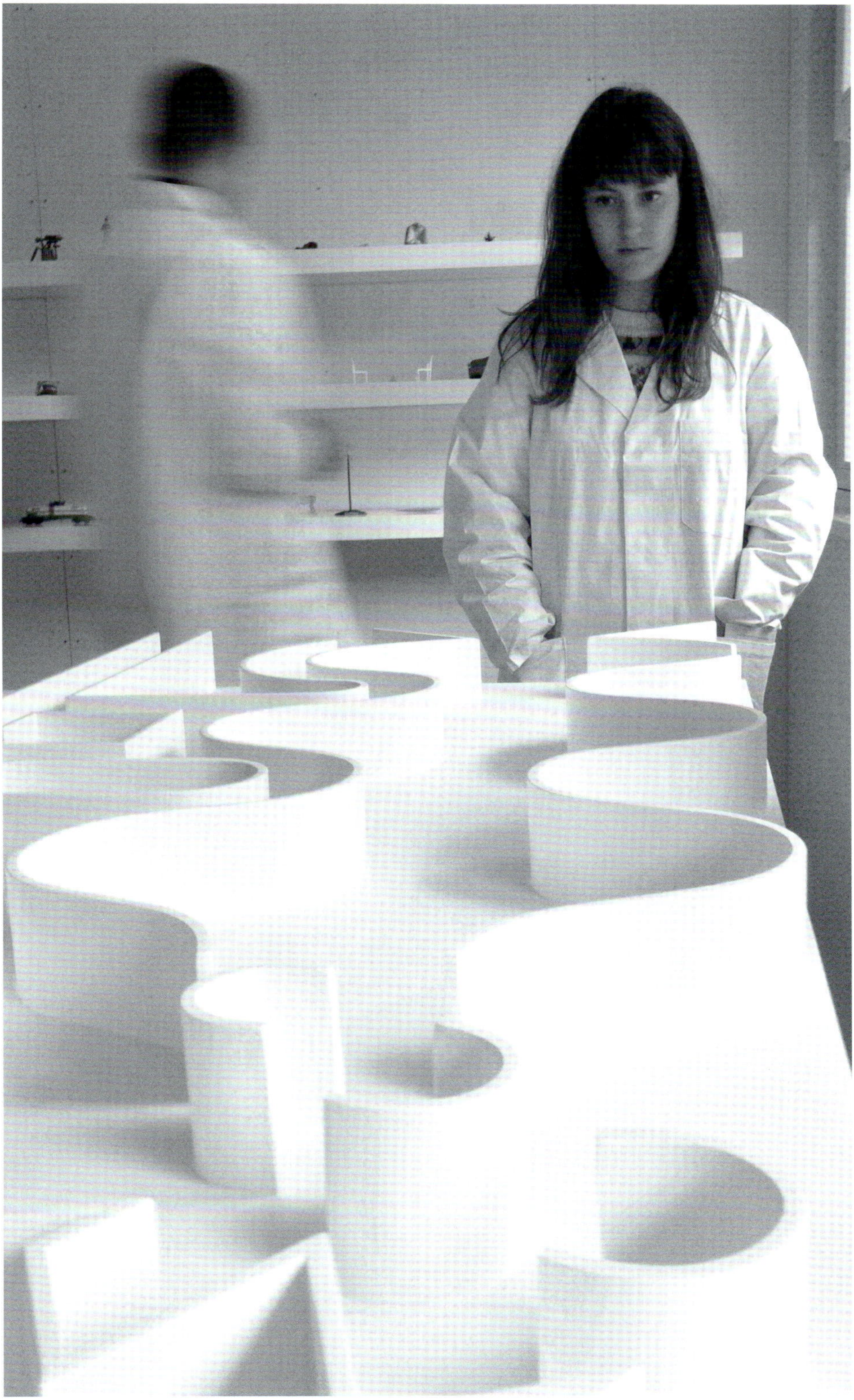

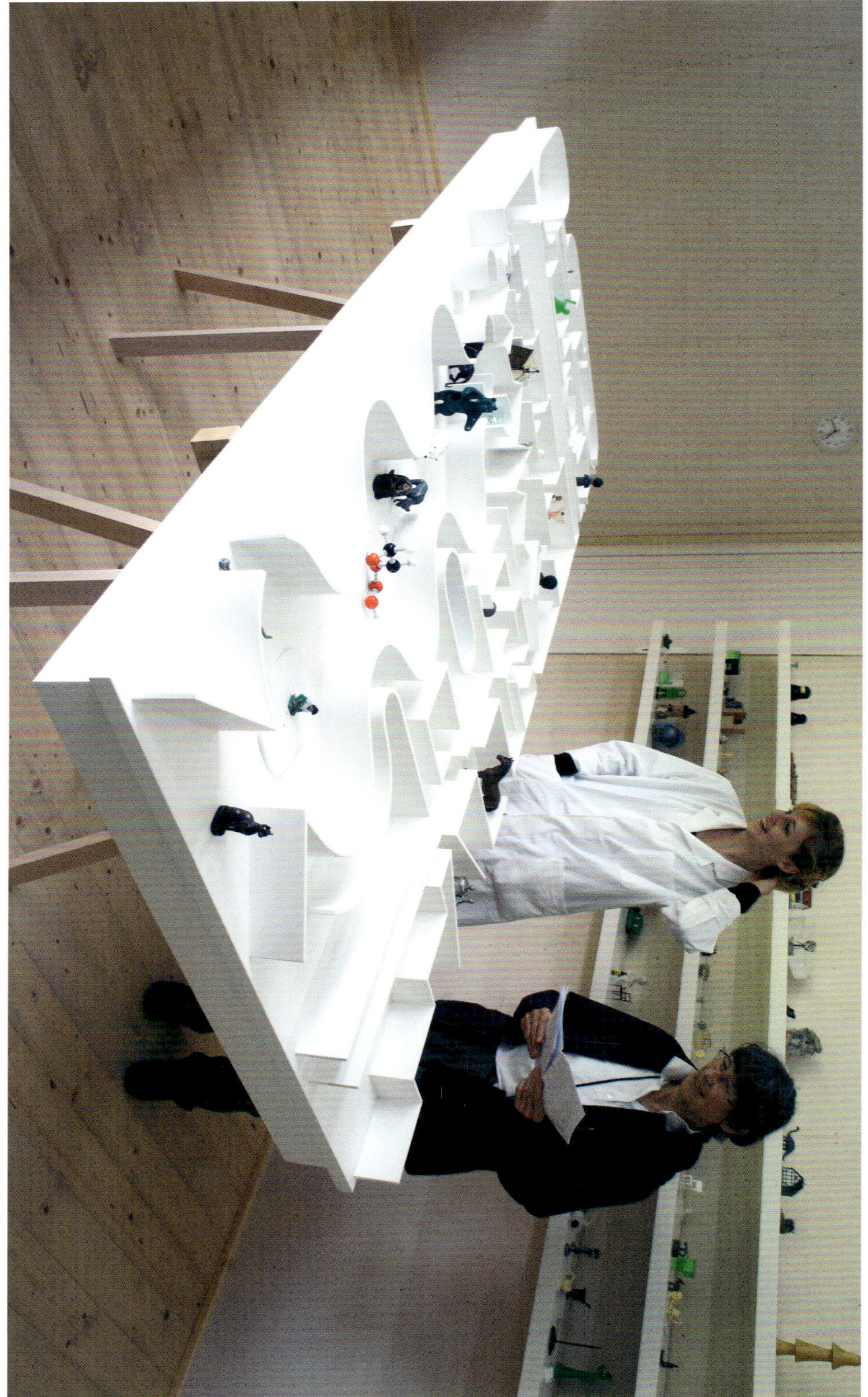

Vaccine against Violence

Number of participants: Individuals
Time: 15 minutes
Space size: Minimum 3×3m
Space requirements: It is convenient to split this space in two sections. The antechamber, where the balloons and markers are, must have enough light for the participant to draw on the balloon, while the chamber will be darker. As people shout during this activity, it is recommended to soundproof the room or locate it far from other therapies. The dummy will hang from the roof or walls, so it is necessary to have special hooks installed for this purpose.
Furniture: A small table
Props: A full-body dummy on a stand, balloons, permanent markers, sugar pills (placebos), placebo pill bottles,
foam to insulate the space, hooks for hanging the dummy
Therapist qualifications: Basic

DESCRIPTION

This is a cathartic procedure. Your therapist will ask you to blow up a balloon and draw on it the face of the person who has hurt you the most in your life. After doing so, you will place the balloon on top of a punching bag shaped as a headless dummy. Your therapist will encourage you to hit the dummy, yell at it, tell this person why you hate them so much and how he or she did you wrong. Get even with the dummy; punch it until the balloon bursts. At the end you will be given a sugar pill, a placebo that is your "Vaccine against Violence."[1]

In our minds a symbolic act has the equivalent power of a real act. Consequently, the symbolic destruction of a person may free us from the drive to act against that person in real life.[2]

This therapy aims to make real acts of violence redundant, to free the subject from long-standing hatred.

THERAPIST INSTRUCTIONS

1. Greet and welcome the participant.
2. Explain the therapy.
3. Help the participant with the props and ask her to draw the face of someone who has hurt her on the balloon.
4. Encourage the participant to explain why he or she hates the person chosen and how that person caused hurt.
5. Once the balloon bursts give the participant a placebo pill; this is the "Vaccine against Violence."
6. This therapy is appropriate for children as participants.
7. Blind visitors will need assistance drawing faces or writing on the balloons, as well as orientation so they can hit they dummy.
8. This therapy is appropriate for deaf visitors if they are provided written instructions or accompanied by an interpreter to facilitate discussion with therapists.

PARTICIPANT INSTRUCTIONS

1. Take a balloon and blow it up.
2. Draw a face on the balloon representing the person who has hurt you most in your life.
3. Tell the dummy why you hate it so much and how much you were hurt.
4. Get even by hitting the dummy until the balloon bursts.
5. When finished, swallow the sugar pill you are given. It is a placebo that is your Vaccine against Violence.

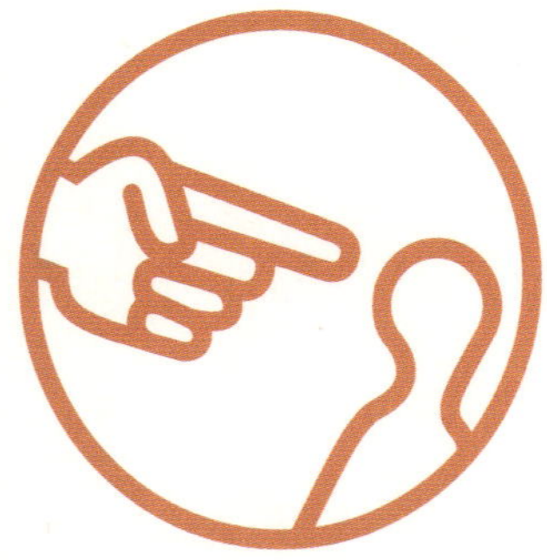

1. This therapy was originally created by Antanas Mockus, the Colombian mathematician and mayor of Bogotá from 1995 to 1997 and again from 2001 to 2003.
2. From a conversation between Pedro Reyes and Raphael Montañez Ortiz, New Jersey, 2011.

What is the Intention of this Therapy?

Antanas Mockus, a mathematician and former mayor of Bogotá, created the Vaccine against Violence to address the issue of family violence during his administration. The following is a transcript of a conversation in which we discussed the origin and development of the therapy.

<u>Pedro Reyes:</u> Can you tell me about how you created Vaccine against Violence?

<u>Anatanas Mockus:</u> The idea for the Vaccine against Violence came about after I read a newspaper article about intrafamily violence. Shortly after I read the article, I met with a psychiatrist and was convinced that although violence has many many causes, the main cause is intrafamily violence. Therefore, if you could only do one thing to reduce the level of violence in any society, it would be to stop the violence trickling down to younger generations.

I invited psychiatrists to a meeting, and over two or three days I asked them to give me information such as the number of children needing professional attention after being victims of intrafamily violence. Astonishingly, the figure was as high as 600,000. There are not enough psychiatrists to treat them all. It was then that we knew that we had to do something different.

Inspiration for the actual vaccine therapy came from a public event called *Años Viejos* (Old years) on New Years Eve, in which people fabricate figures (normally someone unpopular) that are then stuffed with fireworks and burned. At the meeting with the psychiatrists, we made our own Años Viejos, dressed them up with balloons inside, and danced with the figures. It was very entertaining because at any moment the balloon could explode! I wondered how we could use this mechanism to allow people to express feelings of being hurt. The psychiatrists came up with a very good idea; they suggested using the balloon as a head and drawing the face of the aggressor on it.

After the festivities were over, we thought we would give it a try. We asked a twelve-year-old boy, who also happened to be the son of a policeman, to come and test the first Vaccine against Violence. He began to speak and confessed that the worst thing that had happened in his life was that his father hit him. Next, he drew the face of his father, the eyes, the nose and so on, onto the balloon. The psychiatrist instructed the boy to say and do whatever he wanted to the dummy. The child had so much anger that I thought he was going to pop his father's head. I actually tried to stop him, but the psychiatrist took my hand and said into my ear, "Sometimes you have to take sides. You cannot remain neutral." The boy did pop the balloon, after which he was a little bit shaken. The psychiatrist assured him that he has not done anything bad and had not hurt his real father. She told him "It's not your father's body," lessening the boy's feelings of guilt.

After our trial we constructed the whole procedure. We prepared for three or four weeks, gathering with the psychiatrics and psychologists and performing a sort of self-training. The first Vaccine was done with an NGO that fought against intrafamily violence. We were enthusiastic; the first Vaccine had 15,000 participants. We used a small space and the procedure was individual. At the end of that Vaccine, the psychiatrists were absolutely exhausted. There was at least one case where the person was so hurt that he shouted, "This is the reason why I killed you!" There were four members of a family there, the entire family, and the father took the hand of one of his children and showed us a scar, saying, "Please cure us from this." So the medical treatment of violence involved in the procedure was to help people seek help for getting it out, for getting rid of violence. I myself did the Vaccine three times, two of the three times with cameras filming. In the first one I remembered a professor, a schoolteacher. I used to wear short pants, and there were only one or two boys with short pants. The teacher made us stand in front of the other students and began to hurt us with his keychain. Another time I remembered an argument between my mother and me. I didn't pop the balloon of course, but I was verbally agressive. But the third time I decided I could not repeat what I had remembered, so I searched my memory and discovered something that I had never told anyone, not my girlfriends or professors, not my parents or friends. It was in an art gallery on a Sunday; the proprietor of the gallery was a friend of my mother, who is a sculptor, so she had also a sort of professional relationship with him. The gallery was closed, but he took me to a room and said he wanted to teach me some wrestling positions. He didn't take off my clothes, but the thing was so strange that I never told anyone about it, in part because I had no language to explain it; at that age you don't have the words. So at the moment of the Vaccine I said his name (not his surname) and

I was very aggressive, hitting the balloon, and I shouted, "If you like men, look for adults, not children, never children."

At first I didn't want to give placebo pills to the people that came to the Vaccine, but there are studies that show people believe a lot more in the vaccination when they received the placebo. The first time we distributed it, it was really successful, and we also gave the people who came a paper printed with information about institutions that help with intrafamily violence. So we told people, if you feel the need, you can go to this institution for help, like a special offer. We used the intensity of people's reaction during the Vaccine as a screening device to refer people to anger management programs.

PR: Screening to identify the people that needed specialized help.

AM: In medicine that has a special name: triage. So we were doing a sort of triage, and about ten percent of the people were invited not only to receive the paper but to actually make an appointment.

The second time there were 30,000 people, a diverse range of people. We also offered a Vaccine by telephone. It was nothing complex; it was just my voice saying, "Thank you for participating in this journey against violence. Who is the person who has most wounded or offended you? If you were to meet with this person, what would you say? After the beep, say what you would say to him." We received about 400 calls, and in many cases at the end of the message people said thank you — to a machine!

PR: You made a recording of those?

AM: Yes, and we made a transcription. But we did not answer the calls. What is amazing is how the Vaccine has been replicated. In a small town of 10,000 inhabitants, 100 km from Bogotá, a single employee of the health system said, "I can do something like that." First, he went to the official medical institute, and the statistics showed that this particular municipality was the most violent in terms of homicides per each 100,000 inhabitants. He published this fact in the local newspaper, that his municipality was the most violent. He began to do a variation of the vaccination, having people write on a piece of paper what had happened in the past that was wrong, and they made a pile of the papers to burn. In a town of 10,000 inhabitants he performed Vaccine on around 5,000 people, half of the municipality. And some of my team members have done the Vaccine in other cities in Latin America, and the psychiatrist that has been helping me had been doing it on a smaller scale in Venezuela, too, so it has circulated.

§

In 2004 I did a piece called Instant Rockstar in which participants were invited to choose a rock song and perform it, playing a surrogate guitar. Each act ends with the cathartic ritual of smashing the prop guitar. This work was partially inspired by Rafael Montañez Ortiz's performances from the 1950s, in which he destroyed pianos with an axe as part of the Destruction in Art movement.

Ralph's performances had previously inspired applications in the field of therapy, such as Primal Scream, as its creator Arthur Janov describes in his 1970 book *The Primal Scream*. In 2011 I spoke with Montañez Ortiz about violence and catharsis; below is a transcript of our conversation.

Pedro Reyes: Why do you think that we need to express, or experience, some violence in our lives?

Rafael Montañez Ortiz: In a sense what you're referring to is the early brain, because our brain architecture is sort of like a ship that builds itself in the ocean, hopefully without sinking. The brain rebuilds itself, with the exception of the previous fifteen models of hominids, which have all exterminated each other. We're on the sixteenth model and hopefully we'll overcome this ancient brain, which is where the chimpanzee begins. Chimpanzees are not these funny little things with diapers on TV, smoking cigars or playing poker. They're savage beasts, they rip each other apart, they're horrible, they're gang bangers from the beginning of civilization. Later on, we build on that, whether it be australopithecine, archaic sapiens, sapiens-sapiens, and in 180,000 years we haven't done much more in terms of our cognitive potential. So within that framework you get a sense of the savage, barbaric potential that we have; it's there built into our architecture. You can see how around the world a culture can focus the whole cultural process and cognition around that architecture. You have some cultures that focus themselves on this ancient architecture, and so they have this ancient cognitiveness, this ancient primalness about the way they solve things. Our culture — a lot of our culture — has the ancient brain. So if we're wondering why we are so savage, how can we be so barbaric, the answer is simple: our culture has opened that possibility and cognition to us.

PR: This reminds me of what you mention in your manifestos as the need for fulfilling that "unconscious integrity." So certainly, within these different architectures, some of them, like the most primitive ones, call for some violence and cruelty in our lives.

RMO: Yes, but it must be displaced in terms of object. In other words, to be conscious of it you have to displace it, you have to take it somewhere where they're objects. It's sort of like play therapy; instead of the children burning the parents' house down, they make little fires and start understanding their relationship to fire and how to control it. It's like the notion of moving from human sacrifice to flowers and butterflies. I believe this very important transition happened in Mexico.

PR: Yes, "Las guerras floridas," wars that were fought by the Aztecs without having to kill people, using non-lethal weapons like sticks and whips. It's like the ancient version of paintball. In some ways, this tradition of symbolic violence has been replicated up to the present. The best example of it was the Zapatistas, who in 1994 had an uprising where they were carrying rifles made of sticks and wood. This proved to be a much more effective form of warfare because the media really caught onto the asymmetry between them and the Mexican army. What I find fascinating is that, for the mind, a symbolic act has the same weight as a real act. So if you have a space where you can kill someone symbolically that might actually prevent you from having to go and kill that person in real life. This is the premise used by Antanas Mockus in Bogotá when he created the Vaccine against Violence.

RMO: Yes, but there has to be introspection, lucid intellect involved in the process. In other words, if the catharsis happens for its own sake, it reinforces the object of catharsis and empathy doesn't occur. You have to have a lucid, introspective, intellectual involvement and say, this is one of my potentials in terms of my human development over this period of evolution over millions of years. There are new ways of reconciling, like you said, even beyond the notion of the paint guns. We can fence with words and language; we can argue. There's a more civilized framework within which we can do all of this. So it's not just simply a question of opening up an arena where everybody can run in and destroy pianos, furniture, and whatever else. There has to be some introspective insight that is more civil than people beating each other up. Because that's the ancient brain, that's the chimpanzee in us.

PR: Freud once said, "The first man who said an insult instead of throwing a rock was the founder of civilization." How did you start to organize your ideas around the idea of symbolic violence?

<u>RMO:</u> The whole organizing aesthetic framework for it came out of my MFA thesis around 1958, where I had to sit down and really think, "What am I doing?" I'd read a lot of anthropology, psychology, and sociology. I did special research into the ancient shamanic rituals — Frazer's *The Golden Bough* (1890) is one of my strong influences. They explain how some cultures moved away from the idea of needing more flesh and blood for reconciliation and instead end up simply cutting down a tree. Finally the notion of moving from killing a human being to killing a chicken is a radical leap, a kind of more civilized notion of redemption within that primitive cognitiveness. In my thesis I recognize that artists were spending all of their time within certain moral or ethical issues — issues of constructing things. But the real critical issue as I saw it was destruction. It seemed to be that kind of razor's edge upon which civilization maintains balance.

THERAPIST REPORT
Anastasia Bruelle, June 2012

Since the beginning of her stay in Kassel, Christina had problems sleeping. She had really bad nightmares every night. She changed her bed's position so it pointed north, as some people suggested, but it didn't really help. The first night she might have felt a little better becase she thought the change would be helpful. It was sort of a placebo effect; it worked because she believed it would. But after that night the bad dreams recurred. She couldn't get any rest, so she was looking for something that could help her and made the decision to do this therapy, just to try. She was well aware that therapy was a symbolic proposal, that it made no promises. She chose to play the game, to project her feelings and to fight against the dummy. I don't re-member what she drew on the balloon, but she popped it. Her nightmares didn't come back.

Sophie came to ask for an appointment; she wanted to do therapy and told me that she had serious psychological problems. I laughed. She insisted and said that she was followed to the Sanatorium by a doctor and really needed to do a therapy. I changed the look on my face, becoming solemn, and asked her to wait for a therapist. During this time I began to reflect on the role of belief in this project. To what extent do people commit their level of belief? What had started as a joke to me became serious. I decided to do the Vaccine against Violence therapy with her. I ex-plained the process and left her alone in the room. I was waiting outside. She started to scream, to talk to herself, and to beat the dummy. I heard the ballon pop and entered in the room with apprehension. Her eyes were full of tears and her whole body was shaking, especially her hands. Sophie looked very uncomfortable. She wanted to leave the room as soon as possible. I proposed a glass of water and asked her whom she had drawn on her balloon. It was her boss. He was the reason for her problems, so she killed him and left.

Dirck didn't know what to draw. He found it very difficult to think about someone in a negative way and told me, "I don't hate anybody." I commented that it was true, to hate is a very strong negative feeling, but it could be someone who hurt you some time in the past. After thinking for three minutes, Dirck decided to put himself on his balloon. He told me that the face on the balloon represented his dark side. In front of the doll, he felt helpless. It was hard for him to make the decision to hit it, to hit himself. Eventually, he did it, feeling that he could only blame himself.

On her first day at Documenta, during the group therapy Frauke shared her feelings. She was frustrated because in the morning she had seen some violent art videos, and she felt disturbed by them all day. When the group therapy finished I diagnosed her and decided to propose the Vaccine. Frauke came in the room, saw the dummy, and started to feel afraid. I insisted on one thing: this therapy seems violent in the first stage of the reading, but it's important to start at a negative point, to go through the process and to finish on something positive. She blew up the balloon but didn't know how to proceed. I told her to think about something abstract, like an idea, and to consider the balloon not like a head but like a round space where negativity is concentrated. She did, and after the therapy she felt much better. She commented that it would be preferable if the dummy didn't look so human, with the figure of a person. It would be more open to abstract ideas.

THERAPIST REPORTS
Mathilde Fernandez, October 2012

Something strange happened when we arrived in Kassel.
We were accommodated in an ex-hospital that had still
been functioning as a children's hospital just two months
before. The strange thing is that a very large number of
students, including myself, had nightmares and slept
restlessly. I had very violent, vivid nightmares every night.
I remembered them in detail, dreams where I was killing
people, dreams where I was killed. I woke up every morning with aches and pains from being so tense as I slept.
Among the bizarre characters from my dreams was a friend
I'd had a few years ago, to whom I no longer speak.
I dreamed of her two or three times a week, and it was
very disturbing. I was violent with her. I broke glass
bottles on her head. I humiliated her and forced her
to pick up the crumbs under the dinner table. Once she
jumped on me, insulting me with hurtful remarks.
The more she appeared in my dreams, the more I thought
about and hated her during the day. I decided to do
Vaccine against Violence. I had never directly tested this
therapy, but I activated it as a therapist twice during
the time I worked. I felt relatively comfortable with this
therapy. I started the therapy as a participant, so I drew
the friend's face on the balloon. My therapist told me
I should do what the ritual requires. So, plunged into darkness, I pushed her face into the ground and hit her.
I made a final kick like in Quentin Tarantino's film *Death
Proof.* Then I took my placebo pills and returned to
work. She never came back to me.

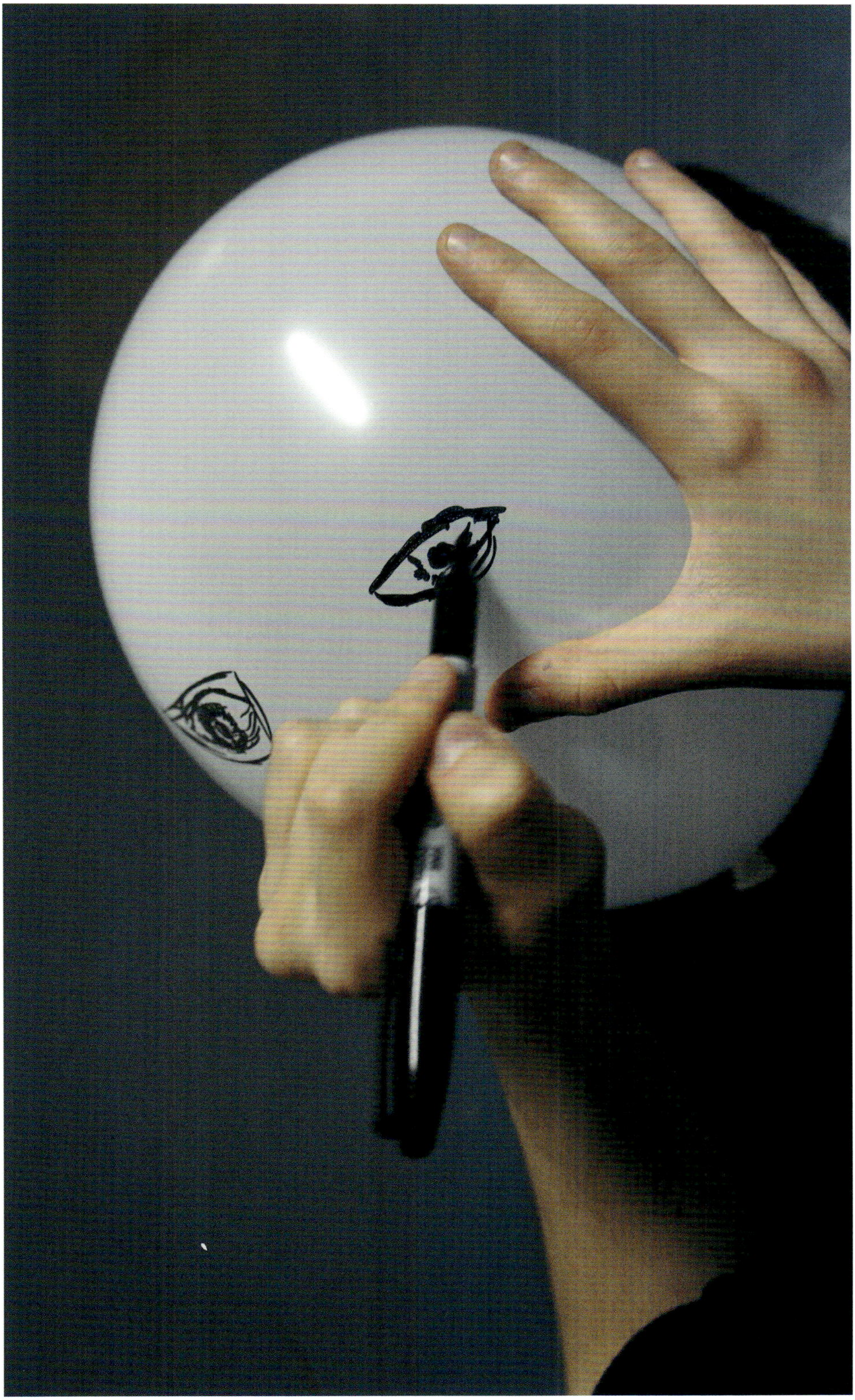

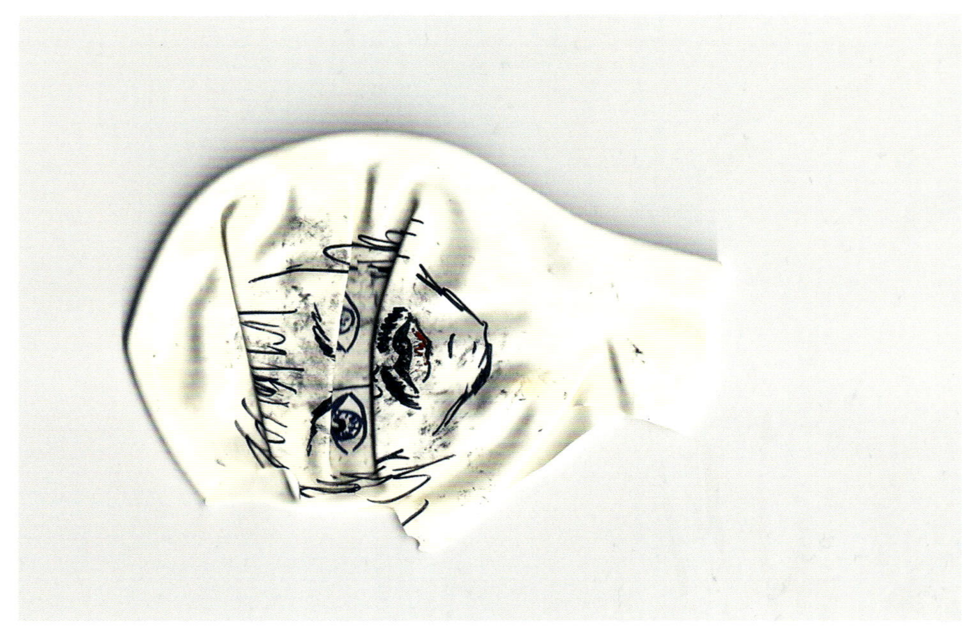

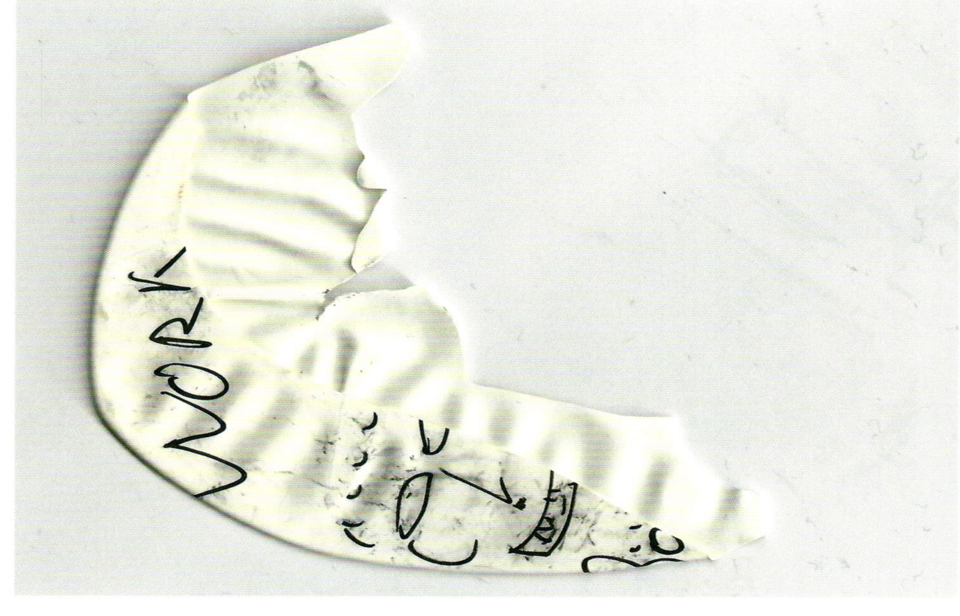
WORK

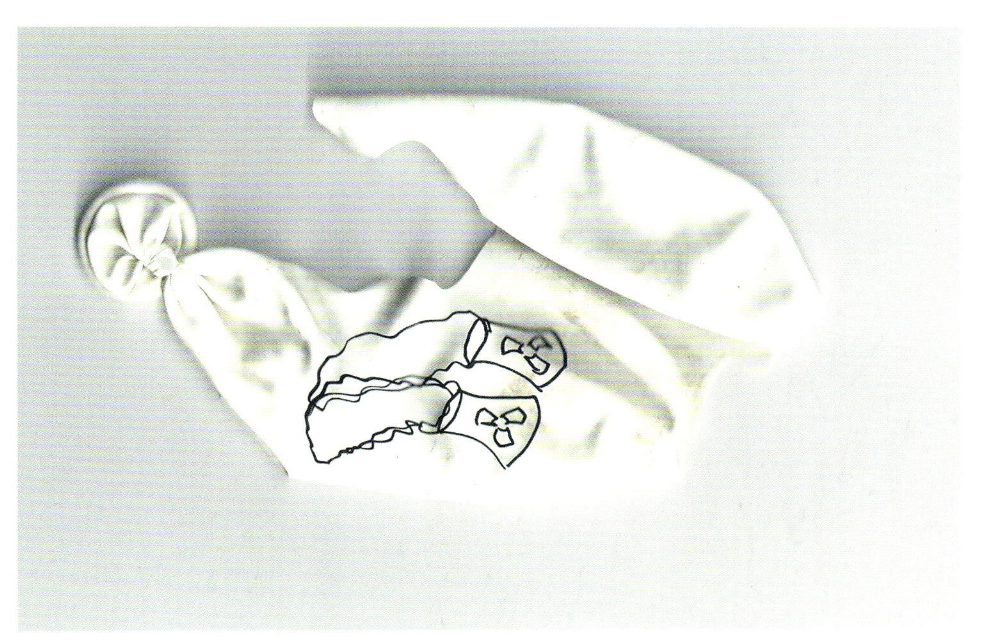
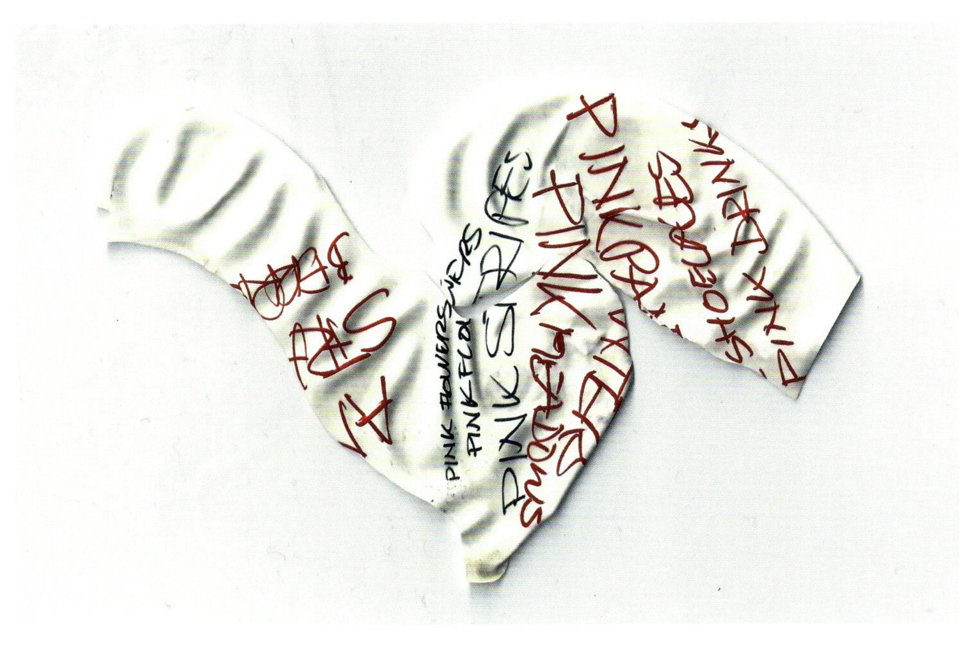

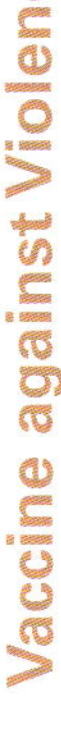

   Vaccine against Violence

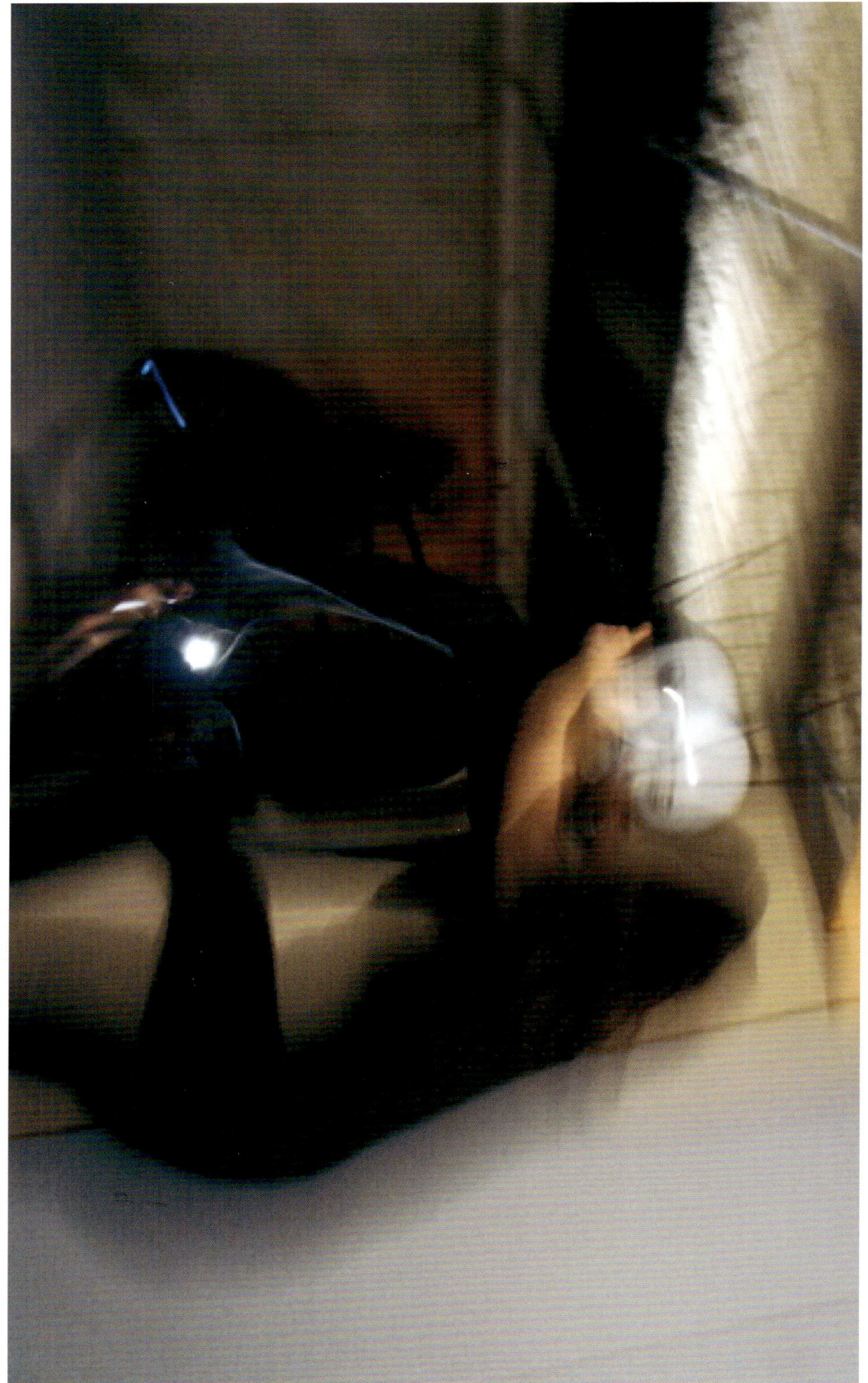

Goodoo

Number of participants: Individuals
Time: 30—40 minutes
Space size: Minimum 2.50×2.50m
Space requirements: This is a very intimate therapy where
participants often cry. We have learned it is better if this space
does not have windows where the participant can be seen by
other people. If the room has windows they must have curtains
that can be drawn. It is important that the table area is well lit.
Furniture: Shelves, table, two chairs
Props: Generic dolls made in advance, small objects or charms
representing a wide range of meanings (see List of Charms for
examples), sewing materials, superglue, wire, pliers
Therapist qualifications: Basic

DESCRIPTION

In popular culture, the voodoo doll
is a surrogate for an intended target
of sorcery. This therapy is a positive
iteration of this doll, thus called
"Goodoo." Here we take a generic
cloth doll and personalize it using
diverse materials.

Think of a person for whom you
would like to do good. Then choose
five lucky charms or tokens that you
will place on different parts of the
Goodoo doll. Think about the meaning of the objects in relation to the
body. For instance, a key on the head
may mean that you wish for the person to open his or her mind or find
a solution, while putting the key on
the hand may mean the person will
open doors, perhaps finding a new
home or job. Objects have different
meanings for each person, so you
must do what feels right to you. Once
you have selected and placed the five
objects, your therapist will help you
attach them to the doll, and at the
end you will "switch on" each spot.
Close your eyes and press each point,
focusing your positive energy there.

Imagine that every time you switch
on these spots they will have an
effect on the real person. Now the
Goodoo doll is working. Take it with
you. You can show it to the person
for whom it was intended.

THERAPIST INSTRUCTIONS

1. Greet and welcome the participant.
2. Explain the therapy.
3. Show the participant the demo
doll with examples.
4. If needed, help the participant
attach the objects to the doll. Make
certain that each object is securely
attached and will not fall off of the
doll, using wire, pliers, or superglue
as needed.
5. Allow the participant to explain
the meaning of the doll.
6. Invite the participant to put a hand
on the doll to fill it with good energy.
7. Once finished remind them the
Goodoo is always working.
8. This therapy is appropriate for
children as participants.
9. Blind visitors will need assistance
choosing different materials
(therapists should describe materials
to them) and making a doll (therapists
will need to do the gluing and sewing).
10. This therapy is appropriate for
deaf visitors if accompanied by an
interpreter to facilitate discussion
with the therapists.

PARTICIPANT INSTRUCTIONS

1. Choose a Goodoo doll from the
stack.
2. Take a moment to think of
someone for whom you would like
to do good. It can be yourself.
3. Choose five objects to decorate
your Goodoo doll. Think about what
they mean and where they belong
on the doll's body.
4. Attach them securely to the doll.
Make sure the doll is exactly as you
want it to be.
5. Explain the meaning of the items
you have chosen.
6. Press each point and concentrate
on its meaning to "activate" it.
7. When finished take the doll with
you and remember: it's always
working. If at any moment you feel
that the doll has lost its power, press
the points again while focusing on
the good they are doing. This will
"recharge" your doll.

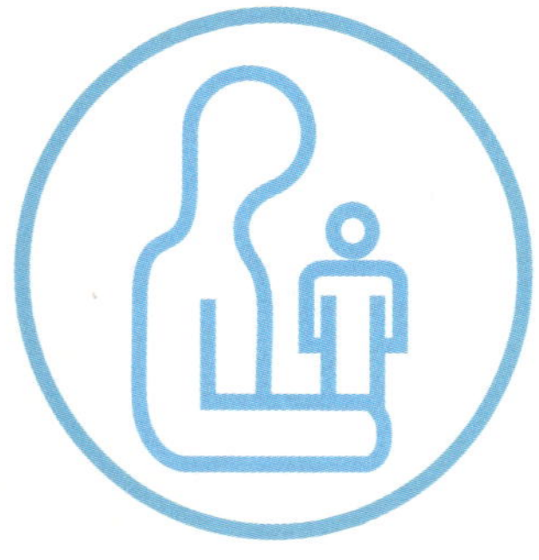

What is the Intention of this Therapy?

The use of dolls — inanimate representations of human beings, animals or imaginary characters — is widespread, timeless and ageless. Dolls are found wherever people are present, and their use is not limited to children. When we are young dolls, are considered toys to be played with; they are babies we pretend to care for, puppets or figures we use to role-play, or companions in our daily activities. Adults use dolls in entirely different ways — often giving them new names in attempt to distinguish them from toys. We enshrine them as saints to be worshipped, we create displays of them in store windows, we burn them as effigies, we travel thousands of miles to kneel in front of them, and we put them in museums once the culture they belong to has become (or is close to becoming) extinct.

The Goodoo doll in this therapy draws on many different traditions of using dolls to express our desires for others, or perhaps for ourselves. The name "goodoo" is a play on the concept of the voodoo doll as it has been portrayed in popular culture over the past century. Here it is important to note that Goodoo uses dolls and charms for their symbolic significance and does not contend that they are anything more. It references the great power of dolls and symbols considered sacred in many religious traditions, with no intent to disparage these traditions, which are excellent examples of the power of symbols as places of pilgrimage.

Here we are "casting a spell" on the person the doll represents, drawing on examples of this kind of sorcery from all over the world, from ancient Africa to medieval Europe to the United States in the twentieth century. Wherever they are practiced, the power of these spells lies in induced autosuggestions, a phenomenon suggesting that when a person is repeatedly told a statement, either by someone else or by that person himself, regardless of its accuracy he begins to believe it. An example would be if someone is repeatedly told that she is clumsy, eventually she begins to knock things over. If someone who is insecure repeats to himself that he is worthy of love and affection, he is more likely to overcome self-doubt. For a spell to have power, its object must be aware of the spell as well as its intention. This is why we encourage visitors to show their dolls to the objects of their Goodoo, but often the process of the therapy itself is enough to create reconciliation within the person present, as is evident in the therapist report from Tereneh Mosely, found in the following pages.

The origins of the symbols are found in the popular tradition of milagritos in Mexico and Latin America. These are small metal charms, often in the form of body parts, that practitioners pin to a wooden object such as a cross or to the robe of a saint to whom they pray. The charms represent a specific desire or petition: a charm in the shape of a leg could refer to a prayer to help someone recover from an injury. A pair of eyes might represent a prayer to heal someone's eyesight, or it might refer to a wish for a saint to watch over him. The intention of the charm is defined by each person.

Just as in the Museum of Hypothetical Lifetimes, the objects uncover mental associations that otherwise would remain hidden; for this reason the therapy must offer a wide variety of charms, tokens, miniature toys, and decorations to choose from. As the intent is always to cause good, these objects should be selected to trigger positive associations. For instance, figures such as guns or flies should be avoided.

The Goodoo doll is a virtual body that stands for someone in the real world who might be known or unknown to the visitor. Some visitors choose to make dolls for themselves. The many possibilities of the virtual body are exemplified by a visitor who wanted her Goodoo doll to represent all of humanity. She pinned to the doll her wishes for every person in the world. She placed an elephant on the doll's shoulder, calling to mind both the strength of the animal itself and the need for us to be strong to shoulder heavy burdens. A light bulb was a crown on the doll's head for enlightenment. A shaft of wheat on the belly stood for her desire for everyone to have enough food to eat.

The last step in the therapy, the "switching on" of the points, recalls the healing practice of the "laying on of hands" in many religions and forms of alternative treatment, in which placing the hands on different parts of the body is believed to allow the healer to channel the flow of energy to cure illness and address emotional traumas. So we perform a sort of acupressure on the virtual body to complete the therapy.

LIST OF CHARMS

Broom	Lollipop	Flower
Mug	Bible	Pig
Flowerpot	Large bottle	Shoe
Watering can	Mask	Pliers
Mirror	Candy	Scissors
Humming bird	Palm fan	Hammer
Sun	Wheat	Jug
Moon	Corn	Potato masher
Virgin	Garlic	Sieve
Pigeon	Egg	Pestle and mortar
Cross	Onion	Cheese grater
Arm	Bread	Bucket
Hand	Basket	Doughnut
Foot	Eyes	Medal
Leg	Glass bottle	Saint Judas
Shell	Stone	Skull
Light bulb	Candle	Scrubbing brush
Bell	Comb	Coin
Star	Tree trunk	Jewel
Key	Coffee cup	Popsicle
Plate of food	Heart	Wicker basket
White dove	Elephant	Bird cage
Baby's bottle	Aeroplane	
Book	Sheep	

Mathilde Fernandez, October 2012

On my second day at the Sanatorium, I was at reception when a Danish woman in her fifties came in with an appointment to make a Goodoo doll. I began the therapy, explaining she had to choose a doll and five small objects to sew to it. She sat in front of me, listening intently. When I asked whom her doll represented, she said it was her son. Right then she began to cry very hard, which worried me and made me want to cry, too. I wanted to do something, to hug her, but that wasn't what I was supposed to do. I was afraid of what she would tell me. Eight minutes later she had chosen her five objects. They were:

- A white plastic dove
- A small toy cowboy
- A seashell
- A wooden cross
- A sun

I was terrified; the combination of the cross and the dove frightened me. I feared this woman would tell me her Goodoo was for her child who died. As she continued to cry I explained that she should find a place on the doll's body for each object. We'd sew the objects on to "switch on" those magic points. This meant she must concentrate and think quietly, and I said I'd leave her alone for this time. When she called me back ten minutes later she was still crying, but she had started to regain her composure. I was still scared but I tried to have an encouraging attitude, despite my anxiety. Timidly she began, "He is nineteen years old…" Then I breathed easier because her child wasn't dead.

She began with the belly, where she placed the cowboy. I held the doll while she sewed. She said, "When he was a child, we did not know how to manage his hyperactivity. He was difficult and agitated, and he fought all the time. One day walking home from the park with his sister and father, we saw a carousel. These rides are very expensive, but of course my son wanted a ride. He became unbearable, crying and making a scene. Nearby, a disabled child was having the same kind of tantrum. My son grew even more difficult, and my husband ended up taking out his wallet. Right then, our son calmed down and looked around him. He realized the other child was crying for a ride, too. My son was little, between nine and ten years old, but he was affected by the other boy. When his father gave him a coin, he took it and gave it to the little boy, so he could ride instead. I chose the cowboy because of this story, to remind me that underneath all his angry behaviour, my son is good."

She placed the dove on the doll's heart and continued, "I chose the dove on the heart so my son can feel freer. Six years ago I left my husband. Our marriage wasn't working at all anymore and we argued about everything. We often fought about the violent video games my husband gave my son, which I couldn't stand. When my husband and I separated, my son felt responsible for our arguments. The dove is for him to know it was not his fault."

We sewed the sun on the doll's chest: "The sun is to make him strong and healthy."

The seashell went between his legs, and she explained, "The seashell is so that my son can live his life as a man, as he wants. He is leaving home to live with his girlfriend. I want him to be happy with this. I hope she will take good care of him, too."

Last, she placed the cross on the doll's head, saying, "The cross is for him to be protected. I would like to still protect him like a little boy, but he is leaving me, and I can't look after him like before."

The woman was dazed as she ended her Goodoo. She had let it all out. I was moved, too, but I stayed attentive and discrete throughout, despite her tears and outbreaks. As she walked to the exit with her doll, she thanked me a thousand times. One of the other therapists who watched me walk her out told me later, "It was like she was going to kiss you on the mouth!"

The day we closed the Sanatorium, I did a Goodoo. I opted to do it for myself. I put a coin on the right foot for financial stability and protection from want. On the right hand, a black fist for power, success, and perseverance. On the left hand, a white fist for strength of mind, intelligence, stability, and peace. On the heart, a golden eagle for charisma, on the shoulder, a daisy for youth as an ally. My head had a bell, for music, joy, good ideas, and laughing. That evening there was a party to celebrate the end of Documenta. I left my bag with my doll in it in a corner, and the next morning I realized my doll was gone. I left it in Kassel and went home without it. Maybe she wanted to stay in Kassel.

A woman came for the Goodoo therapy. I had been asking people about whom the doll is for and what the charms symbolize. They could talk about this while they were putting the doll together or wait until after they finished. She decided to wait until it was done, when she finished she said, "This doll is for my mother, my birth mother, whom I've never met and whom I don't know. I don't know where she is. I don't know if she's still alive." That changed everything in my mind, but I just listened to what she said and she went on to start describing the different charms.

The first charm she described as the Madonna, a medallion that she put on the womb as the symbol of motherhood and giving birth.

The second charm was a key on the doll's hand, because the woman was starting the process of trying to find her birth mother. As her birth mother had to be willing to be found, she felt that her mother had the key to reunite mother and daughter.

Then she put the dove on the heart because she hoped that her mother was at peace with the decision that she made to give her daughter up for adoption. And then she put the wheat on the arm as a symbol of home. Even though she didn't feel like she had a home, this was the symbol of home she carried with her.

She put the skeleton as a necklace, as a charm, because she said she read that parents who give up a child for adoption feel like the child dies or that there is a death of their parenthood.

The last thing she explained was the mirror [on the face] because the only reflection she had of her mother was her own face, and she may actually resemble her mother.

As she described this I actually started crying because I'm estranged from my mother. I feel like I lost my mother and that my mother gave me up because she was very physically and emotionally abusive to me. So I was feeling very connected to this doll because it was something that I wouldn't have done; I would not have made my mother a doll. But then I realized that this doll was partly mine in a way.

As we finished the client got up and left the doll at the table. I said, "Wait, this is your doll. Everybody is taking their dolls." She said, "I don't think I want the doll." So I said she could leave it here and if she changed her mind she could come back and get it.

She went to try out the other therapies, and I watched her out of the corner of my eye. I also wrote down what the doll's symbols were in case the doll got left and no one knew what it meant. But as the time went by, I realized that I didn't want her to come back for the doll, because that is the doll that I should be making for my mother. I felt like this woman made the doll for me and for my mom, and for herself and her mom, because in some way we both lost our mothers. She was actually brave enough to make this doll, and so in leaving it she left it for me, because it's something that I needed.

She didn't come back for the doll. Now I have it and it's something that's good for me to have, I think. It's the first time since I was abused as a child that I've ever really, truly thought of giving something positive back to my mom. I always think of her in either neutral or negative terms, so this has been part of my own healing.

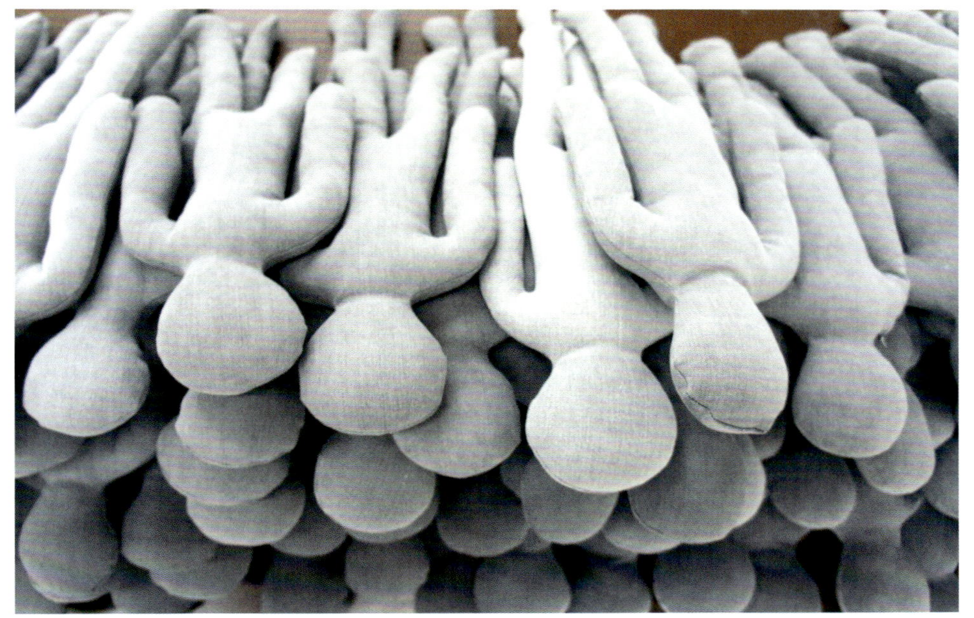

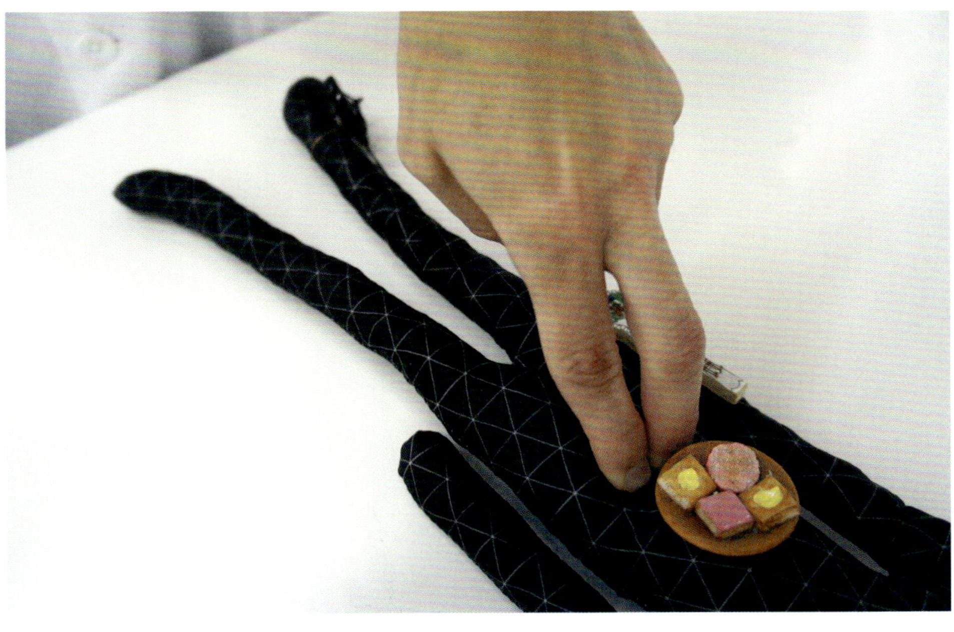

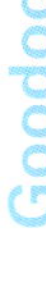

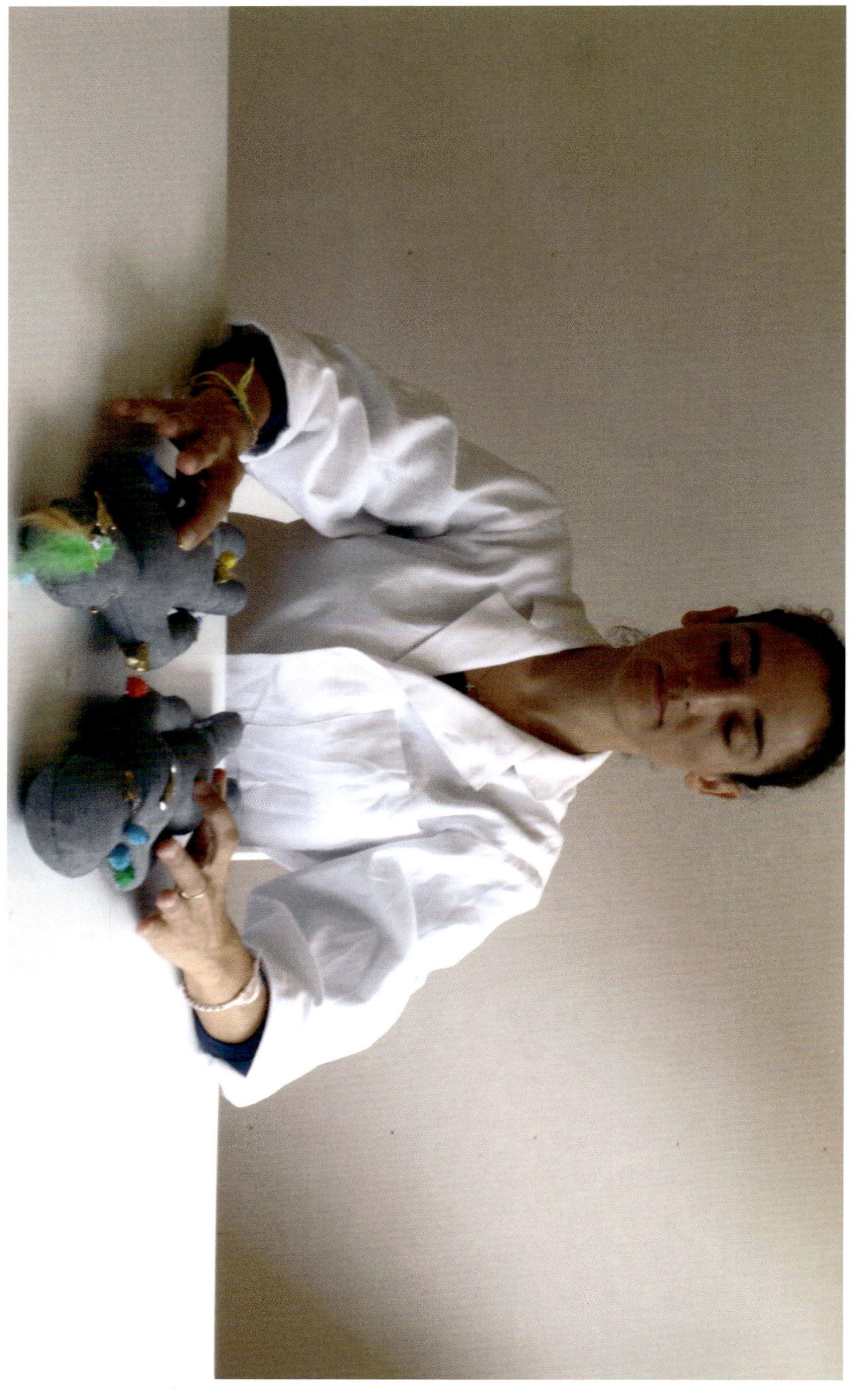

Citileaks

Number of participants: One to five people
Time: 15 — 20 minutes
Space size: 3×4 m
Space requirements: Basic
Furniture: Shelves, table, five chairs
Props: Empty glass wine bottles, tub, paper, pens, string
Therapist qualifications: Basic

DESCRIPTION

In this activity the therapist asks you to think of a secret. The therapist will cover his or her eyes while you write your confession on a piece of paper. It is very important that you omit personal names or details that could jeopardize your reputation or anyone else's. Once finished, roll the paper up and use a string to fasten it shut, leaving one end of the string about forty centimeters long. Place the roll inside one of the glass bottles, keeping the long end of the string outside of the bottle. Lastly, place a cork in the bottle and your bottle into the tub.

In exchange for writing your secret, you are given the chance to read someone else's. Pick one bottle, remove its secret, and read it.

THERAPIST INSTRUCTIONS

1. Greet and welcome the participant.
2. Explain the therapy.
3. Ask the participant to think of a secret.
4. Cover your eyes while the participant writes down the secret.
5. If this therapy is to be offered to children or visitors under the age of sixteen, it is important to provide a separate area or "zone" of bottles containing only the confessions of young people. Care must be taken to ensure that no child visitors read the confessions of adults.
6. This therapy is not recommended for blind visitors.
7. This therapy is appropriate for deaf visitors if written instructions are provided.

PARTICIPANT INSTRUCTIONS

1. Write down a secret on a piece of paper.
2. Roll it up, place it in a glass bottle, and put it in the tub of water.
3. Take another bottle from the tub and read the secret from the bottle.

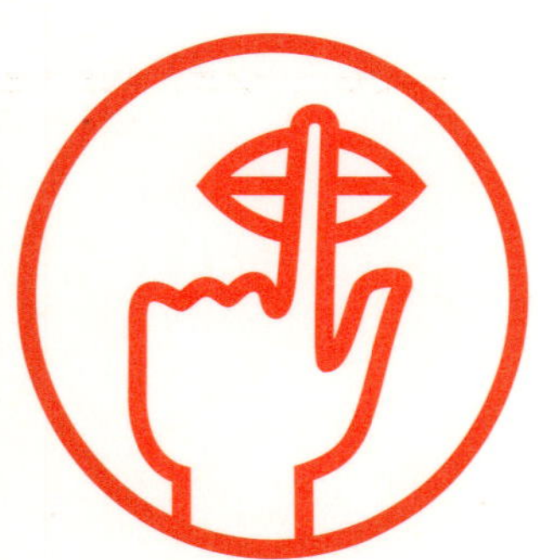

What is the Intention of this Therapy?

Citileaks is a cathartic procedure. The root of the word "catharsis" means "purification" in Greek: to expel a toxic substance from the body. In our daily lives we experience a number of toxic interactions; they leave certain traumas that are part of our autobiography, but we hide them in order to fit in. So the act of confession relieves us of the burden of carrying these secrets. This is different from the tradition of confession in Catholicism and from that found in psychoanalysis. Here the process is done in absolute anonymity. Literally, it's a message in a bottle. What I find fascinating is that it is a mix of extreme anonymity and extreme intimacy. You are requested to write your most intimate secret, something you don't tell even your best friend. This honesty is sought-after at the Sanatorium as a place for encounter. There may be better opportunities to open up with total strangers than with people you know, precisely because you are free from the pressure of the group.

Another element in Citileaks is non-commercial exchange; there is a price, but it is not money. You can only read someone's secret if you've previously paid the price, which is to write one yourself. I am very interested in accountability, in having precise means to measure participation. In a way, this is very similar to Web 2.0 or anything that is based on user-generated content, but it also goes beyond the mere number of exchanges. There is an element of reconciliation.

When I interviewed Alejandro Jodorowsky (see page 197) he mentioned something that is crucial here. He says that actually there is no "someone else," that there is no "other": "The other is a disguise of yours, and you are a disguise of theirs." So in our interaction with others we are actually looking for ways to reconcile with ourselves, and according to Jodorowsky, "There are people that awaken your consciousness and people that close it, that steal it from you." The confession aims to make connections among the individual experiences of catharsis. The catharsis felt by the person who wrote the secret you later read will create its own echo in you.

When in Citileaks we say, "We care about the sin, not the sinner," it produces a certain pleasure, too, not so dissimilar from the pleasure that we take in gossip. Gossip is a guilty pleasure because we are talking behind the back of someone we know. Why do we like to gossip? It gives us a certain feeling of relief when we comment about someone else's failure, because seeing someone else fail relieves the pressure and fear we have of failing. Yet the secrets in Citileaks have been inoculated. There is no risk because no one knows who is confessing, and the pleasure doesn't have to be guilty. Paradoxically, it creates a place where we can let down our façades of confidence and be vulnerable.

One day, a French couple came for Citileaks. They each wrote a secret while I was blindfolded and they thought it was great fun. Their bottles contained two rather amusing secrets. The first told of a man's shame from when he was caught stealing candy as a little boy. The other was the confession of an *au pair* at a large house in England. One evening, taking advantage of the owners' absence, she invited over the neighborhood drug dealers. She said she drank, used drugs, and had sex with them. The French couple was surprised and entertained, asking lots of questions and discussing the principle of patient empowerment. They were so excited that I suggested they exchange other secrets, which they did. I put on my blindfold and when I removed it the woman had not folded her secret. It was written very big and red and I read it by reflex. She didn't hide it; she just folded it it while saying it was a lie.

After that we spoke about the act of lying. With Citileaks, we agreed that lying didn't matter; it was the same as if you didn't lie. Your contribution on paper had the same impact as if you told the truth. Still, I didn't see what would be interesting about lying. The secrets could not be traced—there was no reason to be afraid. What was interesting was observing people's level of shame. If you didn't want to tell too big a secret, you could tell a little one, like "I stole candy." After this conversation the French couple left.

More than a week later an older woman came to reception, insisting on having therapy. I had fifteen minutes to spare, so I offered her Citileaks and she agreed. While I was blindfolded she took five minutes, a rather long time, to write her secret. When she said, "Finished," she had already rolled her secret up well. I put it in the bottle and took another bottle from the basin. As she gently unfolded the secret inside, I realized she had the lie of the French woman: "I WOULD LIKE TO KILL MY MOTHER," a big lie written in red. She grew mysterious as she held it. She said, "It's funny and ironic to get this one. I hesitated initially when I wrote my secret. I wanted to write this same thing, but finally I found something else."

One evening I spoke with Daniel, an art student in Kassel, about the Sanatorium. He told me he wanted to do Citileaks, but he hadn't come because he didn't know what secret to choose. He had too many. He said it was the first time a work of art made him think in advance of experiencing it.

CONFESSIONS

I am dating my supervisor, which is against the rules. My supervisor makes the schedules and I know he favors me. No one knows we are dating.

When I was six years old, I used to fight with my girlfriend—physical fights with punches and kicking. I really liked it. I don't think there is anything wrong with this.

I hope that a certain teacher dies a slow and painful death alone.

I am getting married this summer overseas, but no one is able to know about it until after I return.

One time when I thought I was pregnant, my boyfriend at the time punched me in the belly as hard as he could. I got my period one week later. I don't know if I was pregnant but it felt weird.

I secretly wish I went to Hogwart's School of Wizardry.

I'm the worst friend on earth. I feel awful. People who have helped me or given me their friendship and support at some point in my life suddenly get no response from me. They call me, leave messages, and never get an answer.

I'm an interpreter and most of the time deal with entertainment (movie) promotion. One day I worked with an actor and he asked me to have a drink at the hotel bar. Then he asked me to go to his room. Then he slept with me and gave me $500. I'm male.

It's becoming more and more apparent that I am part of the problem and not the solution.

I'm in love and it's too late. And I drowned an injured squirrel to be humane, but I kind of liked the sadism.

One night my friend and her boyfriend and I were drinking in the park. He got us so drunk from the cheap vodka we bought that we were puking up blood. Before I got sick I drunk dialed my ex-boyfriend and this boy that I was in love with who raped me. I was in denial for years.

I pretend to like guys just for the attention. It makes me feel wanted.

I'm not truly in love with my husband and sometimes I wish we had never gotten married.

Fifteen years ago I killed my sister's hamster, but she thought it died because it was sick.

I don't know whether I should tell her as she was so upset at the time.

I would like to take some time off from my marriage and have a romantic relationship with someone else. And then maybe someone else after that.

I enjoy nude yoga—a society of gay men practicing yoga in the nude. While my instructor has an intense attraction towards me, I have no desire to reciprocate, but I enjoy the extra attention and as a side bonus I have great posture now.

During the construction of the museum, archeological findings were not reported to avoid delay-ing construction.

I have herpes.

I once sat on a pencil and the tip broke off in my skin. If you know where to look you can still see the lead!

I eavesdrop on my neighbors constantly.

I am staying in a relationship because neither of us can afford to rent on our own.

I sometimes wish I were a lesbian so I wouldn't have to deal with men's bullshit anymore.

I saw my mom dating a guy who is married. My mom has been single for over twenty years. I was happy when I saw that even though it was not ethical.

I just stopped waxing my "lower region," and it's been liberating.

I pick my nose and eat my boogers.

My secret is that I think I am smarter than all my friends. It probably can't be true but I believe it. I'm sure some of them know that I think I am smart, but the belief in my superiority is embarrassing!

Though my confidence appears limitless, I am in fact quite self-conscious.

I believe I will never recognize or find my place and space to live an authentic life.

I cheated on my girlfriend and lied to her about it.

I am afraid of loneliness, being hated, and losing my people.

I don't shave my armpits.

I stole my friend's paycheck and destroyed it, and she didn't receive the money for a long time.

I have unprotected anal sex
with numerous people.

Sometimes when my mind is
blank I stare at people. I think
about how their voices sound,
and more importantly how
they would be kissing, fucking.
Good or bad? I can't help it.
The funny thing is that it's nothing to do with attraction. I don't
even have to think the person
is compatible with me. I just wonder how they would be in bed.

I cheat on tests sometimes.

My deepest secrets are totally
sexual. Our Latin lifestyle in
Mexico isn't so conservative.
When I was twenty years old I
had sex with two friends in the
same night in the middle of a
party. I've been with fifteen men
in my life — I don't know if that
is too much but at least five or
eight of them I wish I had never
slept with. I'm not a lesbian but
one night a friend put her hands
inside me.

I will never forgive my father
for his negligence during my
childhood.

I lost my virginity at twenty-five
and the boy I lost it to has no idea.

Sometimes when I've said
"I love you," I didn't mean it.

A while ago I was playing with
my three-year-old cousin in
the pool and when I reached behind me to grab the camera,
she slipped under the water and
nearly drowned. She was safe,
but I still think about what
could have happened every time
she is in the water.

I wish I could forgive her.

I have herpes. It is a source of
shame for me, and I have tried
telling lovers with poor results,
so now I don't tell and take care
of myself and hope for the best.
I am always worried about in-
fecting others and causing pain
and humiliation to someone
I care for.

I want to go back to my home
country and get married to him.
I always say I don't want to get
married though.

I always wished I had tried shop-
lifting, but I have never tried it.

My aunt has been married three
times, and her daughter doesn't
know about two of them.

I have left my thirty-year marriage, and my husband might or
might not have realized I am
gone.

When we were four or five years
old, my best friend (at the time)

and I used to explore each others' privates.

I'm incredibly scared to get married, but I've spent my whole life telling people how hard it is to find the one. When my finance proposed, I honestly didn't realize what was happening, this moment I had been waiting for so long. But I'm acting like the eager bride-to-be and hiding a strong feeling of dread and biting my tongue, when I want to put a stop to it all.

In first grade I ate too much candy and threw up in someone else's locker—I didn't tell anyone.

I engage in many secretive activities, ranging from night-walks with my dog to engaging in sexual activities in public places such as rooftops and taxis.

I don't think I deserve most of the good things in my life. I have gotten most of it out of luck.

I thought my grandmother was scary looking—like a witch!

In sixth grade I stole my father's Playboys and sold them.

I'm the same weight as I was in eighth grade. I've fought ano-rexia for ten years. I wish it would go away — I don't like feeling like this. I blame my illness on my upbringing as a ballerina.

I have reason to believe both my parents have had numerous affairs. That does not bother me in the slightest as long as it makes them happy.

I tell people I'm vegetarian when I am not.

I get super stressed when I need to speak in public.

I think I'm falling for you, but I haven't told you yet.

I made a four-year-old child eat dirt. I told her it was chocolate and it wasn't.

I'm addicted to the Internet and will spend days on my computer with no physical human interac-tion and still feel fulfilled.

My secret is that I feel very little guilt and shame in my life. I'm bisexual; I steal things regularly; I hide things about my life from my mother; I enjoy kinky sex; I've done lots of drugs. I don't feel any reason to have any hesitation about living life fully.

Once I wrote a suicide letter and went out to go to a bridge to jump, but I lost the letter at my school. I was so afraid that someone would find and read it.

I had to search for it and found
it after a while. Then I decided
to stay.

A guy followed me in the street
and tried to rape me. To defend
myself I kicked him in the balls.
He bent over, and I pushed
him to make him fall down so
I could run away. When he fell
he hit his head on a stair. I was
scared that he would get up
again, so I ran away and don't
know if I hurt him.

I had sex with a man while his
wife was watching us. She was
very happy to see her husband in
this position.

I wanted to fuck a dog when
I was fourteen years old.

I lost €30,000 with speculations.

I changed my identity after the
death of my sister.

I haven't told anyone the concrete
circumstances of my dwelling.

I invented another life and I mix
it with my real one. Everyone
is involved, there isn't a single
person in the world with whom
I've been completely sincere.
It's made of lovers, friends, and
places. It's not better than my
real one; it's just an extension
I use to test my memory and
creativity. Thanks to that, I've
discovered a lot about myself and
lived some experiences twice.

It's a constant challenge, and
sometimes I fear it could take
over my real life emotions. I feel
trapped a bit in this amusement
game I created myself.

My most hidden secret concern
is about what I most like to do,
which is painting women. Unfor-
tunately I'm shy about the results, and I never ask someone to
sit as a subject for a portrait.
Also I paint very slowly.

I'm short of money.

I broke a piece of art by an artist
from my gallery. I repaired it
without telling him.

I think I may have been abused
by my father's wife when I was a
little child. I'm not sure because
my memories are not good
enough, so sometimes I feel like
I invented everything, and I feel
disgusted by myself. My therapist wants to have sex with me.

I tried to kill myself because I
felt so much pain and I wanted
the pain to stop.

I am a twenty-two-year-old girl.
As a kid, maybe eight years
old, I had a dog, a Chihuahua.
I tortured the dog just for fun.
I put him in a bag and turned it

around as fast as I could. I'm so sorry and embarrassed about it. One day my boss told me how he tortured his cat as a boy. He said that was normal for children at one point. I told him I had never done harm to an animal. That's a lie. Now I feel sorry for both not telling and torturing a harmless creature.

I'm lonely.

I should have loved my sister. She died without knowing my love.

I want to be/play on stage as a musician, as an acoustic guitar player. I wish I had an audience of 10,000 people.

I'm twenty-five and never had sex.

Sometimes I am too lazy to go to the toilet and I piss in a cup. But just at night. The way to the toilet is long.

One day in Sydney, from across a room I saw a man so handsome he took my breath away. Although we exchanged glances we never spoke a word. The next day I attended a conference about an hour outside Sydney, there in the hotel — to my amazement — was the same man. After three days we found ourselves in bed together on the last night. Five years later only you and I know that this man and I remain secret lovers, meeting in other cities across the world. Both of us are in important relationships that have not suffered, both our lives are complex with our careers, and time is limited. There is nothing more I want of this secret relationship, but it brings me great joy for what it is. I am happy with the fact that no one else knows.

It would be more interesting for the reader to read something sexy I think. I want to be a journalist and am trying really hard, but I have the feeling that I am not very good at writing, or reading for that matter. It's kind of a weakness, and I am afraid that I can never be what I truly want to be.

Kassel is a scary place for me.

I still pretend that I want to be a writer, but I know that I'm not able to do it, and I don't even want to anymore.

I once stood between some of my students, farted, and walked away. Then I watched them blaming each other and laughed my head off.

I love a man who is married.

I'm on my way to the south and I don't know what destiny

and love will bring me, because I'm actually in contact with a couple of different men … and I don't want to decide or to start a story with someone until something special will happen to me.

My secret is hard to think of — perhaps that I often used to undress when I knew or hoped the neighbors could see!

Once I cut myself to calm down after my parents had a fight. After that I painted a blood picture.

Sometimes I hate my patients.

I worry that I might still be crazy and not have control over my life. I have been crazy before.

I fell in love with a married man, even though I'm in a long-term relationship with a woman.

I'm still in the closet.

Although I'm an adult I still like eating the nose bubbles.

Sometimes when I'm at home alone in the evening and I'm kind of bored, I drink one or two shots, then join a chatroom and amuse myself with the typing mistakes I make when I'm a little tipsy.

My self-esteem is entirely predicated on the acceptance of attractive women.

Nobody knows that I was gay fifteen years ago, but I changed! I get an erection when women need to sneeze.

He doesn't know that that man isn't his biological father.

I wished all my life for the death of someone I lived with. He died four weeks ago, and I can't help feeling guilty and relieved at the same time.

Everytime I am invited to some friend's place I steal. I steal each time everywhere, and even if I know it's hard, I continue. I don't feel guilty, but I never told anyone else.

I hope that my daughter has a family and children, because she loves to have a family so much.

At some point not long ago, I seemed to have a little money to continue with the project I had been invited to do with friends and fellow artists. I am clever, convincing and trusted. I (mis-) used these qualities to "frame" a commercial client from the business I sometimes work for — and stole €10,000.

I am terrified that I will disappoint my family. I am nineteen and still have no idea what to do with my life.

When I was a child (five years old) my mother died of cancer. Now I don't remember anything about her, just her beauty and kindness. I feel ashamed of it.

One Allan is an electric tantric lover and makes my body sing, the other Allan puts my sexual energy to sleep with boredom. I am manifesting my next lover and my body is expectant with desire, impatience, and lust! What would my great-grandchildren think?

In the past I had good dreams about the man who abused me!

I'm a gay guy and I really badly want to have bareback sex, even though I know about the risks. First with my new boyfriend. Then with strangers, maybe in a sex-club (a gang bang with people watching). Ultimately with my step-dad. He has aged and he's not that hot anymore, but I used to jack off while thinking about him A LOT. (But actually I'm a very responsible, smart, not-so-crazy guy. Whoops.)

I once beat up a guy to such an extent that he needed medical attention. I left him on the street bleeding.

In Germany there is a village, and there is a treasure under the biggest tree in the street: Wilhelmstrasse 3.

While I love them both very much, I'm relived my dad has the terminal disease and not my mom.

One time I took the largest dump in a public bathroom and tried to blame it on a Mexican worker.

Sometimes when my students are acting up, I play a song in my head that involves great distances and calming seas.

I poured a laboratory radioisotope into the Boston Harbor.

I once flushed a baby alligator down the toilet.

Sometimes I imagine that my partner dies in some horribly tragic way and I start dating others, mostly men of color, specifically the actor who plays Carlos the Jackal in that miniseries that started the other day.

I "borrowed" several thousand dollars from a past job, which "funded" the down payment on my apartment.

I feel like I am spiraling downward. I have given into tempta-
tions… I am having sex with
random strangers. My favorite
story is that I recently met a guy
in the subway and went back
to his place for sex. I'm not sure
if I have a problem because I am
acting like this or if I am proud
of this story. Last night I went
home with an unmarried man.
I feel I might be drinking and
fucking to excess, but on the
other hand is there really ever to
much? I think I would stop if
the sex were bad.

I told a man I had slept with that
he had gotten me pregnant, even
though I knew it was unlikely it
was his. I did this because he was
a minor television celebrity.

The man who thinks he's going
to marry me (and who everyone else thinks will marry me) is
coming to see me for the first
time in months. But last week I
kissed my best friend, and I can't
stop thinking about it. I want
to do it again. But I'm too chick-
enshit to tell either of them.
My mother abused me as a child.
I secretly fear I'll do the same to
my children.

I find Alexander Hamilton
weirdly attractive in a crazy
historical crush kind of way.

Last night I snuck in to a church-
yard and just sat there for an
hour at 12:30 a.m. I wanted to
go in, but I thought I had to
climb the fence. When I realized
the gate was unlocked, I was
so happy; I thought maybe I had
found God. I was very drunk.

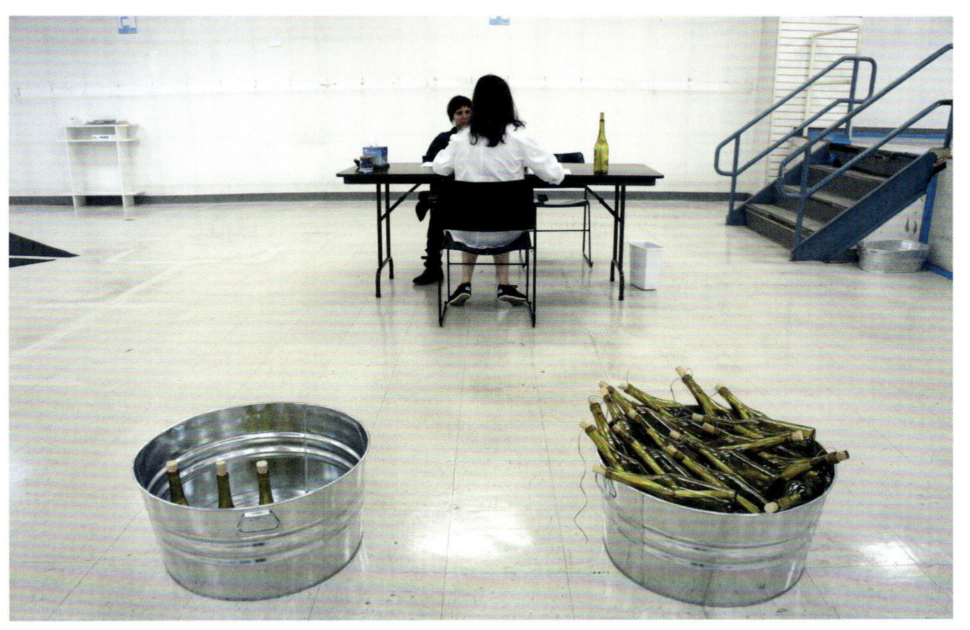

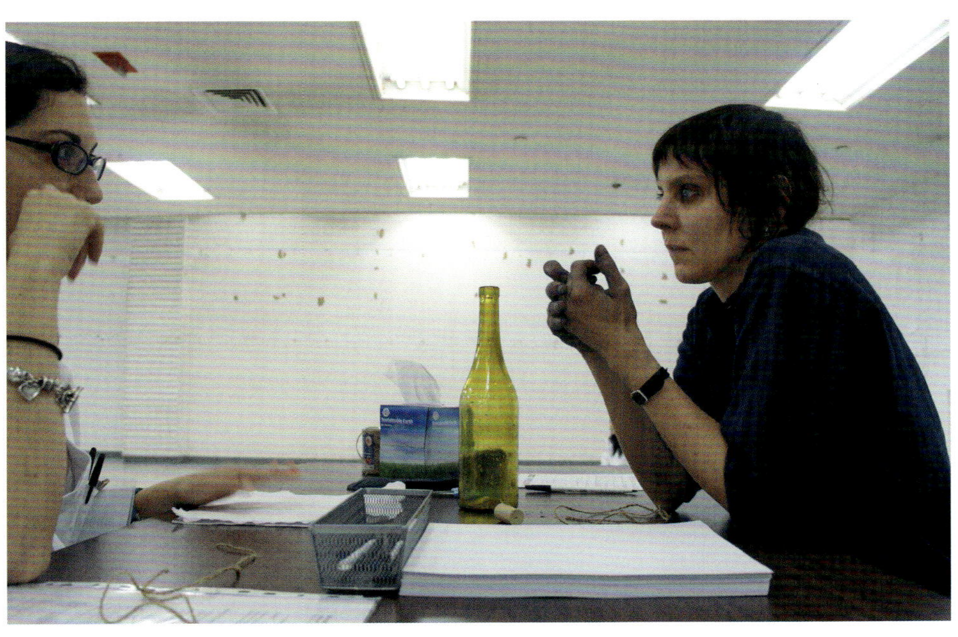

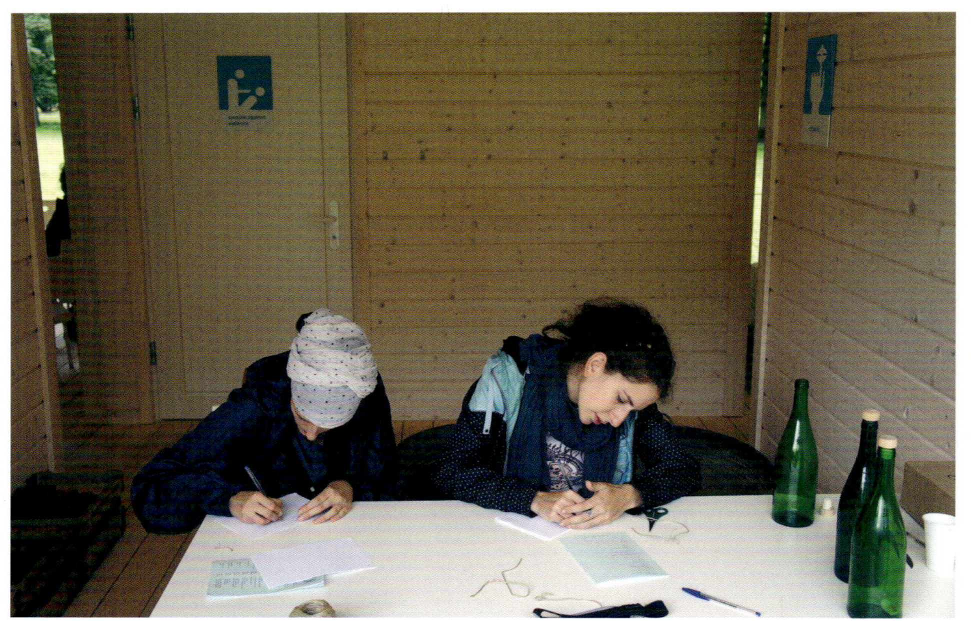

Ex-voto

Number of participants: Individuals
Time: 30 minutes
Space size: 2×2.50 m
Space requirements: The ex-votos are to be hung on the wall, so there must be a space where the paintings can be tacked or nailed. The space must be well lit.
Furniture: Two chairs, a desk or drawing table
Props: Cardboard, paint, brushes, pens, pencils, paper (colored and white), thumbtacks, newspapers, scissors, glue, tape
Therapist qualifications: Basic, although it is preferable if the therapist has basic drawing or painting skills

DESCRIPTION

Ex-votos are devotional objects from the past that can be found in churches and chapels where worshippers wished to give thanks for an event they considered miraculous. Though ex-votos take a wide variety of forms, they always include a text and an illustration describing someone's recovery from an ailment, rescue from danger, moment of joy, etc. We may consider them a sort of prayer.

There are two common kinds of prayers. The first is a petition, when we ask for something. This is probably the most typical prayer, for we often live with a sense of dissatisfaction, feeling that something is missing from our lives. The second kind of prayer is an expression of gratitude. It's easy to lose sight of all that we have. Assessing our lives to look for what we have to be grateful for is a powerful way to acknowledge the good around us.

This therapy requires you to think of a special moment for which you feel grateful. Perhaps you got over an illness, survived an accident, got an unexpected promotion, or found the love of your life. Making an Ex-voto is an opportunity to express your appreciation for this. Tell your therapist what happened and illustrate the scene with a painting or collage.

THERAPIST INSTRUCTIONS

1. Greet and welcome the participant.
2. Explain the therapy.
3. Listen to story of what the participant is grateful for. Draw or paint a picture to depict it. If preferred, therapists can make collages with colored paper to represent the story.
4. When finished, help the participant hang the Ex-voto on the wall.
5. This therapy is appropriate for children as participants.
6. Not recommended for blind visitors.
7. Not recommended for deaf visitors unless accompanied by an interpreter.

PARTICIPANT INSTRUCTIONS

1. Take a moment to think about an event in which you experienced gratitude. Write down a brief description of what happened.
2. A resident painter will paint your story or make a collage to illustrate it.
3. When the painting is finished, the painter will help you choose a place on the wall of the room to hang the painting along with your written description.

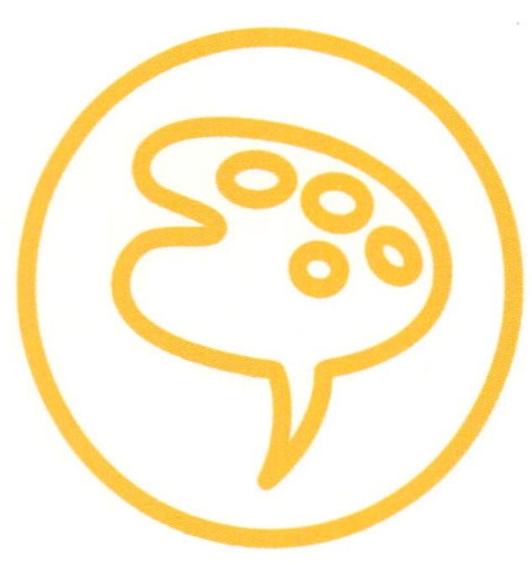

What is the Intention of this Therapy?

I once read a Jewish story by a famous mystic rabbi; I'd like to cite his name here, but I seem to have lost the book. The story, however, has stayed with me. The rabbi said that when we complain about our problems to God, he can respond by sending us more trials and difficulties to make us realize that we didn't have much to complain about before. And conversely, that when we give thanks for our blessings, he will send us even more blessings to show us how much more he has to give us.

This story outlines two basic kinds of prayer. One is to ask and the other is to thank. In the context of psychology, therapy often leans towards the first kind as a space for airing our disatisfactions rather than our contentment. The general assumption is that if you are happy you don't need to go to therapy. In this activity you'll find yourself placed in a state of happiness by recalling concrete events for which you are grateful.

This idea is at work behind the Ex-voto therapy. Part of the effect that the rabbi describes has to do with how we perceive what is around us. When we focus on our problems and complaints, we are more likely to notice things that we have to complain about. Ex-voto is about making ourselves aware of what we have to be thankful for, an exercise that can in turn open our eyes to other good things in our lives.

Ex-votos are commonly found throughout Latin America; they are a tradition with European origins that blended with indigenous systems of votive offerings in Mexico and Central America. A worshipper would go to a painter and tell him a story of a "miracle" for which he felt gratitude: the healing of an injury, salvation from an accident, a marriage, etc. The painter would depict the stories in full color, painted on a piece of wood or tin, and the worshipper would bring the painting to the church or saint's chapel as an offering of thanks.

Wherever the Ex-voto takes place, the walls will start to fill up with other prayers of gratitude. It is not a chapel, but it will become some sort of sanctuary full of the happiness of others.

I remember two Ex-voto anecdotes. The first is a about a
fifty-year-old woman who came with her very young son.
I suggested that the child could also do an Ex-voto; he could
draw while I wrote his story, and meanwhile his mother
could write her story so we can do a regular Ex-voto.

> The child tells me he has been camping for a week in
> the countryside with his mother. They rode horses and
> roasted marshmallows. He drew a horse and colored it
> with watercolors.

His mother took a moment to write her story, so I left her
alone in the room for a few minutes. I preferred to leave
the participants alone with themselves when they needed
to think and find the best story.

> When I came back she read what she had written. She had
> always been alone in her life and had had a very sad
> childhood and youth. She lost her mother when she was a
> child; her father remarried and was completely absent;
> she grew up in the care of people she did not really know
> and she never saw them again. Her older brother, who
> was much older, had disappeared.

She did her Ex-voto to thank the energy that she had
found, rather late, to live her life. She had a child by herself
and now lives in Kassel with her friends. Telling me this
she shed a few tears that she cried for happiness. I drew a
flying carpet. She left, satisfied with the drawing.

> The second Ex-voto participant I remember made the
> appointment for the therapy but did not really know what
> Ex-voto was. He had already come to the Sanatorium
> the day before and did Philosophical Casino. When I ex-
> plained that he was to share a happy event of which he
> has good memories, he looked strange. He did not expect
> that. I left him alone for ten minutes and then he called
> me. He wrote in German, but I read in French. He said,

"Eight years ago I visited an empty workspace in Paris. I told myself that if I had the opportunity to have a space like that, I would be the happiest man in the world. I was finally able to occupy this space and it became an artist's squat, 'The C', where we showed dance, music, performances, and exhibitions."

Fascinated by this story, I wondered aloud what was going on there now. The man's eyes went dull and he told me that "The C" had burned down two years before. He lost everything. This was a beautiful story that ended badly. This man found himself by chance doing an Ex-voto, and it allowed him to view the drama of his life from a different angle. He just had to cut out the tragic part, leaving only what the beauty and magic. The Ex-voto, a multi-colored collage of his text, represented the happy part.

NOTE FROM PEDRO REYES
We can take an unpleasant event in our past and begin to change
details in order to turn the bad memory into a good one. As George
Gurdjieff said, "A man will renounce any pleasures you like but
he will not give up his suffering," so it's not easy for some to let go
of their bad memories.[1] However, Milton Erickson would heal some
patient memories under hypnosis, for example, a man who re-
sented the absence of his father during his childhood, especially
when the father failed to attend a baseball game he'd played in.
Under hypnosis Erickson would take him back to the day of the
game, and he would point to the audience, showing the man that the
father was actually there, then taking the father's role in cheering
for the son. Coming out of hypnosis, the man would have a completely different memory of the event.[2]

1   P.D. Ouspensky, *In Search of the Miraculous: Fragments of an Unknown
    Teaching* (San Diego: Harcourt, Brace, 1949).
2   Milton Erickson, *Mind-Body Communication in Hypnosis,* vol. 3, ed. Ernest
    Rossi, Margaret Ryan (New York: Irvington Publishers, 1986).

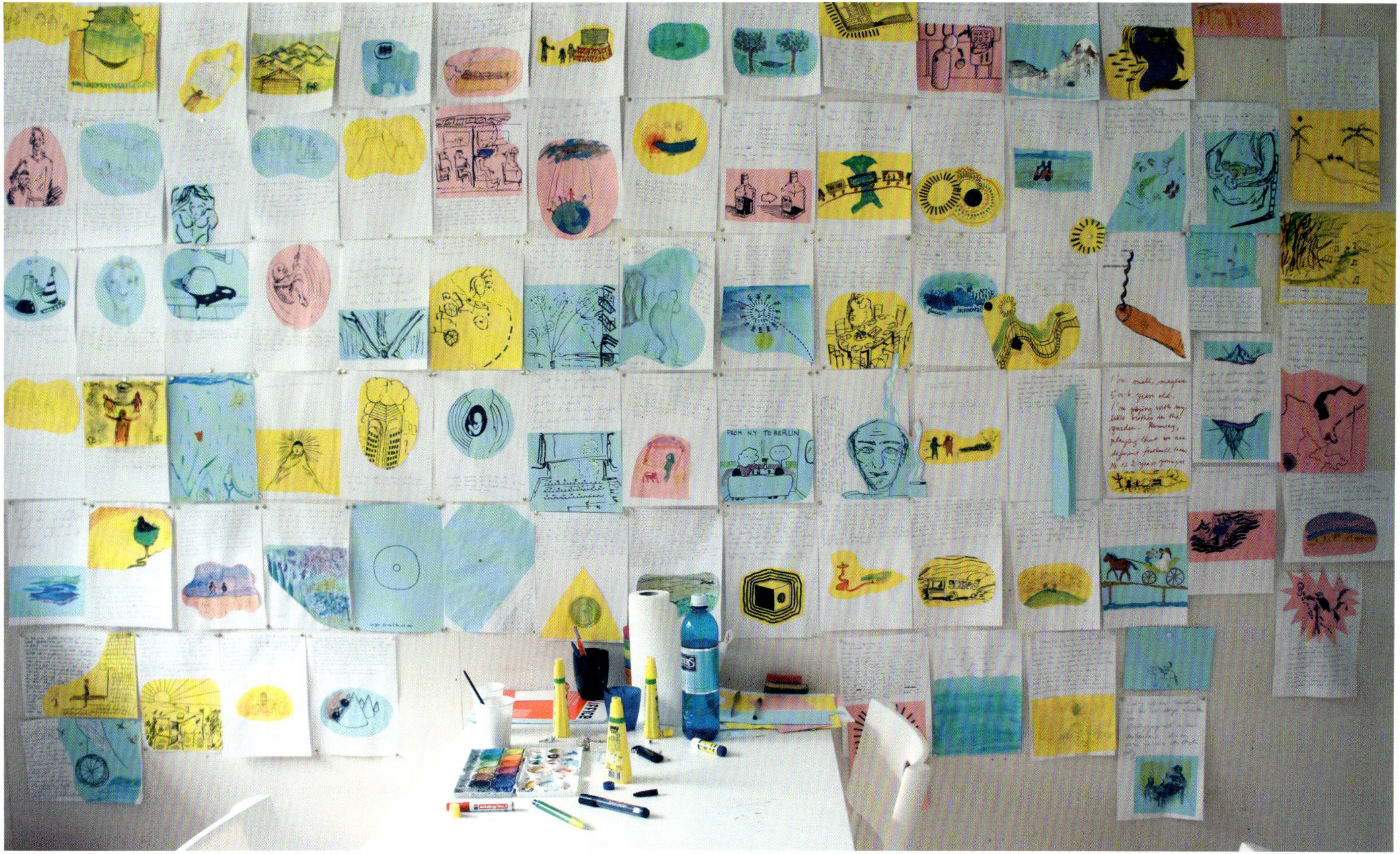

Ex-voto

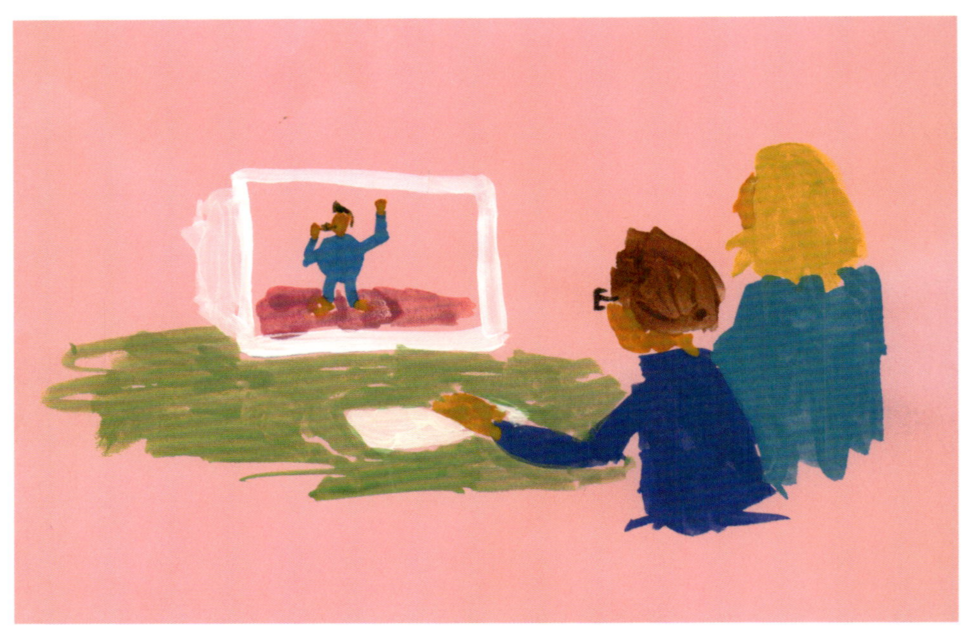

EX VOTO 1
When I was thirty-one, I was directing a music video, a kind of
expensive one (I think) in L.A. I couldn't continue another project,
so someone else took over for me. She turned out to be this
beautiful young girl, and she became my first girlfriend.

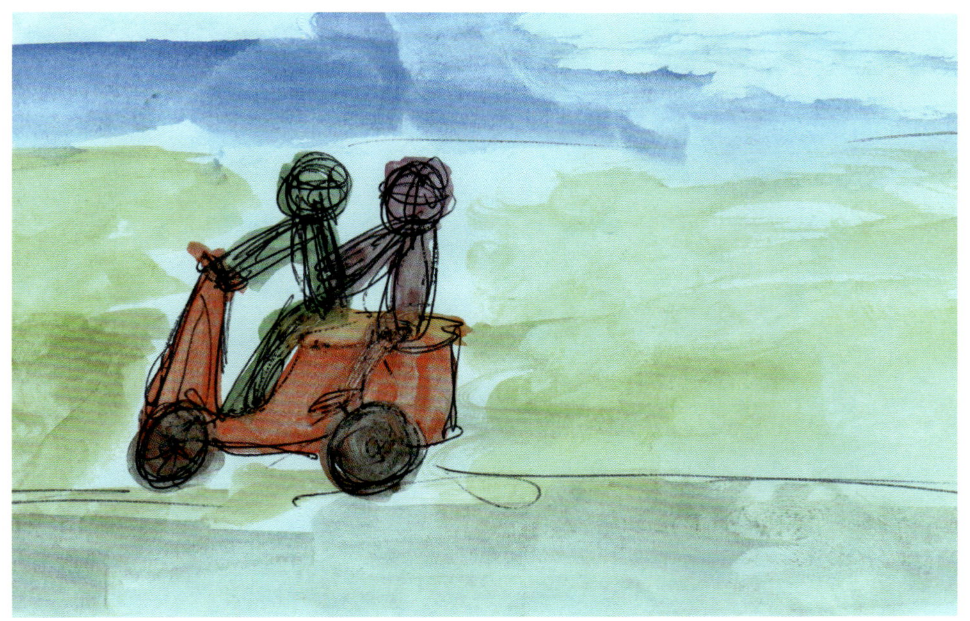

EX VOTO 2

My good memory: Driving a Vespa together with my girlfriend
on the Amalfi Coast. Seeing all the beautiful small places with a
special person. Happiness is only true when shared.

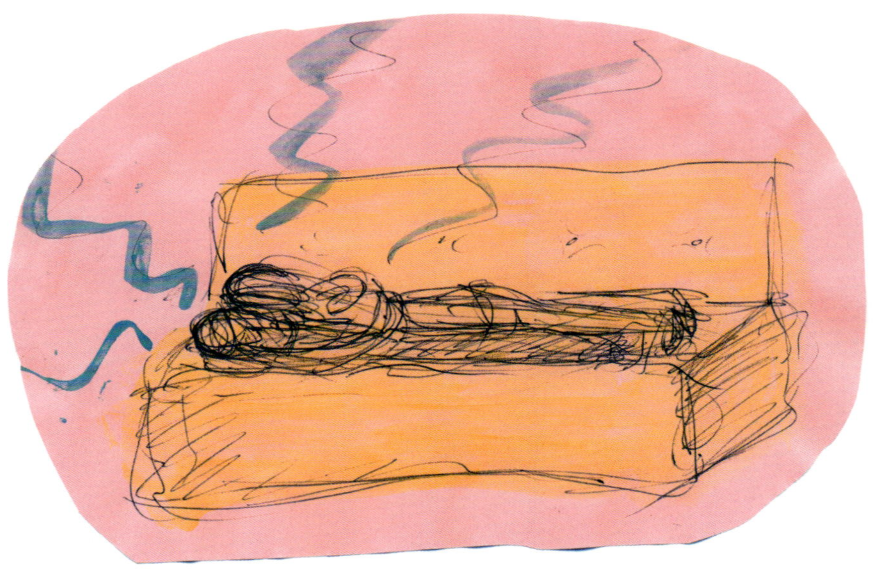

EX VOTO 3

A moment when I felt near to my fifteen-year-old daughter, who
came to me (I was laying on our sofa trying to relax) before we went
to bed and she lay on my body, covering it with her long and thin
body. I got a feeling of her, as she was as a small kid, a baby.
This was a good moment, feeling relaxed and connected, peaceful.

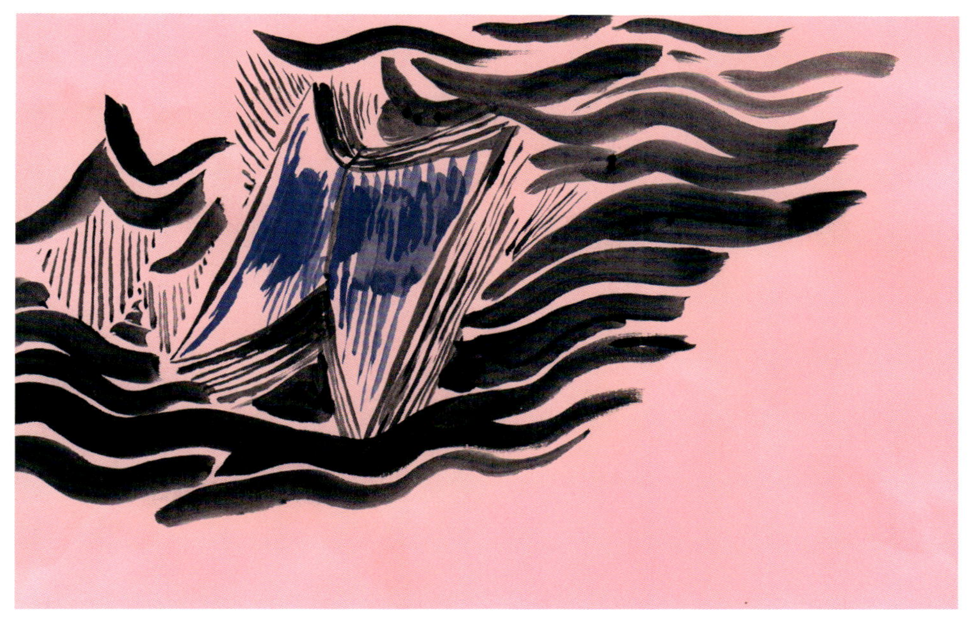

EX VOTO 4
A recent happy memory is: My first front page photograph
for a newspaper.

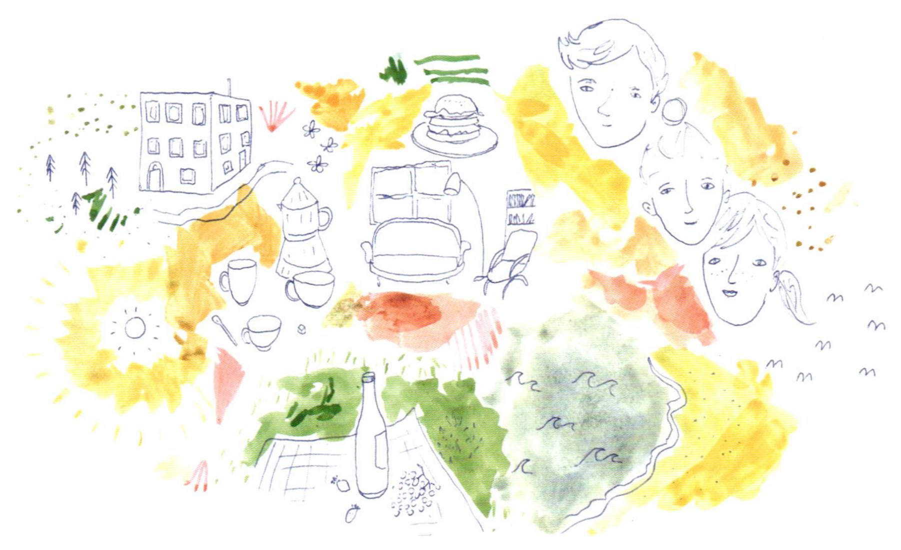

EX VOTO 5
Recently my friend Tilly and I spent a week in Lund. We stayed with
a boy I had met a few weeks prior, while waiting for a bus from
Paris to Berlin. I mentioned I was soon to go to Stockholm, he said
"I live in Lund. Come and visit, it's nice." So, after our ten minute
meeting, I did visit and brought Tilly with me.

We then had a delightful week together, staying in his lovely apartment, meeting his lovely friends, exploring his lovely town, as well
as the nearby city of Malmö. We went swimming at the beach, had
picnics in parks, made pancakes at four in the morning, stared up
at the sky trying to see the polar star, went to a nude bathing house,
drank coffee together every morning, smoked cigarettes out the
window of his apartment, and more besides.

Lund was peaceful and beautiful, the sun was always shining
(but was never too hot), and all memories of this week are for me
bathed in a wonderful golden light of contentment. Time seemed
to exist at a standstill, but still passed far too quickly, and I was
very sad to leave. However, I am glad to have such pleasant and
happy memories from our week in Lund.

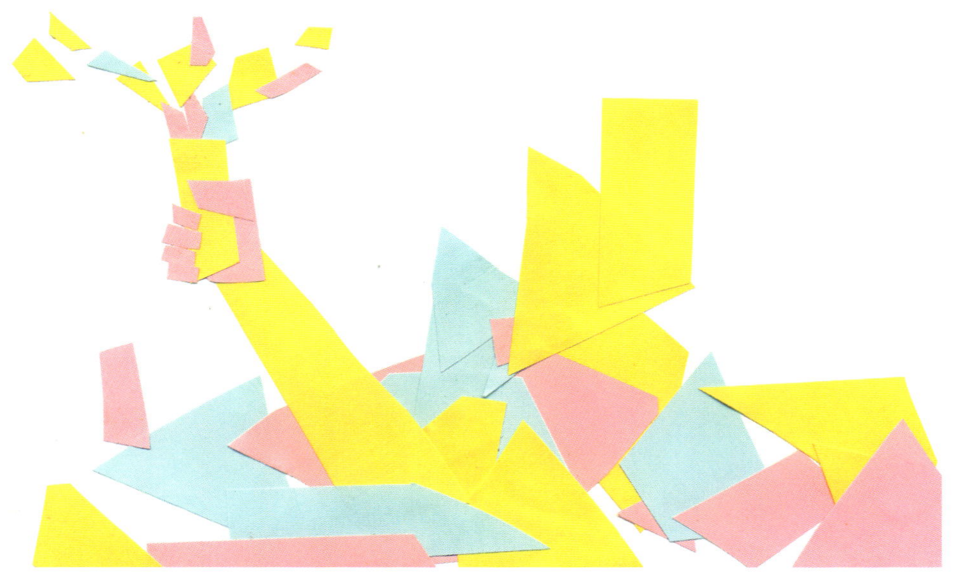

EX VOTO 6

So, about five years ago my life was falling apart. I lost my job and I was married to a man who did not treat me well. And then I got very lucky. My husband misjudged and behaved so badly that I had to leave him, and because of that I wound up living in New York City, where I always wanted to live. I had friends there, I found an apartment and I found a job. The job was only temporary, but because of it, I found another job, and then another one, and now I have a wonderful job that I love. I am living where I want to be, and I have a great life in New York City with all my friends there. I feel very lucky and I'm grateful for all the opportunities and support I have received.

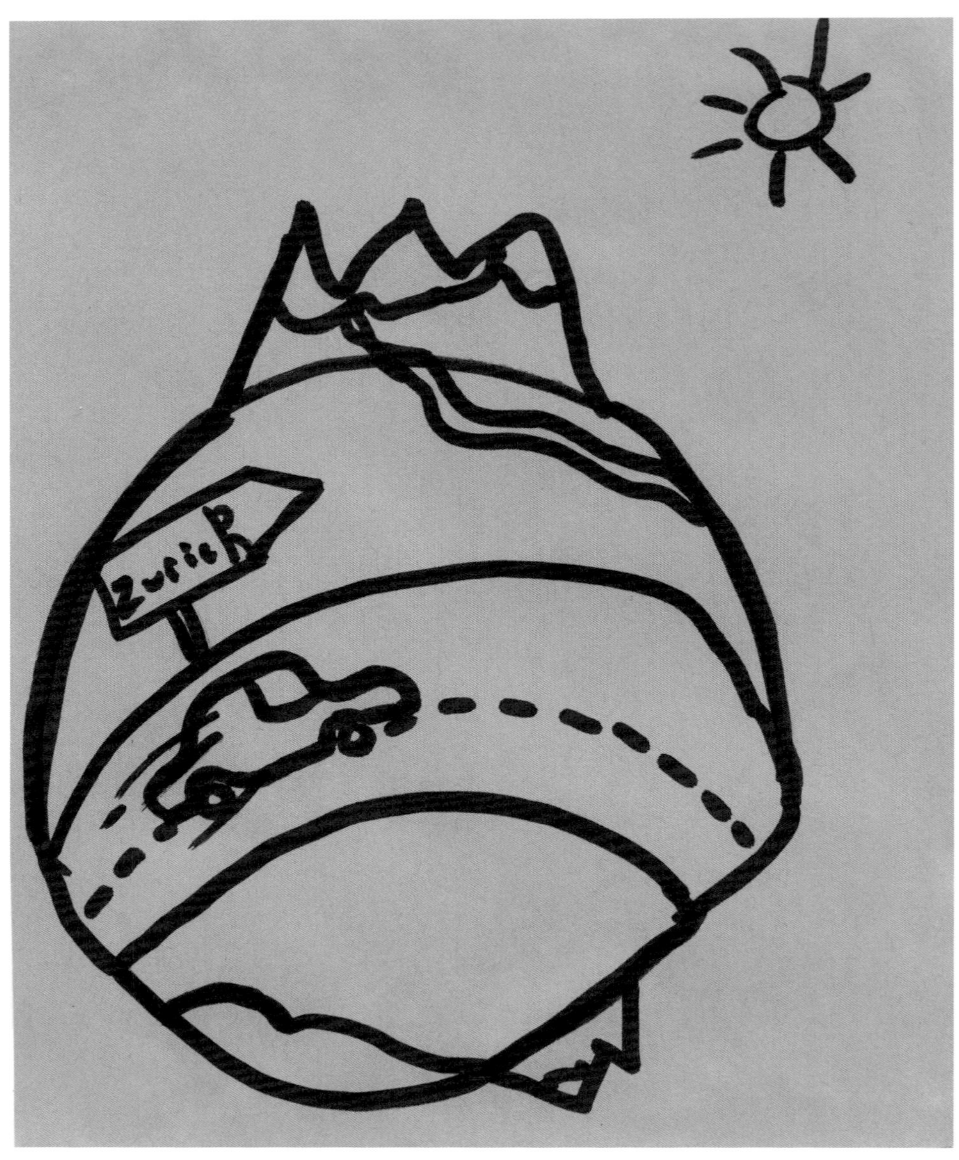

EX VOTO 7

I went to meet a pretty girl a couple of days before leaving to study abroad. It was a really good date and I regretted having to go for a long time. But everything had been set, and it was important, so I went. But a few weeks later she came to visit me there! It was a complete surprise! The best ever! We soon became lovers. It was one of the best surprises I've ever had.

Compatibility Test for Couples

<u>Number of participants:</u> Individuals or couples
<u>Time:</u> 20 minutes
<u>Space size:</u> 3×3m
<u>Space requirements:</u> It is very important to have a sink, as the blender and utensils must be washed often. If the Sanatorium is installed for a short period, it may be possible to use a space that has a nearby kitchen or bathroom. However, it is preferable for this space to have its own sink.
<u>Furniture:</u> Table, chairs
<u>Props:</u> Variety of fresh fruits and vegetables, blender or juice extractor, cutting board, knife, drinking glasses, cleaning supplies
<u>Therapist qualifications:</u> Basic

DESCRIPTION

The objective of this therapy is to discover one person's compatibility with another. To test this, couples can take part in this experiment, in which they choose fruit to represent themselves and their partner and then make juice from their selections.

THERAPIST INSTRUCTIONS

1. Greet and welcome the participants.
2. Explain the therapy.
3. If the participant is on her own, have her select the fruit or vegetable that best represents her. Then ask her to choose the one that best represents her partner. Encourage her to explain her choices of the two fruits or veggies.
4. If there are two participants, have each of them select the fruit they identify with, as well as the fruit they identify with their partners. Encourage them to explain their choices; they will choose a total of four fruits or veggies.
5. Slice the produce and blend it to make juice. Couples may decide to make one juice for each person based on the individual selections, or they may combine their four fruits into one juice. Have the participants taste the juice or juices and judge their compatibility accordingly.

6. Before making juice ensure that fruits and vegetables, as well as juicing equipment, are washed.
7. Keep the juice station clean and wash the blender thoroughly after each use.
8. This therapy is appropriate for children (families) as participants.
9. This therapy is appropriate for blind visitors.
10. This therapy is appropriate for deaf visitors if provided with written instructions.
11. If someone who is single wishes to do this therapy, suggest that he chose another relationship in his life to test: a family member, a friend, or a co-worker.

PARTICIPANT INSTRUCTIONS

1. Choose the fruit or vegetable with which you most identify.
2. Choose the fruit or vegetable with which you most identify your partner.
3. If your partner is present he or she will also choose the fruits or vegetables that represent you both.
4. Cut slices from your fruits or vegetables and blend them to make juice.
5. You can make two separate juices from each of your selections or mix all the juices together into one.
6. Judge your compatibility as a couple by the juice blend's taste.

What is the Intention of this Therapy?

In the late 1940s and early '50s, poets in Chile wanted to take poetry beyond the pages of a book. Vicente Huidobro, not satisfied with the mere act of writing lines such as "Why do you sing about the rose, oh poet! Make it grow in the poem," covered the floors of the rooms in his house with soil and planted a hundred rose bushes. Another pair of poets decided to walk through the city in a straight line; no matter what obstacles they encountered, they found a way to advance: climbing over trees, jumping walls, ringing doorbells, and passing through people's homes with as little explanation as possible. Another similar act involved a poet's decision that money could be transformed and his subsequent act of offering boiled shrimp instead of cash to pay bills (this plays on Chilean slang for money). A bus driver was so surprised he simply accepted the shrimp and let the poet ride.

Called *actos poéticos* (poetic acts) these actions showed the unpredictable nature of reality and challenged these poets to think in metaphors not only in their writing but in their actions. Alejandro Jodorowsky, one of the Chilean poets who developed the concept of poetic acts, says that these actions intuitively led him to discover that the unconscious accepts metaphorical acts as real ones. For instance, walking through a city in a straight line without allowing obstacles to make him change course helped his mind to learn how to overcome challenges by incorporating them into his art.[1]

In this activity, choosing a fruit as a metaphor for yourself and for your partner is the first step; the second is to mix them together. Carl Jung said that relationships are like chemistry: if two substances make a reaction, both are transformed. Blending the fruits and/or vegetables you've selected lets you experience the reaction and the transformation.

1   Alejandro Jodorowsky, *La danza de la realidad*, (Mexico City: Editorial Grijalbo, 2001).

We appreciated having fresh fruit at the Sanatorium every day; it was a great source of vitamins and happiness on rainy days. I enjoyed doing the Compatibility Test with families, who were thrilled to get their children interested in contemporary art.

I kept a few recipes from the compatibility test:

A family of two artists and a cucumber-loving four year old: Apple, ginger, pear, strawberry, cantalope, and a cucumber slice

Characteristics: Sweet, refreshing, pleasant, conventional, sensitive, considerate

Suggestion: Needs vodka

Two photographers: Apricot, radish, mint, yellow bell pepper

Characteristics: Fresh, confusing, undefined. Would make a wonderful gazpacho, chunky salsa, or salad.

Suggestion: Needs ginger, hot pepper, or orange juice

The Compatibility Test for Couples is for me the most obscure part of the Sanatorium.

This story of lovers choosing fruit seemed to me the most interesting when an older couple came to the test. They said funny things like: "I choose the apple for you because it's a classic. You are not eccentric; you are someone safe and I count on you because you are healthy and stable. You are always tempting and beautiful."

Once a young couple chose only lemons and a green apple. The juice blend was completely undrinkable, but they drank it all. They liked it and were delighted. This therapy is good for forcing couples to remember that they are in love.

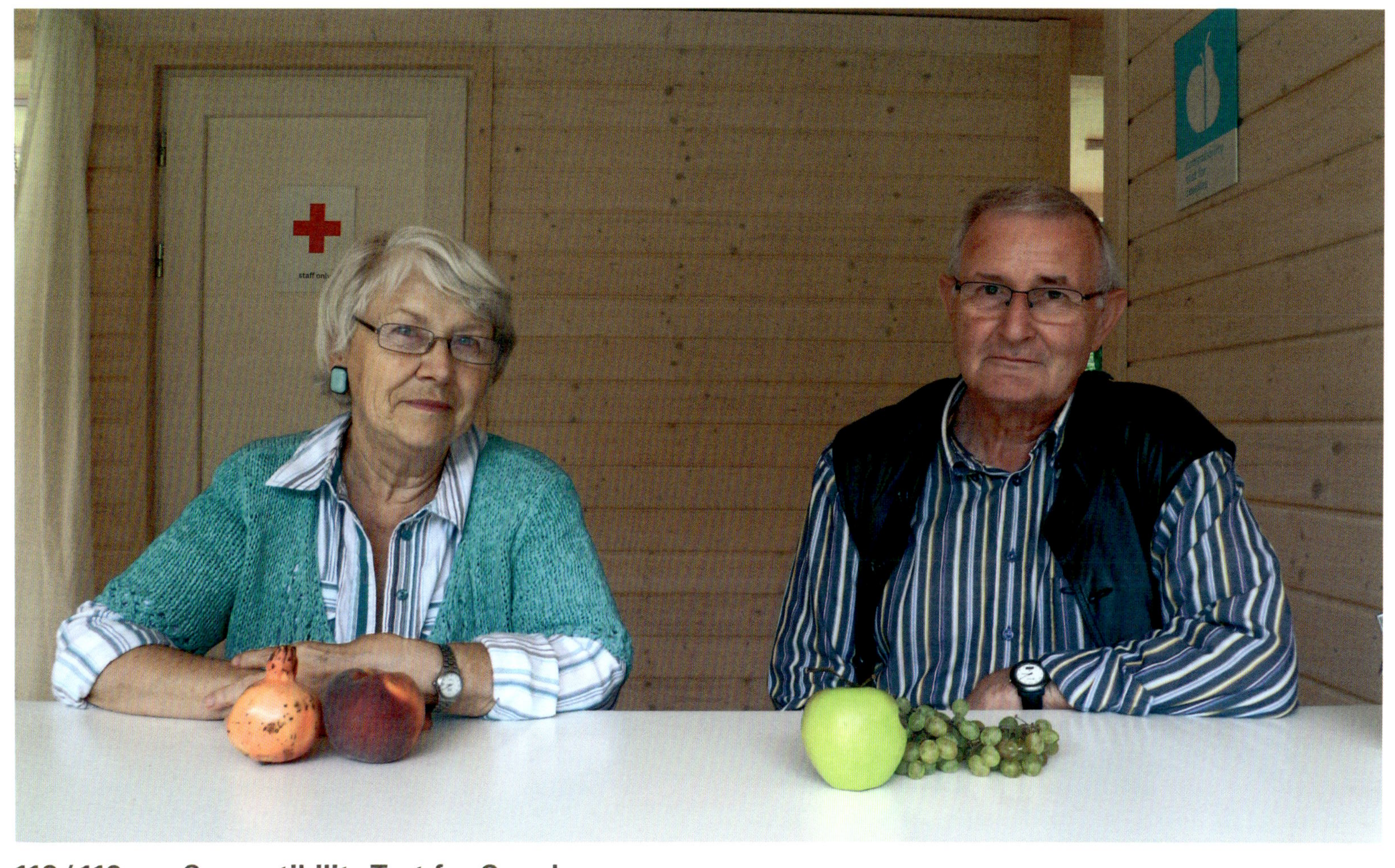

  Compatibility Test for Couples

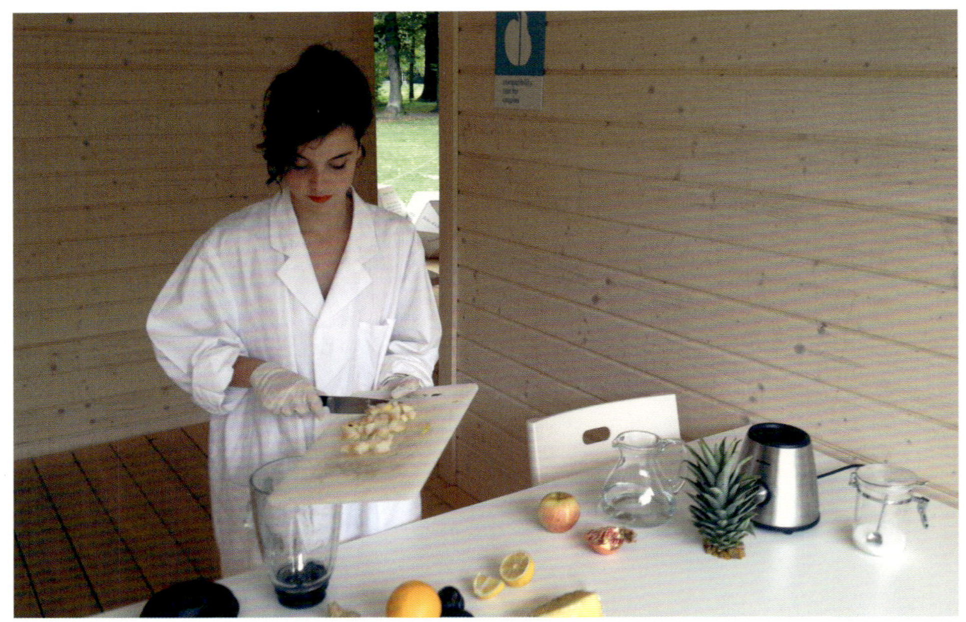

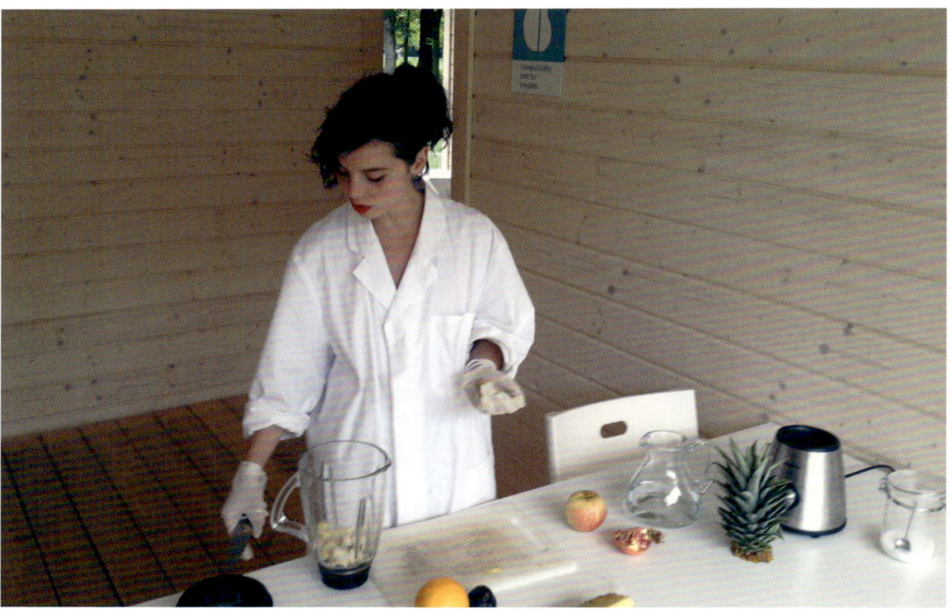

Mudras

Number of participants: Up to ten (can be more if desired)
Time: 30 minutes
Space size: Minimum 3×3m
Space specifications: This activity is conducted with participants sitting in chairs, forming a circle. Since it is a meditiation a quiet environment is recommended.
Furniture: Ten chairs
Props: None
Therapist qualifications: Basic

DESCRIPTION

Mudras are a symbolic gesture involving the body; most are performed with the fingers and hands. Often employed in the iconography and spiritual practice of Indian religions, they are used to guide the flow of energy in the body and to the brain. Research has demonstrated that hand gestures stimulate the same regions of the brain as language. In this therapy you will be taught several mudras that you may find useful. After practicing these, you will invent some mudras of your own. Think of an issue that you would like to address, visualize how to improve or change it, and translate what you see and feel into a gesture using your hands. Incorporate other parts of your body if you'd like. Share your new mudra with the group and practice it together.

THERAPIST INSTRUCTIONS

1. Greet and welcome the participants.
2. Explain the therapy.
3. Demonstrate some mudras, then ask participants to practice them with you.
4. The therapist will introduce the second part of the therapy, saying for example, "I'm going to show you a new mudra I've invented. I've been having a hard time sleeping and I want to create a mudra that will help me find deep rest." Then he will show a mudra that relates to sleep, or to another example.
5. The therapist will say to the person to his left, "Is there anything that you would like to improve about your life right now?" After the participant responds, the therapist will say, "How would you translate that into a mudra or a hand gesture?" If needed, participants can use something other than their hands.
6. Each person in the group will be asked to make her own mudra and teach it to the group. The whole group imitates the mudra before moving to the next person.
7. In this therapy, the second part in which participants invent their own mudras is very easy for everyone to access. However the first part requires some practice for the audience, for which reason it is recommended that therapists rehearse in order to project their knowledge of the mudras.
8. This therapy is appropriate for children as participants.
9. This therapy is appropriate for blind visitors if accompanied by someone to assist them. It is preferable to have blind visitors participate in small group settings.
10. This therapy is appropriate for deaf visitors if they are accompanied by an interpreter.

PARTICIPANT INSTRUCTIONS

1. Work with the therapist and other members of the group to practice mudras together.
2. After you have practiced the mudras, you will be asked to create your own.
3. When you have finished show your new mudra to the rest of the group. Teach it to them and practice the mudras they have invented.
4. Thank your group members for sharing their mudras.

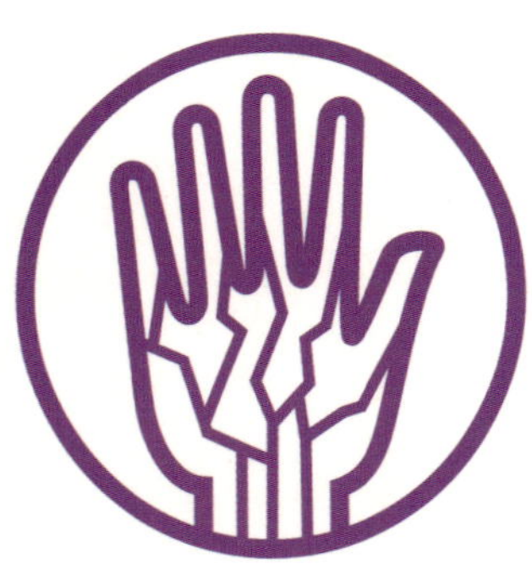

Traditional Mudras

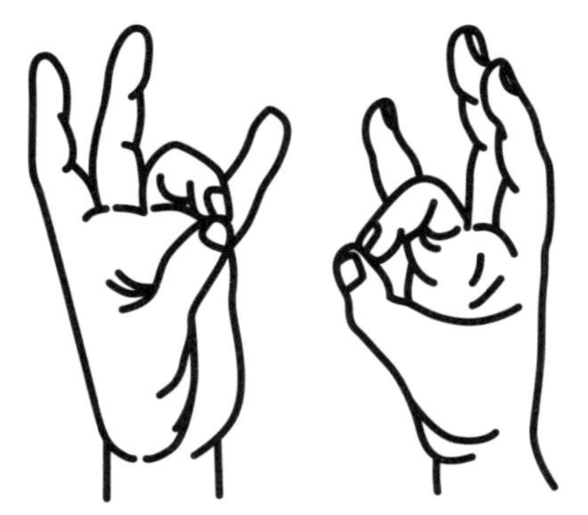

PRITHIVI MUDRA
Formed by touching the tip of the ring finger to the tip of the thumb. This mudra is said to increase vitality, strengthening the body and alleviating fatigue. It also helps to open the mind and frees it from irrational prejudices and beliefs. Practicing this Mudra helps to foster self-confidence and belief in the self.

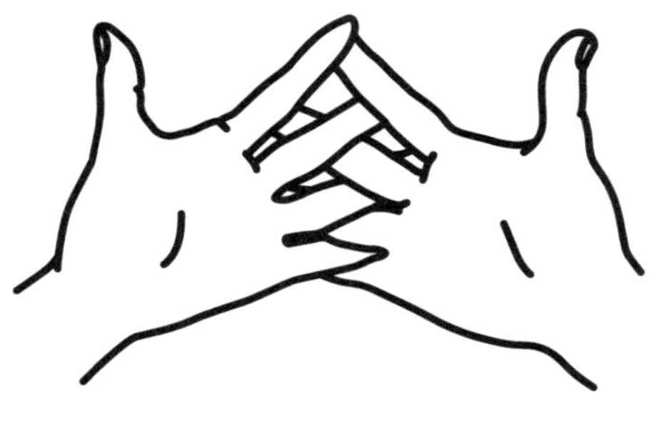

VAJRAPRADAMA MUDRA
Interlace the fingers in front of the chest with the palms facing toward the heart and thumbs facing upward. Open the hands away from each other, creating a gentle stretch to fingers. This mudra represents unshakable self-confidence and inner strength. This mudra is practiced to open the heart and increase compassion

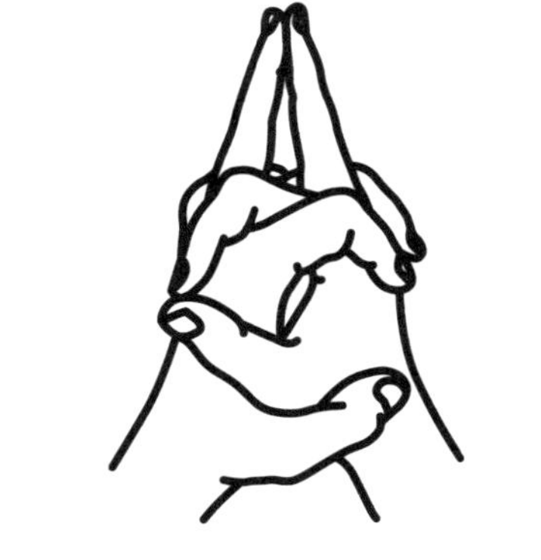

MATANGI MUDRA
Fold your hands, point both middle fingers and place them against each other. This mudra is performed to strengthen the breathing impulses in the solar plexus and balance the energies in this area. It is said to bring harmony, internal balance, and inner strength.

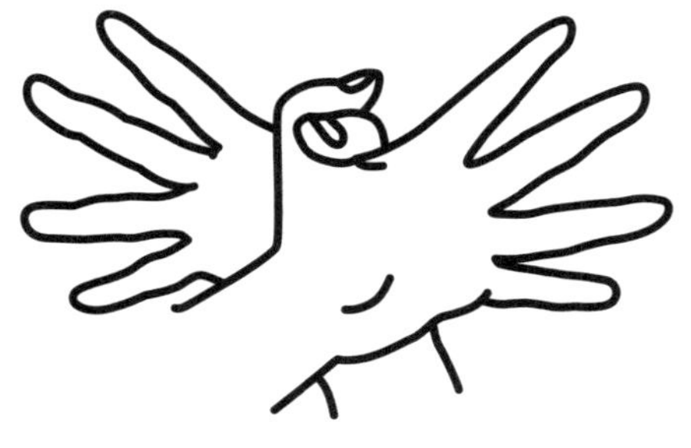

GARUDA MUDRA
Cross the arms in front of the chest, with the left arm in front of the right arm and the palms facing the heart. Hook the right thumb in front of the left thumb to form the shape of dove's wings. Garuda is performed to promote balance and a sense of freedom from boundaries and limits imposed by others or by ourselves. This mudra is said to activate blood flow and circulation and balance energy on both sides of the body.

What is the Intention of this Therapy?

Our mind is in constant flow. We frequently swing from one mood to another. One idea behind this activity is to give physical form to a particular thought or feeling, in order to make it easy to return to it later. By focusing on the feeling or mental state that you would like to achieve and translating it into a gesture using your hands, fingers, or other parts of your body, the brain must visualize what it desires and manifest it with the physical motion. By repeating the motion and continuing the visualization, the aim is to "fix" the gesture as a pathway to this desired state, creating a meditative shortcut to help us access this feeling or thought when we find our moods changing or our minds preoccupied.

The group aspect of this therapy is critical. Participants sit in a circle to give the activity a horizontal structure in which everyone participates. After practicing the traditional mudras, the therapist begins the process of inventing and sharing the personal mudras. It is important that she be the first to disclose her own desire in order to help the group warm up to the activity.

The sharing and practicing of each participant's mudras is an exercise of our mirror neurons, a neural mechanism that enables individuals to understand the meaning behind movements made by others — the intentions and emotions that drive others' actions. It does so through activating the individual's own internal representations coding those movements. That makes the other's movements easier for the individual to physically imitate, and also produces in the individual an imitation of the emotion the other felt while moving.[1] When we are children, mirror neurons help us to learn by observing what our parents and other people around us do—walking, talking, eating, getting dressed, etc. As we grow up, our mirror neurons let us develop empathy, our ability to relate to the feelings of other people. So the activity of listening to each group member's desire and practicing the mudra he invents leads us to exercise our empathy as well as to consider our own relationships to the desire he expresses.

I discussed the phenomenon of mirror neurons with neurologist and Sanatorium advisor Dr. Alice W. Flaherty. An excerpt of the conversation follows.

<u>Pedro Reyes:</u> It's an interesting point that some contexts make changes easier than others, to the degree that sometimes you have to change your context for the personal change to take place.

<u>Dr. Alice Flaherty:</u> Yes. Willpower is typically a weak force, but it is usually strong enough that it can get us to an environment that can make us do things. Often what is most helpful is when that environment already has a lot of people doing what we are trying to do, like going to the library when you're going to study, right? Your mirror neurons respond to the sight of those rows of heads bending over their book, and it's easier to keep your own head bent on your task. I can't study in the kitchen. My willpower is sort of worthless there.

<u>PR:</u> What is that phenomenon called where you start with an action that then produces a feeling?

AF: Like when you imitate crying, it makes you feel sad? Your action changes your brain's physical environment in a way. From your mind's point of view your body is a part of the environment, and if the body is making a sad face that is evidence to the brain that something is sad.

PR: Tell me about the "wiring" that makes that happen. Actors do this; they have command of their feelings through gestures as a feedback loop.

AF: The mirror neurons are involved, though there are other systems too. Mirror neurons give us a bit of an urge to imitate actions we see others make. We tend to dismiss the urge to imitate other people as really primitive. But it's produced by high-level brain areas and is very important for learning. Although we say "monkey see, monkey do" because chimps imitate more than other species do, kids imitate way more than chimps do. They need to. Learning by example is much more efficient than trial and error learning. Mirror neurons are essential for learning language. When the mirror neuron system doesn't work well, it's very hard for babies to learn speech

That is a problem in autism. Autistic babies' mirror neurons are under-active, and they don't imitate their parents' speech sounds. They don't babble. For the average baby, if you go, "goo goo gah gah," it says "goo goo gah gah," When their mother sweeps the floor, autistic kids don't pretend to sweep the floor. They don't have imaginative play. And they have trouble imagining what other people are feeling because they never pretend to be other people.

PR: Like Albert Bandura's idea of Modeling Behavior and the Bobo Doll Experiment. It's this classic experiment from behavioral psychology where a kid is shown a movie with an adult hitting a doll. Then he is left alone in a room with the same doll. The kids that saw the movie hit the doll and even invented new ways to harm the doll, while the kids that didn't see the movie hugged the doll.[2]

AF: Yes, mirror neurons can make bad emotions contagious too, not just make everyone more sympathetic. Doctors use the word very narrowly; they mostly talk of feeling another person's pain. In fact, empathy was originally an art criticism term (*Einfühlungsvermögen*). It meant the experience of seeing a view from the perspective of a figure in a painting, an imaginary character.

When doctors took the word "empathy" out of the world of the imagination and into the real world, things got visceral. Our brains have images of our bodies, but the image is made with nerve bodies, not paint or pixels. Mirror neurons put another person's body map into your brain, on top of your body map. That changes your brain and also your body. If you watch somebody being injected with a needle, most normal people tense up the same muscle that is getting needled in the patient. Your body is physically changed by what that person is going through. It's kind of cool that there is a visceral way that people's selves merge to some extent.

PR: I think this is extremely relevant regarding change. To improve human relationships, which are often thought to have been motivated by honest and pure intentions…

AF: Honest desired exchange. You believe that, yes.

PR: No, it's the opposite. It's more about the basis of action. Modeling our behavior on another person lets us work on actions previous to the belief and adopt a habit even if it hasn't been internalized yet… to do the right thing even if you don't feel like it. This is the reason why manners and etiquette were invented; the form sometimes may precede the content.

AF: "Fake it until you make it," as they say, though that's a snarky way to describe such an important process. Some of your collective rituals change people that way. The Sanatorium mudras do. And your *Palas por Pistolas* (Guns for shovels, 2008) project in different cities. Even if I didn't have a strong urge to melt down my boyfriend's guns, but all my women friends are getting rid of their husbands' guns, I'm more likely to want to do it. Then once I've done it, I can start to feel pleased that I have done this good, life-affirming thing. That's what makes a community; empathy for good emotions can be as contagious as bad ones. Actually, more contagious. A researcher named Nicholas Christakis showed that people are more likely to "catch" happiness from contact with happy people than they are to catch sadness from contact with sad people.

So in your *Pistolas* project, when you organize the tree planting and you get all these people together doing the same thing, it's an important force that not only every individual person does this, but 1,500 people are doing it together. I think it's great that this supposedly low urge to imitate can really be so powerfully elevating.

1   Giacomo Rizolatti and Laila Craighero, "Mirror Neuron: a Neurological Approach to Empathy," *Neurobiology of Human Values*, eds. J.P.Changeaux, A.R. Damasio, W. Singer, Y. Christen (Berlin: Springer, 2005) p. 107.
2   Albert Bandura, "The Role of Imitation in Personality Development," *Journal of Nursery Education* 18, no. 3 (April 1963).

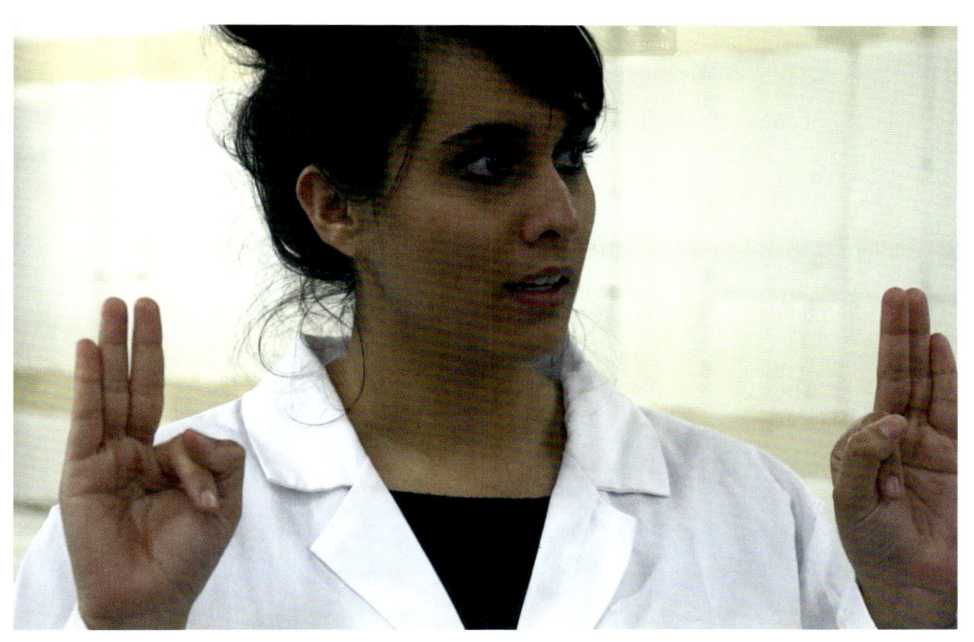

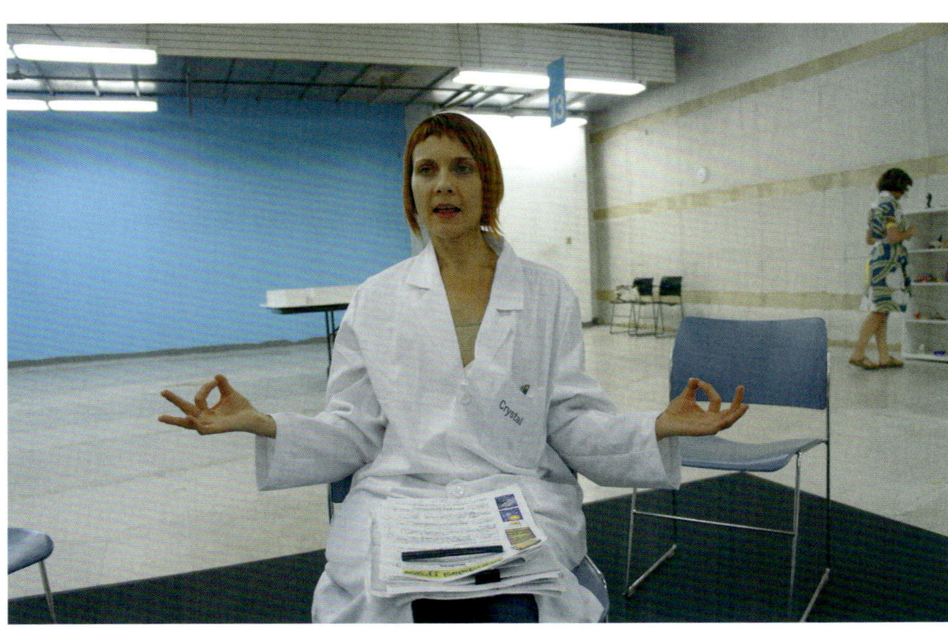

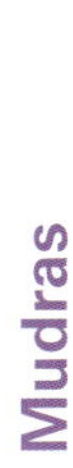

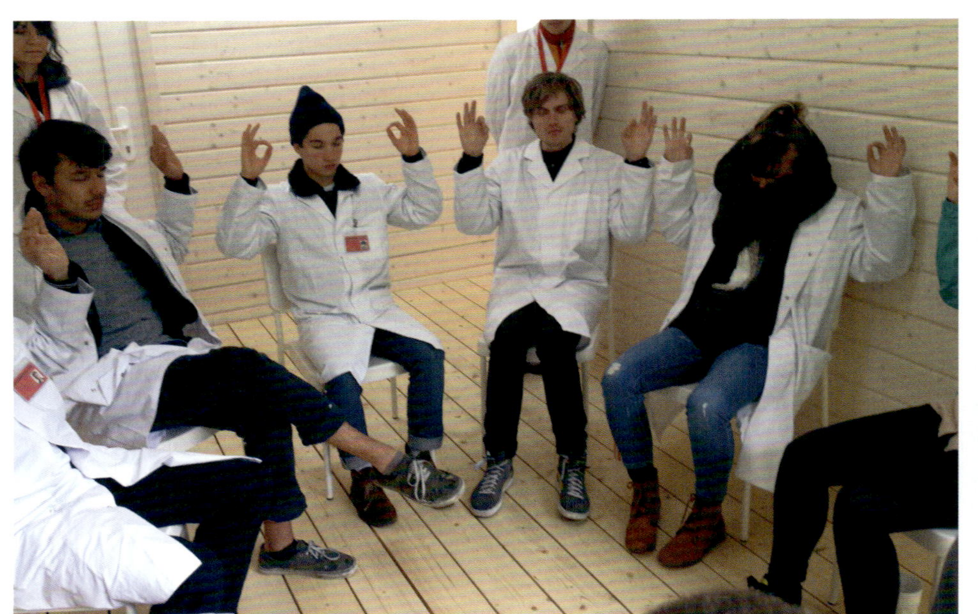

Philosophical Casino

<u>Number of participants:</u> Small groups of three to five people
<u>Time:</u> 30 to 40 minutes
<u>Space size:</u> Minimum 3×6m, ideal 4×8m
<u>Space requirements:</u> Carpeted floor with some kind of padding to absorb the impact of the dice
<u>Furniture:</u> Table, chairs according to number of participants
<u>Props:</u> Five oversized fiberglass dice featuring selected quotes silkscreened on each side, notecards, pens or pencils, a box to collect questions
<u>Therapist qualifications:</u> Basic

DESCRIPTION

Philosophical Casino works like an oracle. You will be assigned to a group. Each person in your group will write down three questions. The questions will be put in a box. You will find a series of dice, each of which features a philosophical quote on each side from one of five categories: Greek, Far East, Renaissance, Nineteenth Century Philosophy in German, and Mid-Twentieth Century Philosophers. Your therapist will ask the group to select one die to roll to give an answer to the question she pulls from the box. How does the quote that comes up shed light on your question?

THERAPIST INSTRUCTIONS

1. Greet and welcome the participants.
2. Explain the therapy.
3. Ask the participants to write down their questions.
4. Have the participants place their questions in the box and select one to ask the die.
5. Have the participants select the die they will use, ask the question and roll the die.
6. This therapy is appropriate for children as participants.
7. This therapy is appropriate for blind and deaf visitors with adequuante assistance.

PARTICIPANT INSTRUCTIONS

1. You may ask any of these oracles one question, with a maximum of five questions total.
2. Think of your questions. Write them down on the cards provided by your therapist and place your questions in the box near the oracles.
3. If your question involves names that should remain secret, use X or Y in your question to stand for the names.
4. Spin the die and read the philosophical quote on the side that lands upright. How does it apply to your question?
5. Your questions are anonymous; they are collected solely for statistic purposes.
6. Not recommended for blind visitors.
7. Not recommended for deaf visitors unless accompanied by an interpreter.
8. Therapists will need to roll the die for visitors with limited mobility.

What is the Intention of this Therapy?

An oracle prepares your mind to assign special weight to a text or a symbol. One mundane example is horoscopes; even if you find them corny, you pay special attention to your own sign and read the horoscopes of other signs according to the people in your life. The same applies to other oracles, from the *I Ching* to fortune cookies.

In the Philosophical Casino, the quotes on the dice are selected to be epigrams, maxims, and sentences that are universally useful and can shed light on most situations that may come up. They are particles of wisdom — a term that seems to be out of fashion, as we've moved from valuing wisdom to valuing knowledge and then from knowledge to information. But we must continue to seek wisdom, judging something wise accoding to its usefulness or capacity to awaken consciousness in the other, to lead to new insights.

In this activity the quotes serve to spark the ultimate exercise of philosophy, conducted very much in the style of the ancient Greeks. The peripatetic practice of philosophy involved a small group walking and conversing or talking while resting under a tree — this is why laurel wreaths were associated with knowledge. When you are in the Philosophical Casino, your question is read and a quote is offered to you as a key to help you see your problem in a different light. The random partners you find next to you can make interventions, suggesting facets of the situation in a light-hearted manner.

"What philosophy is and how much it is worth are matters of controversy," said German philosopher Karl Jaspers. He continues:

> *One may expect it to yield extraordinary revelations or one may view it with indifference as a thinking in the void… One may take the attitude that it is the concern of all men, and hence must be basically simple and intelligible, or one may think of it as hopelessly difficult. And indeed, what goes by the name of philosophy provides examples to warrant all these conflicting judgments.*[1]

The attempt in Philosophical Casino is to offer the tools of philosophy in a casual yet meaningful manner, avoiding these extremes, as one of philosophy's main questions since ancient times has been simply "how to live?"

1   Karl Jaspers, *Ein Chrung in die Philosophie*, trans. Ralph Mannheim (Zurich: Artemis Verlag, 1949).

THERAPIST REPORT
Mathilde Fernandez, October 2012

We organized group sessions of Philosophical Casino. When the group was too large, we separated participants into two teams and asked each to agree on two questions. This technique worked quite well because we had a better chance of getting more thoughtful questions that fit well with the answers.

I remember an individual session of Philosophical Casino with a middle-aged man who came alone from Berlin. I explained the therapy and asked him to write three questions. After five minutes I came back and he had only written two questions. The first was, "Will my wife and I stay together after the departure of my son?" The answer on the die had absolutely nothing to do with the question. I saw from his behaviour that it weakened him. We tried to twist the response to apply to the question, but nothing happened; we could not link the two.

For the second question he asked, "Will my son and I keep the same relationship we have despite his departure?"

The response fell on Rabelais: "Life is not a vase to be filled but a fire to be lit."

The answer was good. It corresponded directly; he interpreted that perhaps he should return to camping with his son in the mountains. We spent a little time talking and he told me that he was twenty years old the last time he came to the Documenta. He had come with his friends and they had camped.

QUESTIONS ASKED OF THE
PHILOSOPHICAL CASINO

Am I close to getting a new job
with one of three agencies
I'm talking to?
Am I doing this correctly?
Am I going to find the way to
a fulfilled, satisfied, produc-
tive, happy life?
Am I making the right choice?
Am I my name?
Am I on the right career path?
Am I on the right path?
Am I really insatiable?
Am I really still in love with M?
Am I utilizing my talents to the
fullest?
Are a cat's nine lives merely its
visible projections into our
3-D universe?
Are gay people born homosexual?
Are love and loss inseparable?
Are things going too easy for me?
Are we meant to stay in New
York for more than two
years?
Are you satisfied with the way
your democratic ideas
are in movement today?
Cake or Death?
Can a circle be squared?
Can I break through my self-
imposed barriers?
Can I live without my parents?
Can I trust future generations?
Can one's search for knowledge
shift between planes of
existence and still maintain
a semblance of some
grounding?

Can the environment recover?
Can there be any mistakes if
something good comes out
of a mistake? How does
it effect my thinking, my
reactions?
Can we change our fate?
Can wise discussion be made
through a dice?
Can you find yourself in a place
you've never been?
How will the EU/UK be benefi-
cial to my career?
Define humanity.
Did I make the right decision
today? Is there a "right"
decision?
Do dreams lead us to believe in
God?
Do I have a duty to try and per-
suade others to stop doing
what I believe is wrong?
Do I have a soul?
Do I just escape from myself or
do I move constantly out of
dissatisfaction?
Do I need a home?
Do soul mates really exist?
Do we make our own choices or
are our paths predefined?
Do you have a soul?
Do you like me?
Do you love Danzig too?
Does being a grandfather mean
you are old?
Does belief in humanity and the
agency it possesses as con-
nected to some form of
rational choice imbue it
with a sort of priori telos?
Does God exist?

Does he like me? Like like like
or just like?
Does John like me?
Does life get better as you age?
Does one have to pursue the best
version of the self to be
happy?
Does the girl that I'm seeing
actually like me or is she
using me?
Does the guy of my life live in
NYC?
How can I accept that which is
beyond my control and has
great power over my future?
How can I afford to live freely?
How can I be a better daughter?
How can I be a good influence and
supportive to my family?
How can I be a good parent?
How can I be happy?
How can I be more kind to my
roommate?
How can I be the most famous
artist?
How can I become better?
How can I experience more joy?
How can I free myself from envy?
How can I get to spend their life
with me?
How can I get more in tune with
my subconscious?
How can I have more energy?
How can I improve my business?
How can I know when it's right?
How can I learn to let go?
How can I make a better use of
my time?
How can I make more money
(and not be miserable while
doing it)?

How can I make the most out of
next year?
How can I overcome the obstacles
that prevent me from creating and publishing art?
How can I prevent myself from
repeating old habits and
negative behaviors?
How can I stop desiring something I don't need?
How can one make the best use
of time, make it longer or
fill it better?
How can one remain calm?
How can people stop wanting to
accumulate things?
How can we receive insight?
How can you accept getting older?
How can you accept that one day
you will die if you know
there is nothing to come
afterwards?
How can you do what you love
when you fear you won't be
good at it?
How could the infinite exist
within us?
How deep is the river?
How did tigers get to be so awe-
some?
How do I access my artistic side
more easily?
How do I be more happy?
How do I be supportive and a good
influence in my family?
How do I become more confident?
How do I become more efficient
at work?
How do I begin?
How do I create meaning and
purpose and happiness —

in this world?

How do I cure my brain tumors?

How do I find love?

How do I get over being insecure about my job?

How do I get over loss?

How do I incorporate the different aspects of myself — or more specifically how I see myself when representing myself in dealing with others — in career and interpersonal relationships?

How do I keep from boring myself?

How do I know if I've made the right choices?

How do I know when it's time to move on from my job?

How do I learn to put others first?

How do I make my life meaningful?

How do I move forward?

How do I move on from feeling guilty?

How do I stop slicing my drive?

How do I stop worrying about stupid shit?

How do I work better and happier with my co-workers?

How do leave my job?

How do you describe "blue" to a blind man?

How do you know?

How do you synchronize a TR-707, TR-727, and a MC-202?

How do you trust?

How does a person stop playing out alternative versions of his life in his head?

How does an individual balance ambition with being satisfied with their current situation?

How does one achieve inner peace?

How does one find inner quiet/ peace?

How does one live a meaningful life in a world of absurdity?

How does one maintain faith as an atheist?

How does your heart know when it is safe to love?

How important is the accumulation of money for oneself?

How is the best way to live our lives?

How late is Starbucks open?

How linked are one's understanding and experience of sociability and humanity?

How long does sadness remain?

How long can people sustain their idealism?

How long should you wait for someone?

How long will I hang onto my apartment?

How long will I live in NY?

How much should I think about the people in my life when deciding where to move?

How should I approach planning my career?

How should I proceed?

How should I read the guidance I receive?

How should I spend my upcoming year of free time?

How to help my children achieve their "dreams"?

How to live for myself?

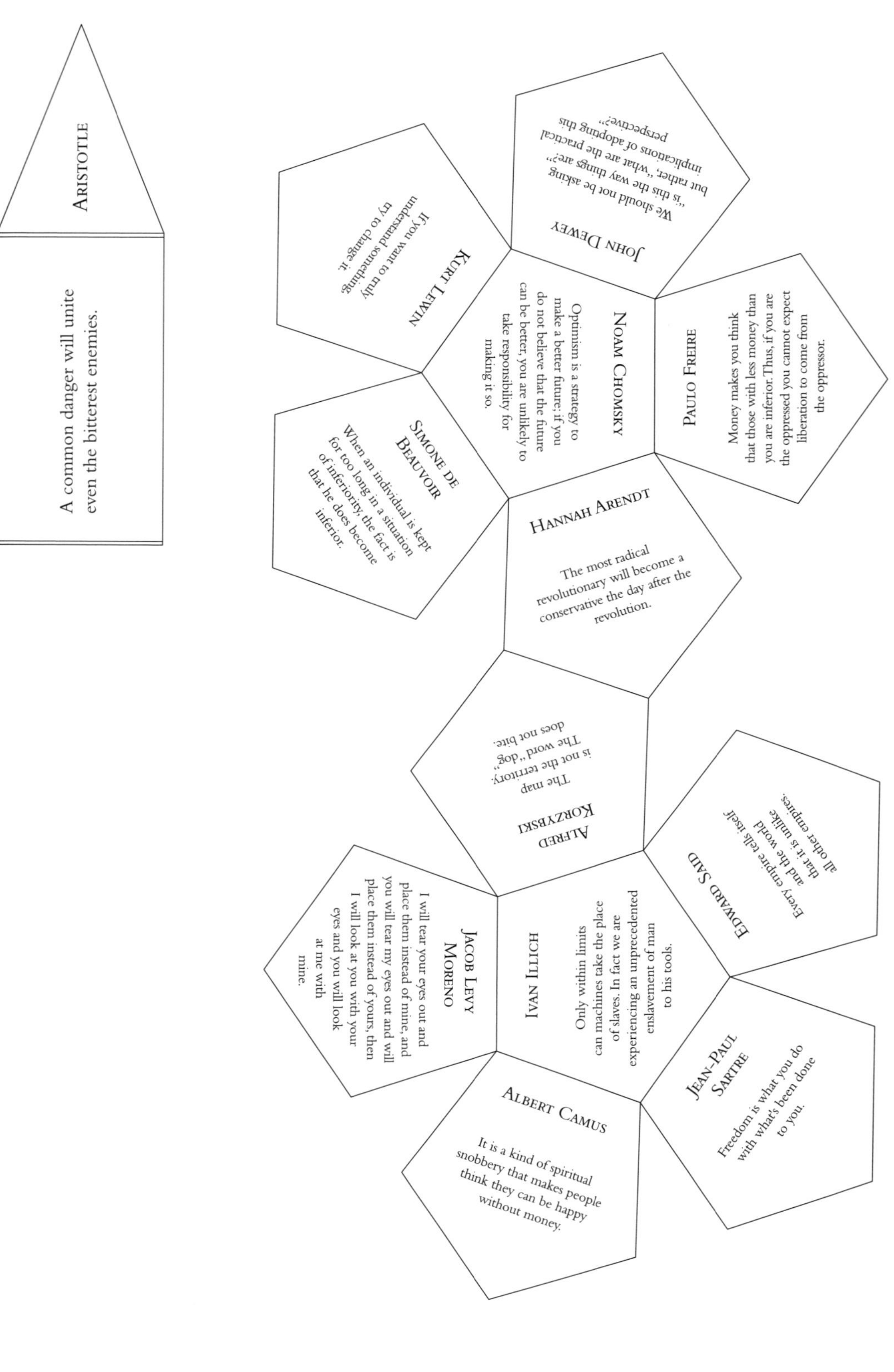

ARISTOTLE
A common danger will unite even the bitterest enemies.

KURT LEWIN
If you want to truly understand something, try to change it.

JOHN DEWEY
We should not be asking "is this the way things are?" but rather, "what are the practical implications of adopting this perspective?"

NOAM CHOMSKY
Optimism is a strategy to make a better future; if you do not believe that the future can be better, you are unlikely to take responsibility for making it so.

PAULO FREIRE
Money makes you think that those with less money than you are inferior. Thus, if you are the oppressed you cannot expect liberation to come from the oppressor.

SIMONE DE BEAUVOIR
When an individual is kept for too long in a situation of inferiority, the fact is that he does become inferior.

HANNAH ARENDT
The most radical revolutionary will become a conservative the day after the revolution.

ALFRED KORZYBSKI
The map is not the territory. The word "dog" does not bite.

EDWARD SAID
Every empire tells itself and the world that it is unlike all other empires.

JACOB LEVY MORENO
I will tear your eyes out and place them instead of mine, and you will tear my eyes out and will place them instead of yours, then I will look at you with your eyes and you will look at me with mine.

IVAN ILLICH
Only within limits can machines take the place of slaves. In fact we are experiencing an unprecedented enslavement of man to his tools.

JEAN-PAUL SARTRE
Freedom is what you do with what's been done to you.

ALBERT CAMUS
It is a kind of spiritual snobbery that makes people think they can be happy without money.

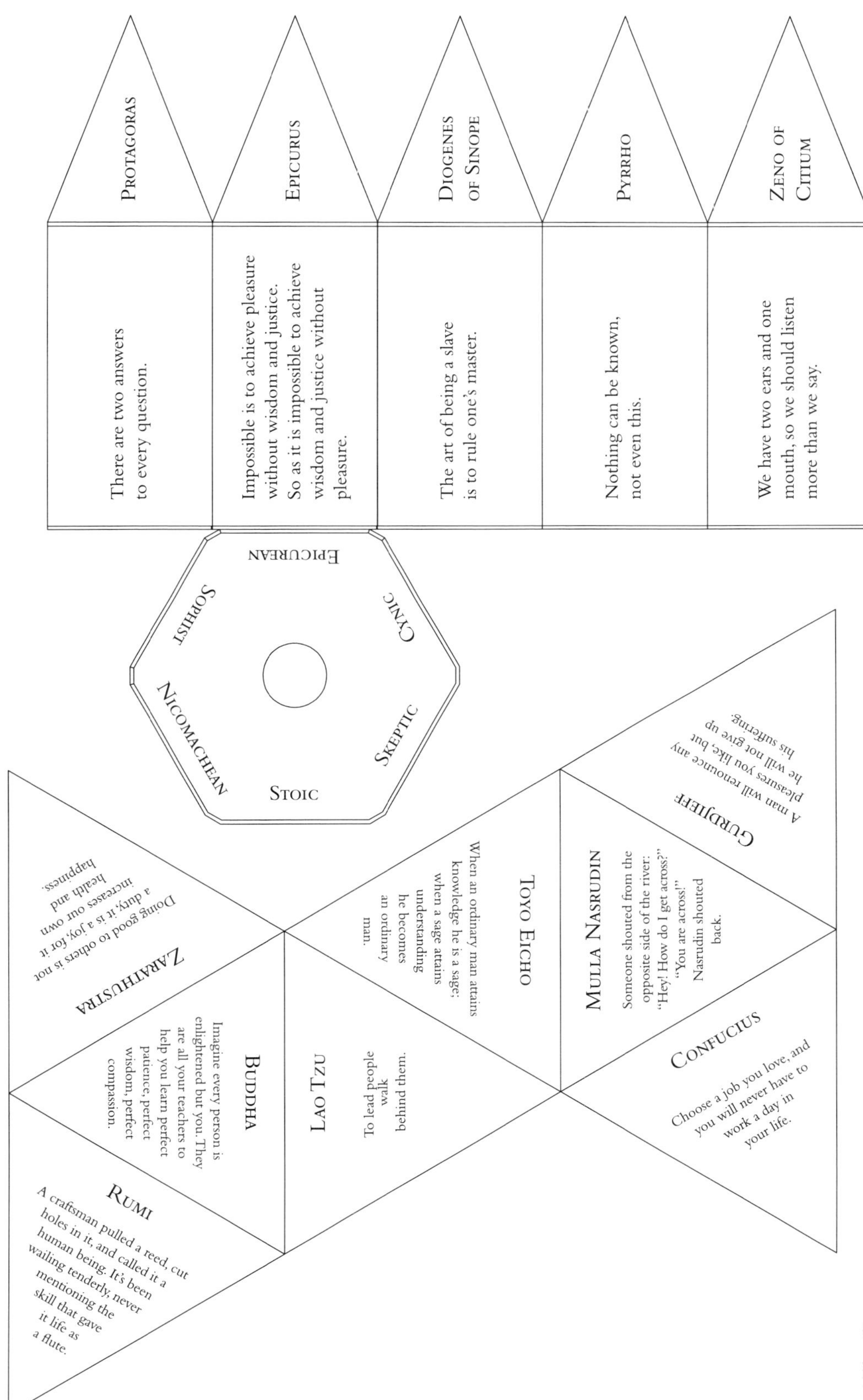

PROTAGORAS
EPICURUS
DIOGENES OF SINOPE
PYRRHO
ZENO OF CITIUM
There are two answers to every question.
Impossible is to achieve pleasure without wisdom and justice. So as it is impossible to achieve wisdom and justice without pleasure.
The art of being a slave is to rule one's master.
Nothing can be known, not even this.
We have two ears and one mouth, so we should listen more than we say.
EPICUREAN
SOPHIST
CYNIC
NICOMACHEAN
SKEPTIC
STOIC
ZARATHUSTRA
Doing good to others is not a duty, it is a joy, for it increases our own health and happiness.
TOYO EICHO
When an ordinary man attains knowledge he is a sage; when a sage attains understanding he becomes an ordinary man.
GURDJIEFF
A man will renounce any pleasures you like, but he will not give up his suffering.
MULLA NASRUDIN
Someone shouted from the opposite side of the river: "Hey! How do I get across?" "You are across!" Nasrudin shouted back.
CONFUCIUS
Choose a job you love, and you will never have to work a day in your life.
BUDDHA
Imagine every person is enlightened but you. They are all your teachers to help you learn perfect patience, perfect wisdom, perfect compassion.
LAO TZU
To lead people walk behind them.
RUMI
A craftsman pulled a reed, cut holes in it, and called it a human being. It's been wailing tenderly, never mentioning the skill that gave it life as a flute.

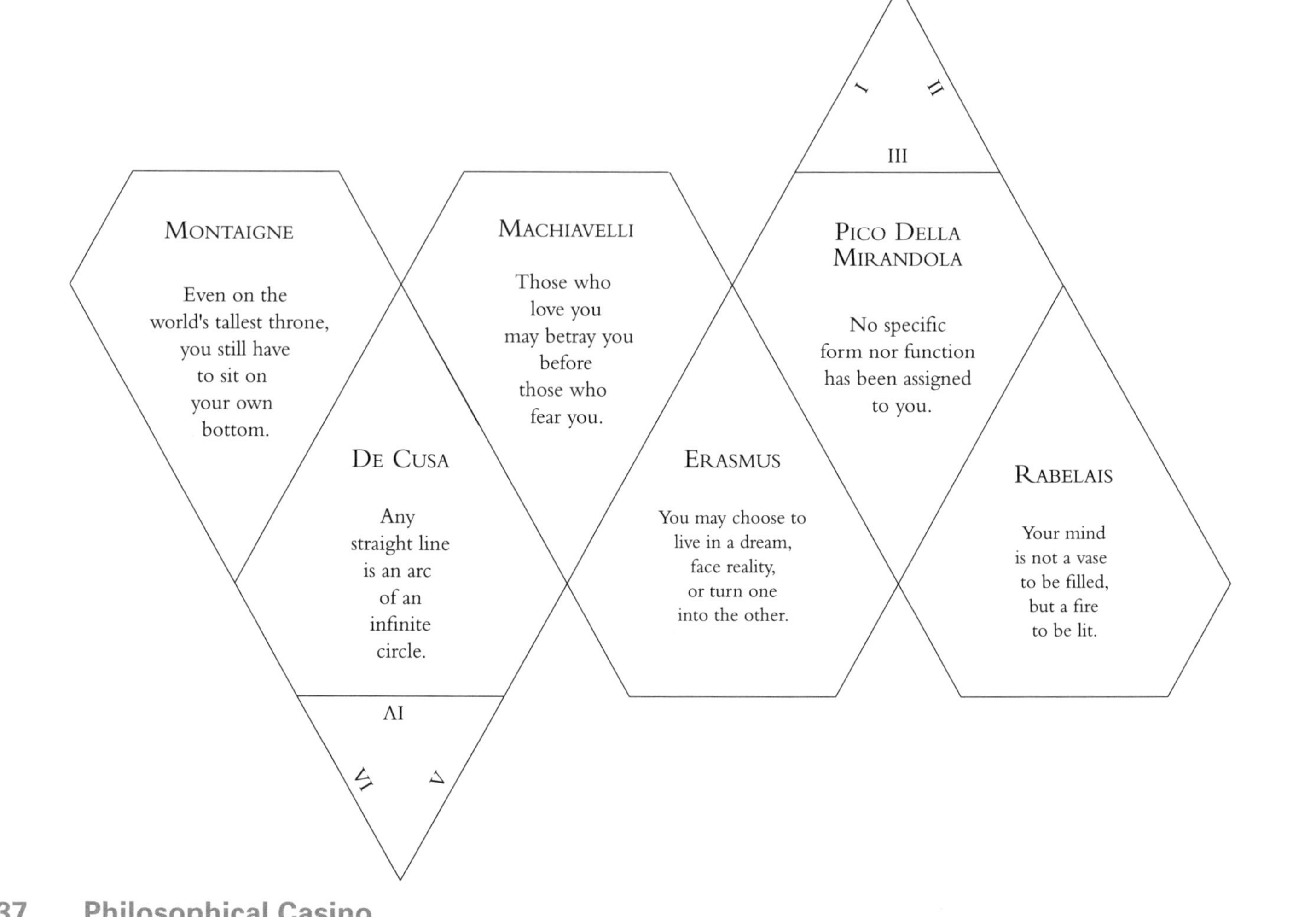
MONTAIGNE
Even on the world's tallest throne, you still have to sit on your own bottom.
MACHIAVELLI
Those who love you may betray you before those who fear you.
PICO DELLA MIRANDOLA
No specific form nor function has been assigned to you.
I
II
III
DE CUSA
Any straight line is an arc of an infinite circle.
ERASMUS
You may choose to live in a dream, face reality, or turn one into the other.
RABELAIS
Your mind is not a vase to be filled, but a fire to be lit.
IV
V
VI

KANT

He who
has made
great moral
progress
ceases
to
pray.

NIETZSCHE

There are
no facts,
only
interpretations.

HEGEL

The owl
of Minerva
spreads its wings
only with
the falling
of the
dusk.

WITTGENSTEIN

Show
the fly
the way out
of the
fly-bottle.

SCHOPENHAUER

Honor
has not
to be won;
it must
only
not be
lost.

HEIDEGGER

Das nichts
nichtet.

FEUERBACH

Truth comes to us through
the other. That which is
true belongs neither
to me nor
exclusively to
you, but is
common
to all.

MARX

Capital is like a vampire,
it lives only by sucking
living labor.
The more labor
it sucks, the
longer it
lives.

NOVALIS

Time
is inner space.
Space
is outer time.

SCHILLER

Man only plays when in
the full meaning of the
word he is a man,
and he is only
completely a
man when
he plays.

How will I know if I have made the
right choices (career, love)?
How will I make more money in
the face of a growing global
economic recession?
How will I realize success?
How will my life and love change
the lives of others?
How would moving affect my
family?
How should I overcome my
shyness?
I've reached a fork in the road
and need to choose a path,
which way should I go?
If E=MC², what is E if C approaches zero?
If I get a dog will I never marry?
If I were to leave my life as-is
tonight, would my life
as-it-could-be make me
happy/satisfied?
If sex is not a sin in God's eye,
why do religious people put
such an emphasis on it?
If so much of what we "know" is
generated by the dynamics
of the organs of the body,
what part of consciousness
can endure after death?
Must it have a memory of
the body?
If the dialectical struggle that
results in the negation of
the terms of existence were
to ever resolve itself, what
comes next?
Will I go back to living in Europe?
If your heart is pure and good,
will good things naturally
come to you, or do you
have to still seek out what
is good for you?
In order to find love, is it more
important to be vulnerable
or to be true to your own
needs?
Invest in photo equipment?
Is a minimal lifestyle sustainable
for me?
Is David dating that ho?
Is dreaming (of future hopes)
a luxury?
Is a threesome going to be an
interesting experience?
Is God cheesy?
Is happiness the most important
thing?
Is ignorance bliss or cowardice?
Is it better to live in the city or
country?
Is it better to stir the pot and
plan or just wait and see
what rises?
Is it better to underuse or
overuse something?
Is it easier to be alone in a crowd
or an empty space?
Is it healthy to remind yourself
of traumatic experiences
from the past?
Is it important to live?
Is it more important to seek
happiness and fulfillment
within one's own lifetime
or to have a lasting and
meaningful impact on
mankind's history?
Is it not a good choice to focus on
making art as opposed to
other more practical areas?
Is it more powerful to do an

action for itself, for its value as an action in its own right, or is it more powerful to do an action successfully, as a means towards an end that is demonstrably good?

Is it ok to be driven by hate?

Is it ok to dislike religious people?

Is it possible to be faithful to your partner always?

Is it possible to truly understand another person?

Is it time for big change?

Is language meaningful in any way? Can it express a universal truth?

Is leaving New York, having kids and living in the suburbs going to make me happy?

Is love important?

Is moving back the right decision?

Is my relationship that was ended because of distance now on an inevitable spiral downward to a meaningless life?

Is my search to find life's path going to lead me further from my current self or closer?

Is perfect love possible?

Is personal vanity a good thing or bad? In other words, is narcissism necessary for survival?

Is spending money on an MSW education a reasonable reason for a lifetime of debt?

Is straight or curly hair more attractive?

Is suicide a human right?

Is the guy I'm going on a date with Tuesday going to be "the one"?

Is the universe only perception?

Is there a balance between art and protagonism?

Is there actually a God and does he watch over us?

Is there life after death?

Is there life on other planets?

Is there such a thing as a true monogamous relationship?

Is there such a thing as life without drama?

Is there such a thing as man's "true nature" or soul? Or do we accumulate our nature as we age?

Is there such a thing as truth?

Is there such a thing as unselfish love?

Is this it?

It is a bit sour but I believe our friendship will survive this.

J + L =?

Meaning?

Now that I'm turning 47 what shall I do with my life?

Petrache rules and I'm happy he got a lot of you thinkers started, but why did it all end up having to be about God?

Queens, Brooklyn, or Manhattan?

Romantically, or in choosing a life partner, how do I focus on who would be the best match?

Shall I marry my girlfriend?
Should I adopt a child in this lifetime?
Should I adopt Jeff?
Should I be single or not and why?
Should I be writing rather than working full-time?
Should I change jobs?
Should I do what he's asking me to do?
Should I eat dinner and if so what should I get?
Should I incorporate more fruit and vegetables into my diet? If so, what fruit and/or vegetables should I choose?
Should I get a pet?
Should I go back to music?
Should I go to film school?
Should I go to work tomorrow?
Should I go to Switzerland next month?
Should I have a change in career?
Should I invite my girlfriend to visit my family in another state even though the relationship is fairly new?
Should I kick one of my brides-maids out of the wedding party?
Should I listen more to the dead or to the living?
Should I make completing certification a priority?
Should I move here in the fall?
Should I move to California?
Should I procreate?
Should I quit my job to go back to school?
Should I quit my job?
Should I relocate in the next year?

Should I send a letter?
Should I start doing yoga?
Should I stay with a caring but emotionally detached person — will I be happy enough?
Should I stick to architecture?
Should I stop sleeping with F?
Should I take care of peanut?
Should I take the job at EH?
Should I try to stay with M+R?
Should I work harder or just relax?
Should I do WWOOF or should I focus on NYC?
Should love be the ultimate goal?
Should we stay on this NYC track or change lanes?
Should I go to PPSC?
So what's next? And perhaps more, tell me something I don't know.
Will I feel satisfied with my adventure in Japan?
What should I do the year after next?
What am I looking for?
What am I meant to do in life?
What am I supposed to do now?
What am I?
What can I do to achieve my personal goals in an effec-tive/non-aggressive, yet not too stressful direction?
What combination of love and career will make me happy?
What do I do in August?
What do I need to know now?
What do I need to work on?
What does it mean to be a good mother?

What does it mean to be a good
person?
What does it mean to be an
individual?
What does it mean to be happy?
What does it mean to come from
a place?
What does it mean to know
oneself?
What does it mean to say chil-
dren are innocent?
What good can come out of the
bad situation I'm currently
in? (the Germans)
What happened to my blue dress?
What happens next?
What happens when we die?
What is "success" in life?
What is beauty?
What is freedom?
What is good?
What is happiness?
What is home?
What is libido?
What is love?
What is more important family
or career?
What is my best use?
What is my biggest personal
challenge?
What is my identity?
What is my lucky number?
What is my purpose in this world?
What is my real passion?
What is reality?
What is romanticism?
What is the best borough and
why?
What is the best path I should
take after I finish my
masters program?

What is the best use of my time
and energy?
What is the best use of my time/
life?
What is the best way to take
advantage of the summer?
What is the deal with dreams?
What is the goal of an ethical life?
What is the key to finding the
right path?
What is the key to happiness?
What is the key to maintaining
perspective?
What is the meaning if all this?
What is the meaning of life?
What is the meaning of life?
What is the meaning of life?
What is the most enlightened
human activity that I can
participate in?
What is the most important
question we ask?
What is the new black?
What is the next step?
What is the origin of war?
What is the real meaning of "soul
mate"?
What is the right date?
What is the right type of work
for me?
What is the role of personality in
art?
What is the source of music?
What is time?
What is true love?
What is wisdom and is it desira-
ble?
What job will I get?
What kind of cheese will I like?
What kind of mother will I be?
What makes a person interested

in attending an installation like this?

What matters to me more than anything?

What motivates us?

What of the next ten years?

What religion is the best, most useful religion?

What should I do with my career?

What should be my moral compass?

What should I be when I grow up?

What should I do as a profession?

What should I do regarding my professional life?

What should I do right…now?

What should I do with my life?

What should I do with the rest of my life?

What should my next move be?

What sort of relationship will I have with my mother?

What vocation should I embark on next?

What will my next job be? And will it be significant in the world?

What will be my legacy? What will the world remember me for?

What will happen when my dad dies?

What will I eat for dinner?

What will I get from New York?

What will it take for me to finish my project—in a way that I am totally satisfied with it?

What will it take to figure things (life) out?

What will lead me to satisfaction (and away from restless-ness) in my life?

What will my love life/family life be like in five years?

What will the future of the monetary world/global economy be?

What work should I do?

What would going back to Buenos Aires imply?

What would make me most content?

What's a way to be happy?

What's best for my dog?

What's love got to do, got to do with it?

What's my dharma?

What's my problem?

What's the next step?

What's the best kind of dog?

Why are languages different?

When am I going to return to Europe?

When faced with a conflict between two options, how does one decide on the best choice?

When I die will it just be "lights out"?

When is the right time to make a commitment?

When should I quit my day job?

When should women serve as soldiers?

When we think do we create our thoughts?

When will humans be replaced by something smarter, stronger and better looking?

When will I die?

When will I marry?

When will I travel again?

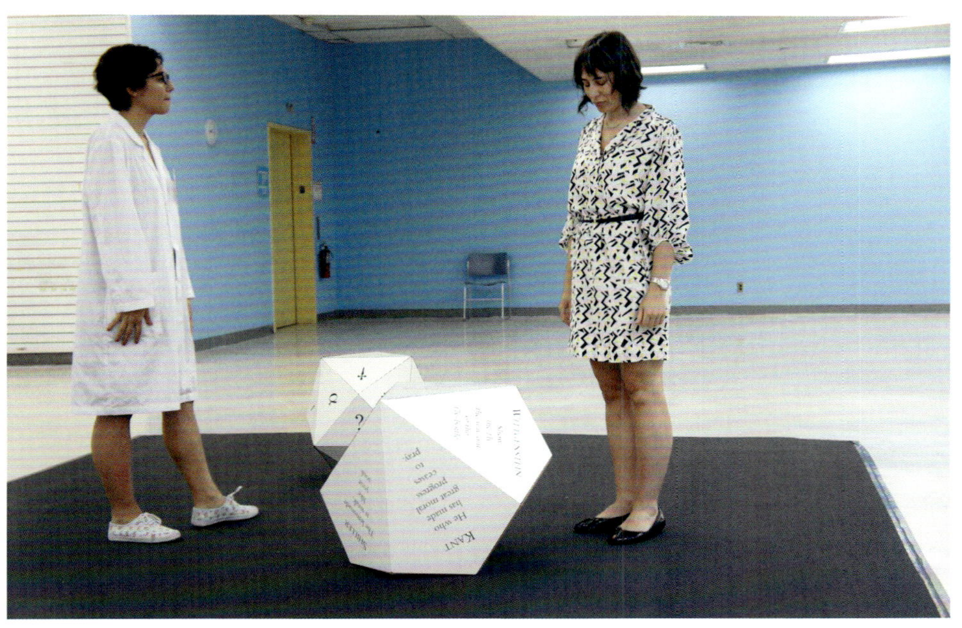

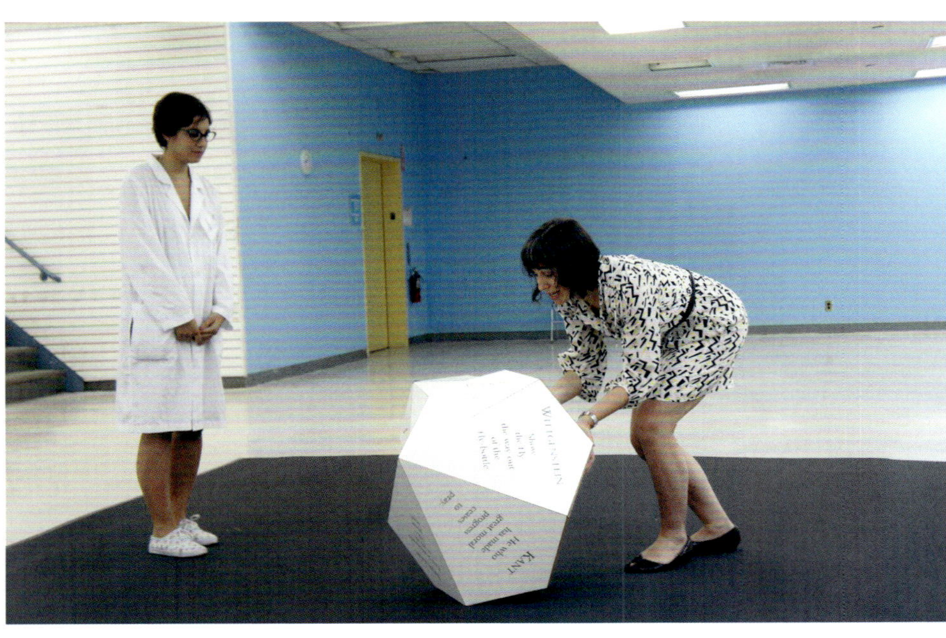

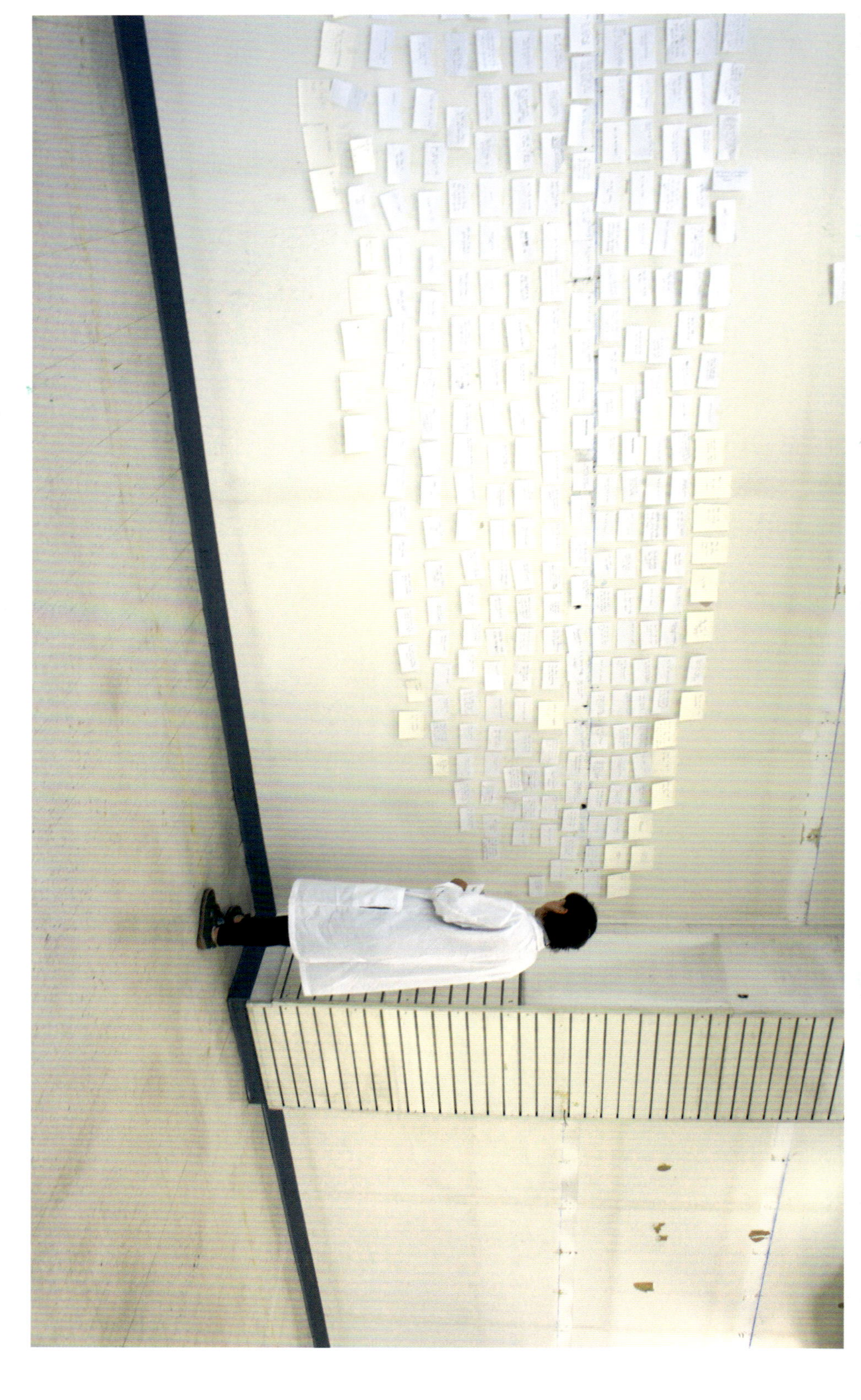

Epitaphs

Number of participants: Individuals
Time: 30 minutes
Space size: 3×3 m
Space requirements: Quiet, intimate. It is desirable to have a control to dim or lower the lights.
Furniture: Carpeted floor or mats, low table
Props: Hammer, letter chisels, notecards, thumbtacks
Therapist qualifications: Basic

DESCRIPTION

In this therapy participants are given the chance to write their own epitaphs, using language as plain or poetic as they wish.

Most people never get to know what will be written on their tombstones, although some — especially writers — leave instructions on what they want said in summary of their lives.

In this exercise you get to choose the words that will tell future cemetery-goers something about you, and perhaps about the meaning of life as well.

THERAPIST INSTRUCTIONS

1. Greet and welcome the participant.
2. Explain the therapy.
3. When the participant has composed an epitaph, he will use the letter chisels to stamp it into a set of two notecards. Show him how to arrange the letters and use the hammer to create the "tombstone."
4. Hang one of the epitaphs on the wall and give the other to the participant.
5. This therapy is appropriate for children as participants.
6. This therapy is not recommended for blind visitors.
7. This therapy is appropriate for deaf visitors if written instructions are provided.

PARTICIPANT INSTRUCTIONS:

1. Lie on a mat or carpet and picture yourself at your funeral.
2. Take a few minutes to compose the words for which you will be remembered. Write a draft.
3. Once you have completed your draft, choose two cards for your epitaph and place them on top of each other.
4. Carefully pick up and place the letters of the metal stamps and hammer your epitaph, letter by letter.
5. Once you have finished the lettering, place your epitaph in the "cemetery."
6. Keep the second copy of the epitaph for yourself.

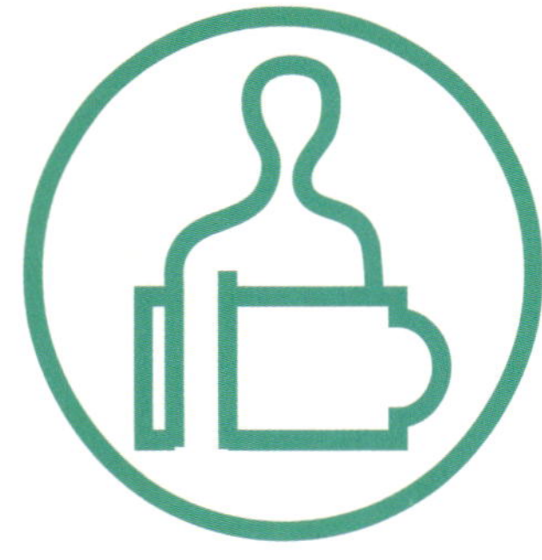

What is the Intention of this Therapy?

The Epitaphs therapy asks visitors to project into the future to a moment when they no longer exist. An epitaph composed by a visitor provided me with a key to understanding the intention of this therapy: "Die before dying."

She explained that the concept comes from Muslim tradition (it is also found in other religious traditions and meditation practices) and states that we must choose to "die," or to give up the tangible world and all that traps us inside ourselves, before experiencing literal death. By recognizing the inevitable end to ourselves and our egos, we are freed to live more fully in the world.

When participants are invited to lie down, they are encouraged to die before dying. Then, writing an epitaph, the words for which one wants to be remembered, requires visitors to reflect on how they would summarize their lives up to now, or how they would like to be remembered for the lives they have yet to live. In order to do this they must embrace a measure of mortality that gives them distance from which to consider the past, present, and future. The benefit in this therapy comes with the insight one gains by finding this perspective, which may help us evaluate our priorities and make changes to ways we're not living the lives we wish for.

Some visitors take this therapy very seriously, while others may use a humorous or silly approach. This can be seen in the epitaphs as well: some will be earnest, some will be literary, some will be funny, etc. All approaches and results are welcome here; Epitaphs is a judgment-free place for people to get comfortable with the thought of the world without them.

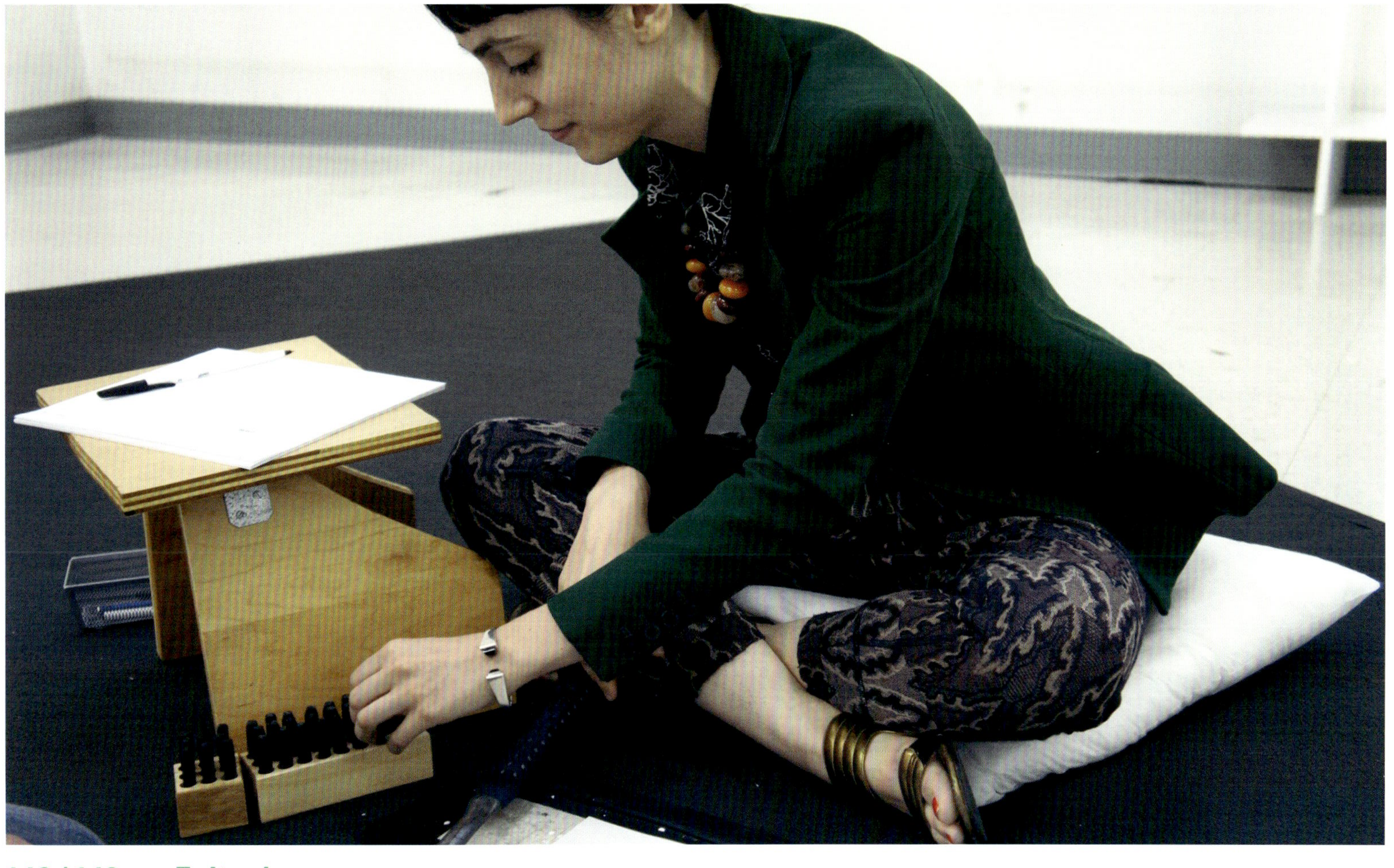

FRIEND
CONFIDANT
LOVER

HE WAS REALLY JUST
A NICE GUY

SHE HAD TOO

MANY DRINKS

AT THE DISCO

DIED HEROICALLY
SAVING FAMILY
FROM SHIPWRECK
IN THE RED SEA
OMANN

GET A

OUIJA

BOARD

GOT PICH

DIED TRYING

Transmigration Express

Number of participants: One to 40 people, depending on room size
Time: 40 minutes
Space size: 6×6m
Space requirements: Carpeted floor, yoga mats or blankets
Furniture: None
Props: Pillows, balloons, eye masks or sandblasted goggles
Therapist qualifications: Conducting this therapy requires a confident guide, especially when working with larger groups, for which reason it is recommended that therapists practice with members of the staff several times before taking on participants.

DESCRIPTION

This therapy is like a poor man's movie theatre. We are going to use our own minds as a projector. It's a session of "inner visioning." Participants are asked to lie comfortably on the floor and close their eyes, covering them with a mask or goggles. Slowly warming up, the participants listen to instructions given by the therapist in a soft voice to help them open up to inner visions. They will be asked to hold a balloon between their knees and squeeze it gently while breathing evenly, concentrating their awareness on the effect this motion has on their bodies and minds; combining the inner visioning with this movement creates a kind of conscious dreaming, a state of creative being. This therapy may bring up memories of experiences, visions, or past emotional states, or it may create insight into the present state of mind.

THERAPIST INSTRUCTIONS

1. Greet and welcome the participants.
2. Explain the therapy.
3. Instruct participants on how to use their balloons. Begin giving them instructions for the inner visioning in a slow, gentle voice.
4. This therapy is appropriate for children as participants.
5. This therapy is appropriate for blind visitors.
6. This therapy is not recommended for deaf visitors.

PARTICIPANT INSTRUCTIONS

1. Take a pillow and a balloon. Lie comfortably on the floor and close your eyes, covering them with a mask or goggles.
2. Listen to the therapist as she gives instructions and suggestions to help you relax and guide your mind.

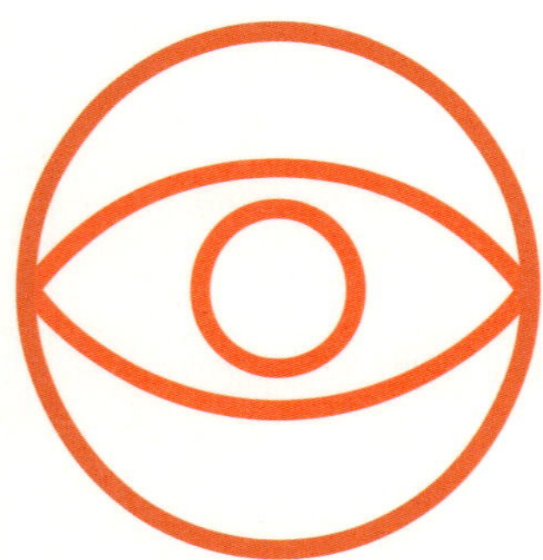

What is the Intention
of this Therapy?

This technique is based on physio-psycho-alchemy, which was a series of inner visioning experiments conducted by Raphael Montañez Ortiz in the 1970s and 1980s. Interested in the potential for healing and reconciliation offered by meditative visits to past lives and parallel dimensions, Montañez Ortiz described his motivation for creating physio-psycho-alchemy in this way:

Whatever our time and place in history or on this planet, we are all of us today as we were pre-historically, as we were in the beginning, dreamers, and as dreamers we have all experienced our transmutations of matter to mind and mind to matter. It is a process we have all realized in every dream we have ever dreamt, it is our process of unconditional imaginative belief, it is when our soul is most spirit, our mind most matter, and all matter most mind. Unconditional imaginative belief is a critically important process within the context of our processes of being and our development because our formless, forming alchemical spirit at the core of our reforming soul, what Jung calls our anima corporalis, makes no distinction beween experience that takes place in what we call our imagination and experience that takes place in what we call reality.[1]

In the spring of 2011 I visited Montañez Ortiz at his studio, where he conducted physio-psycho-alchemy sessions with me that were recorded and which became the blueprint for the following meditation. Having learned his method and watched tapes of his experiments in the 1970s, I tested the method during the first iteration of Sanatorium in New York City, with overall good results. I found out that despite the fact that everyone in the group was wearing sandblasted goggles and we were doing the session with as little light as possible, some women felt ashamed of doing the workout of squeezing the balloon with their knees while using skirts. Because the pelvic movement is critical to this activity (a technique indebted to Kundalini yoga), it is recommended to advise participants that it's preferable they wear pants (unless they don't mind). Also, requesting that people imagine "past life experiences" triggered richer fantasies, which is why I named the therapy Transmigration Express.

1   Rafael Montañez Ortiz, *Towards an Authenticating Art, Vol. 1 and 2* (New York: Columbia University Teachers College, 1982) pp. 21 — 22.

TRANSCRIPT OF A TRANSMIGRATION EXPRESS SESSION

Here are the steps to follow.
You are going to work on relaxing. This doesn't mean you will
immediately relax, but you are
conscious of the fact that you are
working on relaxing. The reason
you are working on relaxing is
so that you can release tension
and the energy in the nervous
system that we must always control because we are constantly
making adjustments for gravity.

So right now you are going to
surrender to your musculoskele-
tar resonance.

What I'd like you to do while
you are squeezing the balloon is
to pay attention to your breath.

Breathe in and then release the
breath completely.

Repeat that—make it a cycle
that keeps going.

While you are breathing I am
going to ask you to pay attention
to your pelvis. I want you to
simply follow the instructions.

I want you to think of a clock on
the back of your pelvis. 12 o'clock
is at the top towards your head.
6 o'clock is towards your feet.
From there you go clockwise,
one two three four…
What I am going to ask you

to do now is to tilt your pelvis
to 12 o'clock.

Now, slowly tilt it to 6 o'clock.

Now, move it as an arc over to
9 o'clock. Continuing the arc,
go to 12 o'clock. Now continue
the arc back to 6 o'clock. Now go
to 12 o'clock, without the arc,
straight back.

You are at 12 o'clock.

Slowly go from 12 o'clock to
3 o'clock in an arc. Now, from
3 o'clock back to 12 o'clock in
an arc. Now, from 12 o'clock
straight to 6 o'clock.

Go back to 12 o'clock.

Do a complete arc from 12
following 1, 2, 3, 4, 5, 6, 7, 8, 9,
10, 11,12; a full circle. Now the
full circle in reverse.

By now you should be in touch
with the pelvis and the idea,
because the energy has released
the pelvis and moved up to your
rib cage and moved up into
the shoulders. Keep the pressure
with the knees. If your legs
tremble, release that tremble.

Take some breaths.

Work on the in-breath.

Release the in-breath.

If you find any congestion in your nasal passage you can continue breathing in and out.

By now your legs should be trembling a little. Let the tremble go.

When you let out the air, the tremble should get stronger.

Put pressure on the balloon.

Let the tremble get to the pelvis and release the pelvis. Let it go up to the rib cage. Release your rib cage. Release your shoulders.

I am going to ask you now to let your imagination take you somewhere. See where it takes you.

[*For increased fantasy*: Let your mind take you somewhere else in time. Go back as far as you want to go… years, decades, centuries ago. You have lived before. Find yourself. What era is it? In which place on Earth are you? What situation do you find yourself in?]

Allow yourself to be there. Experience there. Experience that place.

Slow down your breath.

Breathe slowly.

[Allow four to six minutes of silence.]

Come back here.

Feel the rug with your fingertips. Now do it with your toes.

Let go of the balloon. Roll to your side in the fetal position. Then slowly sit up.

Turn to the person next to you and take turns telling each other where you went.

[For smaller groups, instead of pairing with partners to talk about where participants went, the group can sit in a circle and go around the group counter-clockwise to share their inner visioning experiences.]

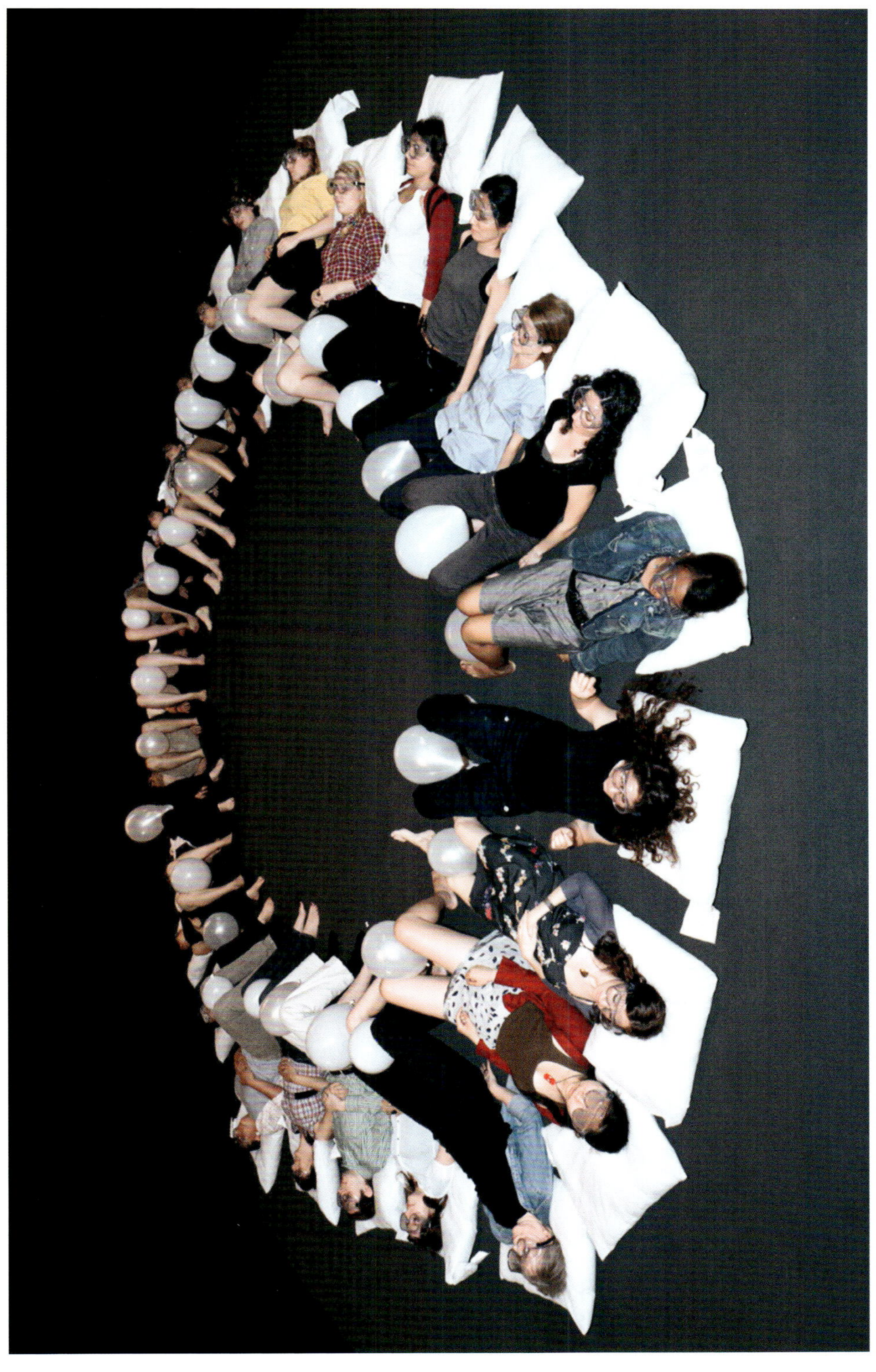

Installation view of "Transmigration Express," Courtesy, Solomon R. Guggenheim Foundation, New York. Photo © Kristopher McKay

Therapy Incubation Unit

THERAPY INCUBATION UNIT
While the Sanatorium creates a
space that is an exception from soci-
etal and cultural norms, it runs the
risk of becoming a rule in itself if it is
operated mechanically, without the
volunteers using their own spontaneity in their interactions with visitors.
To ensure that the volunteers would
engage and seek out moments for
innovation, the resident volunteers
in Kassel were encouraged to develop therapies of their own. This section includes descriptions of the
volunteer's experiments. They went
through different degrees of development; some activities happened
only once, while others were tested
on several occasions. Still others
are simply proposals that the volunteers made based on their experiences conducting therapies.

The volunteers in Kassel brought
their own creative impulses to the
Sanatorium. One person decided
to use all the leftover fruit from the
Compatibility Test to make preserves, creating a symbolic extension of the therapy by blending the
fruits representing all the many
participants into one result. Another
pair of therapists, Pauline Cazorla
and Mathilde Fernandez, wrote the
lyrics and music of a song about
the Sanatorium. Both of these are
examples of experiments that don't
necessarily lead to a new therapy
but nonetheless become an important component of the Sanatorium.

On Serendipity

In the following conversation Neurologist Dr. Alice W. Flaherty and I discuss which environments are more likely to welcome new ideas and the difference between being and becoming.

Pedro Reyes: Yesterday I was watching a movie by Jean-Luc Godard. It was talking about exception and the rule. And he was saying, "Culture is the rule, and art is the exception."[1] Talking about a rule as something bad and exception as something good. However, I do believe that for change to happen you need to craft exceptions that may become the new rules.

Alice W. Flaherty: If you are making a scientific discovery, you may find many unusual events, but that is not progress until you see that there is a pattern.

PR: But what about the difference between who you are and who you want to become?

AF: Recently I had an experience that made me wonder if that question might distract people from developing. I was in a panel for medical residents on alternative careers in medicine, the ones that didn't fit the usual patterns. There was a doctor who had done a lot of television work, one who had become a social activist, someone who was the administrative head of a big hospital, and me, a writer. We were all pretty different from each other, but when a resident asked us how much effort it had taken to plan our unusual careers, each of us rejected the idea of focusing rigidly on a set long-term goal. When something serendipitous comes along, you shouldn't feel bound to ignore it because of a goal you have for your ideal self.

Therapists sometimes promote having a strong sense of self, but that sense can limit you.

It interested me, the idea that those creative people didn't have a self they were aiming towards. Donald Winnicott, the child psychologist, used to say, "I don't look for a child until it's there to be found." We may want to cultivate, for example, a young person we think is artistic. We have the idea that he's going to be an artist, and we try to help him by sending him to after-school classes and art camp, but maybe if we had let him develop more flexibly, he would have ended up in something else.

PR: Like many people who are trained in a musical instrument, and they drop it at the first moment they can.

AF: It makes sense to give opportunities to people so that some of them take it from there, but there has to be room to take advantage of serendipity. When I think about what my own children are like, I have to stop myself and remember Winnicott and think they are not like anything in a way. My sister, too. I always had this idea of her as mildly melancholic. But what I supposed was her temperament has been very different ever since she moved away from the East Coast to California and has had the freedom to go in new directions.

So when people think too hard about who they want to become, it almost makes me worry a little bit. It can distract you from seeing your opportunities. It separates you from being "in the moment," which is where change actually happens. It seems like the longer term your plans are, the more they become a little artificial because they're neglecting the fact that you and the world are going to change. I'm not trying to say people should just drift around and not work towards something. It's just that working for something means a constant series of choices each moment, not ignoring the moments because you are looking so far ahead.

PR: Don't you think that it's good to have multiple goals? As the years pass I think it gets easier to combine ideas and activities that seemed very distant from each other.

AF: Yes, that's true. My medical goals are kind of related to why I'm here talking to you. Is that what you mean? And they both relate to how I take care of my kids.

PR: Also in terms of education, instead of pursuing specialization it could be very interesting to pursue integration of seemingly unrelated interests.

AF: It's inspiring to meet people who have a very narrow focus on one particular interest, and yet that interest relates to every single thing that they meet. They are interested in everything in the world, through that particular lens.

I went to a talk recently that was on the development of the human brain. It was a beautiful talk, literally, because the scientist had found a way to give individual neurons hundreds of different colors in a living brain. Each neuron had a protein that would fluoresce a different color— blue, red, mauve, chartreuse, hundreds of combinations—when exposed to light. The scientist put a plastic window in the skull so she could shine a light on the brain, and a rainbow would shine back.

But the colors weren't the point, that was serendipity. What the scientist wanted was a tool to see which neurons die as you learn things and grow up. In a praying mantis, every neuron stays alive for the entire life of the insect, and it can't do without any of them. But human neurons are a redundant mess. The human is born with trillions of extra connections between neurons. It's great for making serendipitous associations between ideas, but most of them are false, delusional. The baby has wonderful, magical ideas. It thinks that opening its mouth causes a tasty nipple to materialize within it. So the baby can't do anything until its brain prunes away some of its creative ideas. It takes years and years for a human to learn to feed himself. And as part of the process of learning about what is true, what works, millions of neurons die.

The scientist said that her children accused her of having very narrow interests because she spends so much time thinking about her research project. They told her, "You only focus on a single thing these days because so many of your neurons have died over the years. Now you have a mantis brain." And she thought, "You know, maybe they're right."

In some ways creative people are like children, but not like the idealized wide-eyed child. They are like real children, their ideas start out messy and sometimes dangerous. Most creative ideas are bad ones. That is why art is such a great, liminal place to explore new ideas, it's safer than the real world. If one of my residents tries her creative idea with a patient, she may kill him. Ideas can come out of your Sanatorium that could not come out of a medical clinic. Creativity is too dangerous. Necessity is not the mother of invention, creativity needs a safe environment and plentiful resources. Necessity just prunes your neurons and some lovely illusions.

1   Jean-Luc Godard, *Je vous salue, Sarajevo*, 1993.

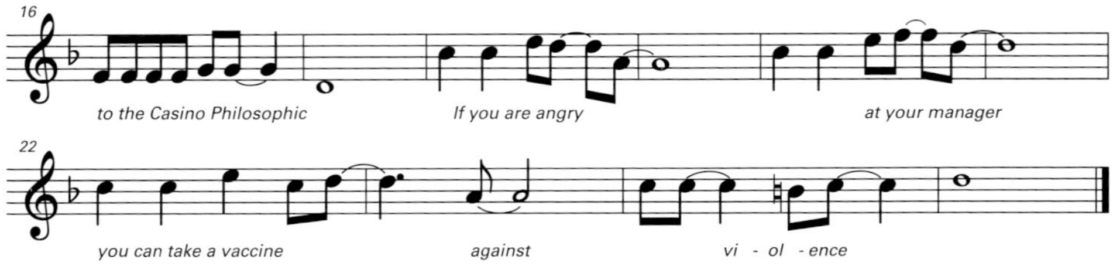

Forget your arguments
Meet your therapists
Nobody's judging
We are no scientists

SOLO 5
If you are grateful
For a memory
Tell it to one of us, we'll make a nice
    drawing

SOLO 6
If you need to test your couple
    compatibility
Come with your partner
We'll make you a juice and see

CHORUS
Let's take an appointment in
    Sanatorium
We're a nice team
We'll cure your deliriums

Forget your arguments
Meet your therapists
Nobody's judging
We are no scientists

SOLO 7
Dig your worst secret
Drop it in a bottle
And you can get a random one in
    exchange

SOLO 8
Figure out your life
Past present future
Curate your own exhibit in the
    hypothetical museum

CHORUS
Let's take an appointment in
    Sanatorium
We're a nice team
We'll cure your deliriums

Forget your arguments
Meet your therapists
Nobody's judging
We are no scientists

The Sanatorium Song

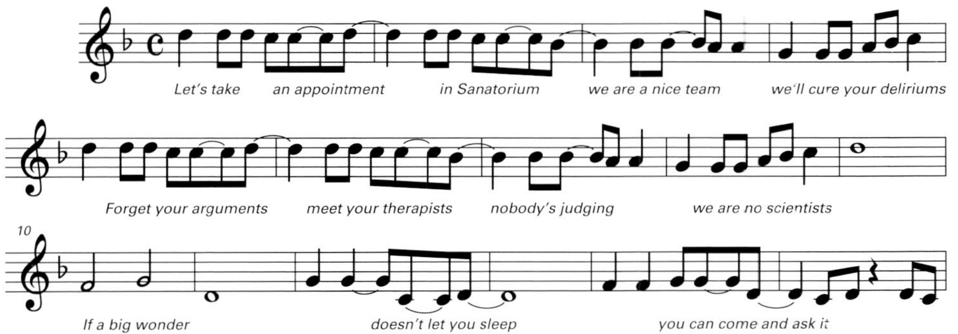

This song was written by a
pair of international Documenta 13
volunteers in Kassel.

By Pauline Cazorla and
Mathilde Fernandez:

Let's take an appointment in
   Sanatorium
We're a nice team
We'll cure your deliriums

Forget your arguments
Meet your therapists
Nobody's judging
We are no scientists

SOLO 1
If a big wonder doesn't let you sleep
You can come and ask it
To the Casino Philosophic

SOLO 2
If you are angry at your manager
You can take a Vaccine
Against Violence

CHORUS
Let's take an appointment in
   Sanatorium
We're a nice team
We'll cure your deliriums

Forget your arguments
Meet your therapists
Nobody's judging
We are no scientists

SOLO 3
If you wanna wish
Great things to someone
You're welcome to choose your own
   Goodoo doll

SOLO 4
If you are over stressed
By your urban life
Think about sharing a relaxing mudras
   with us

CHORUS
Let's take an appointment in
   Sanatorium
We're a nice team
We'll cure your deliriums

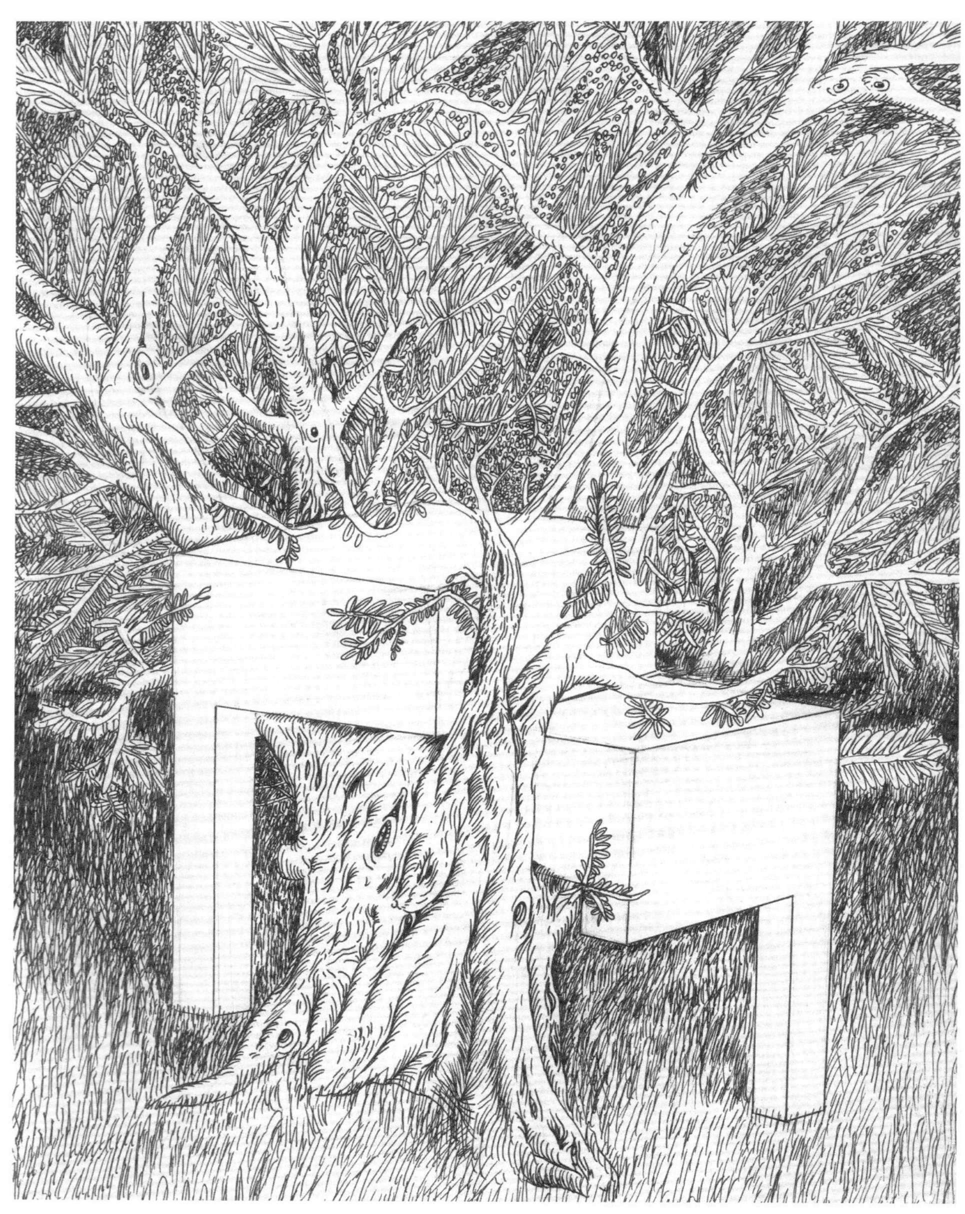

Illustration by Leo Sexer

Dream Dwelling
Leo Sexer

Here the term "dream" is taken in the sense of a wish, what we would like to have. To dream about something is, the first necessary step towards achieving this thing, and without the dream it is impossible to think about how to reach this goal. Putting one's dream into words gives it a greater chance to eventually be fulfilled. For a prophecy to be self-realizing, it first needs the space to manifest itself as a prophecy. In *Social Theory and Social Structure*, Robert K. Merton developed the notion of the self realizing prophecy, which he describes in this way: "a false definition of the situation evoking a new behavior which makes the originally false conception come true."[1]

"Dwelling" means living space. It is a concept used by Martin Heidegger in a text entitled "Building Dwelling Thinking" from the book *Poetry, Language, Thought*[2] Dwelling is an experience, it cannot be disconnected from subjectivity. The word "dwelling" includes the notion of a building and of a home, integrating both the building and the emotions related to it. In this therapy I ask people to think about the house of their dreams. If there are two people, they have to collaborate to create this house. I tell them the house is like a metaphor for their own psychology and social and personal ambitions. I let people draw their houses, allowing a wide range of expressions and styles.

I had very interesting patients. Two girls, when I said they had to live together in their dream house, both shouted, "I never want to live with her!" But they still managed to make their house, which looked like a tennis court divided in two parts but with some links and bridges between the two sides. I also had interesting individual cases, such as a self-confident man doing a house inside the earth, in a mountain, and afterwards an introverted guy who did his house in the air. The common point of six therapies I did one day was the participants' interest in light. I would expect this from an architect but not especially from this therapy.

This relationship between architecture and emotions has a story. In Mexico in the mid-1950s, a group of architects founded a movement called "emotional architecture" a departure from the functionalism dictated by the reign of architectural modernism. They thought that modernism was overwhelming humanity in the twentieth century. The concept of a building in emotional architecture becomes poetic, sometimes directly coming from a narrative instead of material constraints.

To propose a therapy for one person only implies different goals. Alone, the one-on-one relationship with the therapist creates a space of intimacy that allows them to properly explore the personal concept of "home." In a group, patients have to reconcile their own desires with the desires of the community, and it becomes a collective creative exercise.

1   Robert K. Merton, *Social Theory and Social Structure*
    (New York: Free Press, 1968) p. 477.
2   Martin Heidegger, "Building Dwelling Thinking," *Poetry, Language, Thought*, trans.
    Albert Hofstadter (New York: Harper Colophon Books, 1971).

Laughter Therapy
Liliane Puthod

The Staff will make you laugh:

Ashamed but curious, they might
    laugh at you.
You don't exactly know the reason
    why, but it happens mostly at the
    reception.
Laughter therapy - for you and for
    me -
Lay down on the floor.
Look at the ceiling.
Another patient (maybe someone
    you don't know) lays his head on
    your belly.
Then it's your turn to lay your head
    on somebody's belly.
Create a reactive chain of laughter.
Start to laugh, you might have to
    force yourself.
Just to begin.
Then, it comes by itself.
Because you look ridiculous in this
    situation, and you know it.
You are also aware that all the
    curious people around are
    watching you.
Because we all look ridiculous in this
    situation, and we know it.

Say WOOF, like a dog.
Say MEOW, like a cat.
You see, you are laughing.
It's a reflex.
Bellies shake heads.
It is contagious.
It is nervous.
This is the social laugh.
Laughter brings laughter.
Sometimes you might say,
    "Welcome," to the visitor
    arriving, and he laughs.
You might explain to him what the
    Sanatorium is like, and he laughs.
You might say absolutely nothing
    and he laughs.
How curious it is.
Actually, how curious we look:
    ten fake therapists wearing white
    lab coats in a fake Sanatorium,
    welcoming visitors and asking
    them if they would like to try a
    therapy for half an hour.
"Are you real therapists?"
Only volunteers.
"Is it a joke?"
Perhaps it looks like one.
This is an anonymous human
    experience, individual or in a
    group.
It's not real, not a spectacle.
This is to try.

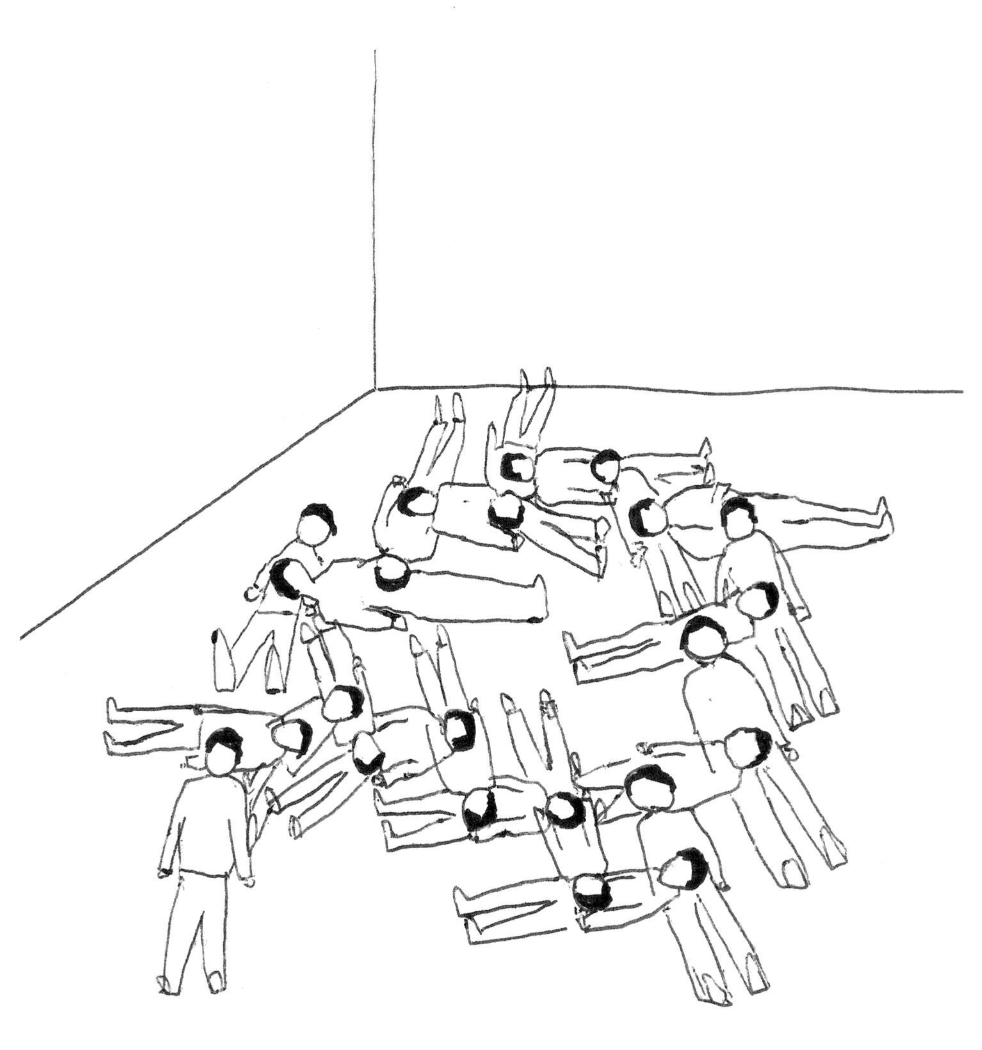

Illustration by Liliane Puthod

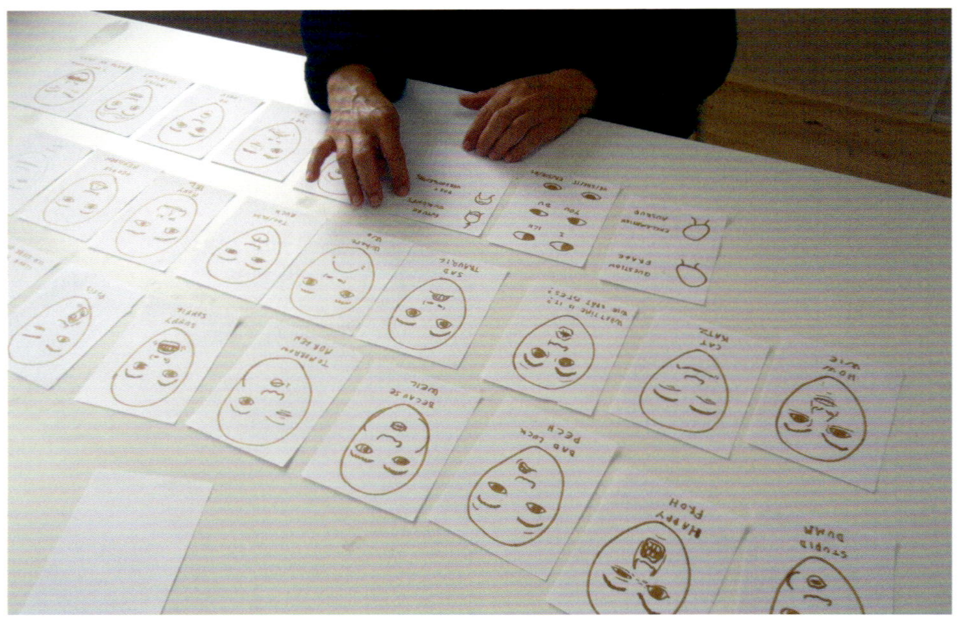

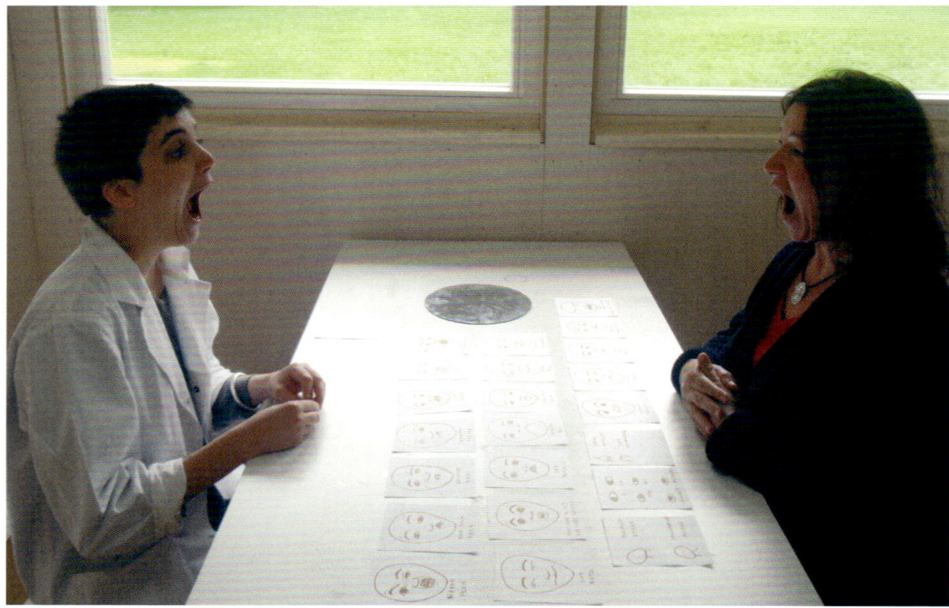

Faces
Johana Blanc

"Faces" is a reflection on language, communication and facial expression. It gathers a small group of participants (from one to five people) to imagine a facial sign language. A thirty-minute session is split in two parts; in the first part, the therapist suggests some face stretching exercises, such as "the mirror," during which participants pretend to be the mirror of another, imitating his gestures and expressions. Those exercises tend to push the patient to look for diverse possibilities of facial deformation and to put him in a confident state of mind without shame and without the necessity of verbal communication.

After this first part the therapist briefly explains the how the facial dictionary works. This dictionary is formed by a number of cards on the table or posted on the wall. Each card presents a drawing of an expression and its translation. An average of twenty basic words is enough to begin. Some cards should also present some basic grammatical protocols, especially punctuation marks and conjugation.

The therapist starts a conversation in this language. At some point in the conversation the existing basic words will not be enough. The therapist will then invite a patient to invent his own facial expression to "say" a new word. Patient and therapist will create a new card they will add to the others, expanding the dictionary. A hand mirror should be available so the patient can look for the appropriate expression or push himself to "pronounce" the existing words/expressions. The facial dictionary should not be inspired by known body language: a smile would not necessarily mean "good,"

frowning eyebrows would not inevitably mean "bad." Facial expressions that are usually used to communicate are limited in number, therefore the therapist should encourage his patients to explore their faces' possibilities. The faces they make should be corrected if they are not quite right. The therapist does not need to know every words in the dictionary, he can learn it at the same time as the patients and also invent words when needed.

The fact that the dictionary is incomplete creates a need that related to the frustration of making an exchange in a foreign language. At the Sanatorium we had to learn to communicate in a language that was not our own. To perform therapies in such conditions could sometime be an obstacle. Some visitors shared a lot with us when we did not understand quite well what they were saying, or sometimes they could not express what they wanted. Due to this language obstacle, I imagined offering the visitors an alternative approach to language. The communication difficulties are embodied in the absurdity of grimaced conversations. I wanted this facial language to be as far as possible form any linguistic reference, so it would ask from the participants a personal and concrete investment into the act of talking.

Faces creates new situations, in which the Sanatorium's visitors are brought to making faces with complete strangers. The face constitutes a primary element in the context of an encounter, and generally it is inseparable from our identities; however, we use so few of its resources as we talk. With this facial language I ask the patients to reconsider their faces. Grimaces become masks, a disguise for words, with which people are invited to play.

Party Therapy

In the evenings during Documenta 13, the volunteers working at the Sanatorium found themselves party-ing. A lot. It was almost inevitable to be drawn into the festivities that were happening every day at a nearby abandoned church, as well as at other venues. When I was in Kassel I found myself going out every evening to participate in the fun, but it was also an important way of digesting all of the intense interactions I had during the day, as well as bonding with the team.

When I asked two of the students, Leo Sexer and Caroline Tripet, why some of the students were having trouble coming up with therapies as I had encouraged them to do, they had two answers:

Leo Sexer: I think just being in Docu-menta, given the size of the exhibi-tion, it was really difficult to create something. For me, for example, I was so full of information from all of the surroundings that it hindered my creativity.

Caroline Tripet: Work took a lot of time and energy, even just those four hours a day we worked. I think also partying took a lot of time!

Pedro Reyes: I remember when we had a dinner at the hospital, I asked the team how many days a week they left the bar when it was daylight outside. My question was very spe-cific. I asked, "How many days a week did you walk out of the bar and hear the birds already singing?" They told me on average it was five days a week! This is more than 70% of the time! Do you think this is accurate?

LS: Yes, we were partying nearly every day.

CT: But it was sometimes necessary.

LS: Yes, because there was a lot of pressure, especially for the first couple of weeks. But I didn't party as much towards the end, as I thought my liver was going to explode! But we needed it. It was an incredi-ble experience.

I have to agree; I can count some of that time among my dearest mem-ories ever. The partying was so therapeutic that one of the students, Stefan Botez, wanted to organize a party one night at the Sanatorium. It was an excellent way to take own-ership of the project. Another stu-dent, Carolina Guillermet, created a party during the day in which the therapists staged photos of them-selves in whimsical situations. The following are photographs from those celebrations.

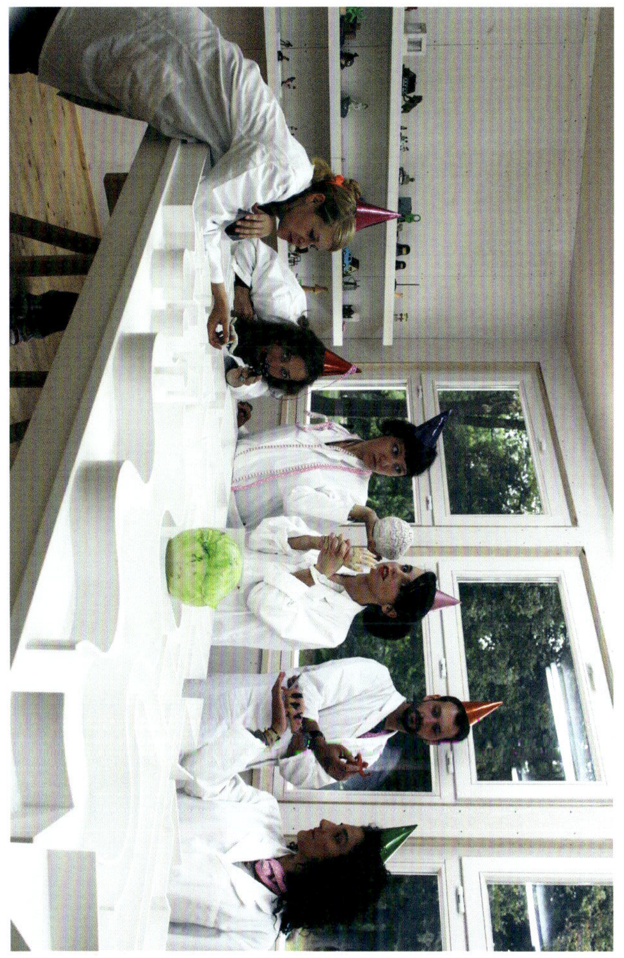

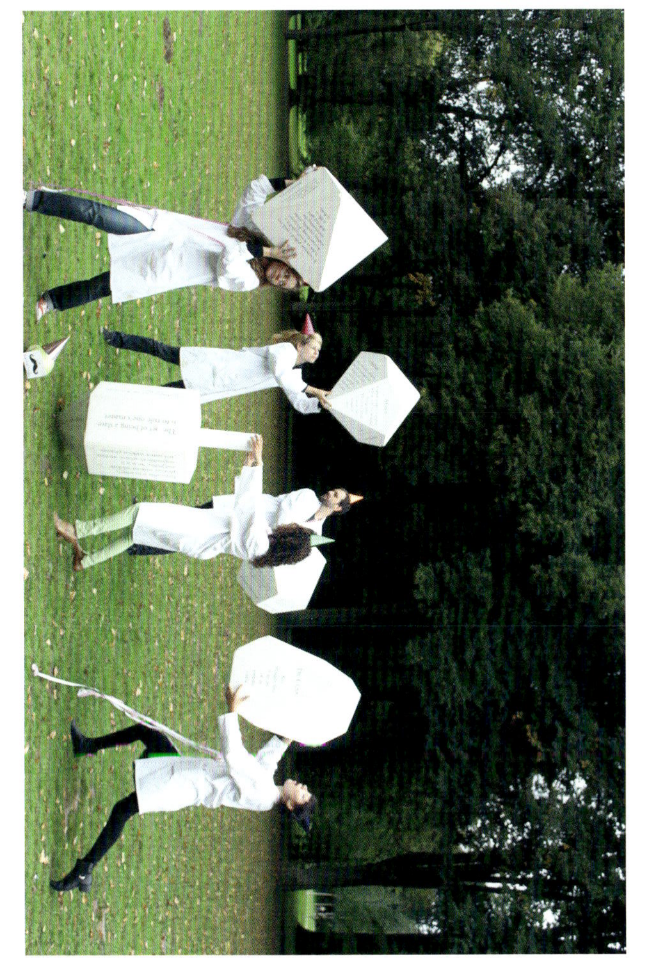

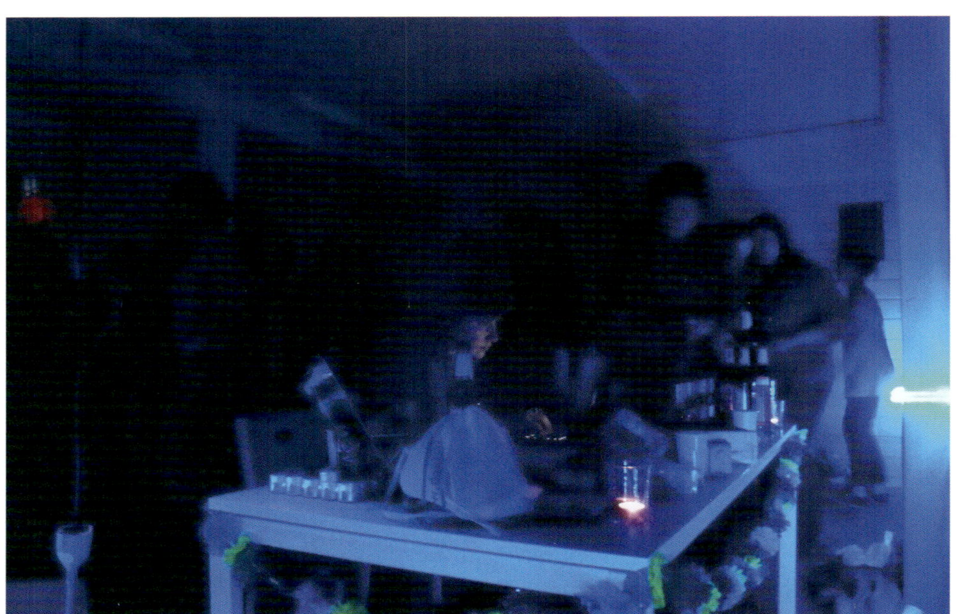

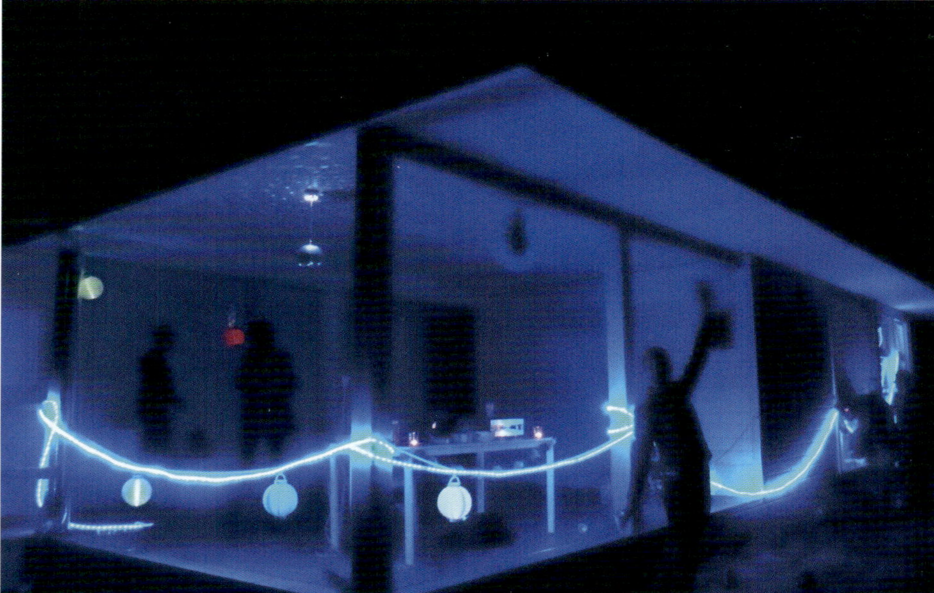

Clinics

CLINICS
Professionals with extensive
experience in their areas of
expertise have visited the Sanatorium to give lectures, demon-
strations, and workshops.
These sessions are intended
for the staff of the Sanatorium,
not for the general audience,
although often some people
from the public have joined in
the activities. This is an area
open for development where
guest lectures can be built into
the program of future install-
ments of the Sanatorium.

Dr. Ludwig Möller

Dr. Ludwig Möller, a professor at Kassel University, visited the Sanatorium to tell me about his Moving School project.[1] While talking we connected over a shared interest in art for social change. When I learned about his experience coaching students, I was happy to discover that he was interested in coming once a week to talk with the volunteers. He set a precedent for the figure of the Sanatorium Coach, which we now know is a very important part of the Sanatorium's operations.

Being a Protestant pastor, he met some resistance from many of the student volunteers for whom religion was an off-putting subject. Yet I felt it was very important to be open to the Western tradition of Christianity as we had also had clinics on Chinese, Indian, and other Eastern traditions at the Sanatorium.

The day of the Blessings workshop was the day before I left Kassel and the Sanatorium, and I was worried about what would happen to the project in my absence. I paired up with Pablo, one of the therapists, who was to give me my blessing. He read a long blessing that we had been given to look for the part he wanted to use, and in the whole text he only found one line that he connected with. He blessed me, saying only, "You do not walk alone." It made me feel reassured and peaceful about my departure.

1   Moving School, http://www.movingschool.eu

DR. LUDWIG MÖLLER
University of Kassel

Why blessings? I think it's the longing for a good word over one's own life. The reassurance that I am not lost in the cosmos, that someone is watching me with a well-meaning look. Although we are living in secular societies, an existential interest in the spiritual world has not vanished.

I told Pedro that I had done workshops about blessings, and he said to me, "Why don't you come to the Sanatorium and show us?" I really liked the idea because I love to be blessed and bless others, but I wondered, is it a therapy? You can talk about it and teach the conduct of it, but do you own it like a method? Can everyone use it or is it a gift only for believers?

Sanatorium is "interested in finding the essence of a ritual so that it can function outside its anthropological specifity. The idea is to strip the procedure of its aura and make it accessible in a secular environment."[2] My experience is that it won't work like that! Stripping a spiritual ritual will change it to a totally different thing. It will loose its identity and power. There is no essence and aura to remove or it will fall apart and vanish, like taking the hydrogen and oxygen from H_2O.

We started the workshop introducing one another, and I asked the volunteers about their own experiences with blessings. It was known that it is a ritual in churches but personal encounters with it were rare. Some volunteers had left the church or considered themselves atheists.

One of the most moving experiences with a blessing I had myself was during my studies in Berkeley when I traveled to Guatemala and El Salvador to visit Christian base communities while a civil war was going on. I had never been to a dangerous area like that. We stayed overnight in Tijuana, close to the Mexican border, in a convent of nuns. Before we left the monastery the next morning one of the nuns touched my forehead, drawing a cross with her finger and saying a farewell blessing. A strong, warm flow of assurance and comfort went through my body.

In the workshop in Kassel we moved to the green behind the Sanatorium in Aue Park where one third of the

Documenta artists showed their work in wooden huts scattered all over the place. I asked the students to move around, looking at each other, saying hello, shaking hands, touching each other. The warm up meant that blessing is body work, affecting the whole human being and not only the world of thinking or faith. Besides the godly touch, it's a human encounter between people. On an intimate one-on-one level of a personal blessing, it is good to recognize our consent to be in even a short-term personal relationship.

Sitting down in the Sanatorium in a circle, I asked the group to find a relaxing position on the floor. I took them on a fantasy journey back into their childhood and from there growing up again. As they moved through these times they were asked to listen to good words and phrases that were said to them by parents, family, teachers, trainers, etc. The aim was to let them discover the good words that stayed in their minds, hearts, and bodies for many years up to now.

Praise and devaluation, positive and negative words of judgment over our lives and actions become embedded. They shape our thinking, sensing, and doing, consciously or unconsciously. Words affect our body: when you only hear about a sweet and delicious ripe red apple someone is holding in her hand, ready to bite into it with relish, your own mouth might water. When somebody only tells you about the sound of the scratch of chalk on a white board, it makes you shiver because you can feel it. The philosopher John Searle wrote about words and sentences as speech acts. Saying a blessing is not just the words; it's acting. Many decisions we make are mainly influenced by speech acts of people I communicate with directly or who are imaginative persons in my mind, like the "little man in the ear" as we say in Germany (which of course could also be a woman!).

After the fantasy journey we shared our experiences of the good sentences, and very different situations came up as stories of encouragement and warmhearted feelings. For some it was hard to remember many of positive sayings. It seemed that the negative words had been much easier to recall.

I chose this walk-through experience, psychological and philosophical reflection, and short biographical work,

for two reasons. First of all, I expected skepticism from
the young artists about a workshop with a religious theme,
or to be more precise, with a Judeo-Christian theme.
Eastern religions seem to be trendier, though ambiguous,
and bad experiences with one's own Christian tradition
seem to be numerous. Organized religion and Christianity
are not "in" for many young people in the West. And as
a participant later told me, some even thought I wanted to
proselytize them. Secondly, it was important for me to
show that religious rites have a strong connection to human
needs and hopes. In secular spheres they pop up again
in different forms. Some show masters in Germany end
their performances with secular blessings like, "Everything will be good!"

After the workshop, Pedro Reyes wrote to me from
Switzerland: "It was very important for me to realize the
role of blessings that you shared with us. Just last week I
was doing a puppet show in Basel and before every per-
formance we held hands and shouted '*Mucha mierda*,' which
is a Latin American custom that actors do before going
onstage. Whenever we forgot to do it, the show was weak!
So it's really important to focus this intention both with
heart, voice, and touch."

Proceeding in the workshop I asked the students
to experiment with touch. To touch somebody during a
blessing is not a necessary part of it, but for somebody it
might be more reassuring and comforting. The task was to
identify which body parts are OK to touch if you don't
know the person doing the touching very well. The students
laid their hands on their partners' legs, different places on
their backs, shoulders, and heads. Different levels of
good feelings were identified and showed a high degree of
consent. These were all Western students, and of course there
are differences and taboos about touching in other cultures.

Next, I passed out the texts of several blessings.
From tradition I choose Irish blessings, which often show
a smile and sense of humor between their lines. St. Bonifa-
tius is one of the most well-known Irish monks.

"May love and laughter light your days,
and warm your heart and home.

May good and faithful friends be yours,
wherever you may roam.
May peace and plenty bless your world
with joy that long endures.
May all life's passing seasons
bring the best to you and yours!"
　　"When times are hard may hardness
Never turn your heart to stone,
May you always remember
when the shadows fall—
You do not walk alone."
　　"May God give you...
For every storm, a rainbow,
For every tear, a smile,
For every care, a promise,
And a blessing in each trial.
For every problem life sends,
A faithful friend to share,
For every sigh, a sweet song,
And an answer for each prayer."

The students could choose a blessing they liked and then had the opportunity to read the blessing to their partner while laying on hands (or not). Some composed their own words for their blessings.

It was later criticized that I "forced" students to read religious texts, which I didn't recognize as a problem in an experiential way. I heard it "through the grape vine" so I don't know the background of the critique. It shows an understanding of the sacredness of these texts or the necessity to believe in them if you use them. Blessings are connected with human experience, but they bring in God as an actor.

Blessings, in that sense, are understood not to be given by the persons saying them; he or she is simply delivering it, being the "mouth of God," to use a human metaphor. Following this understanding there can't be a misuse of blessing. Everybody can try it. Do it! It is a gift and no one has a say in its effect. But I have seen many, many people leaving calm and joyful after receiving their blessing.

1　This refers to a text in the Sanatorium brochure at Documenta 13.

Dr. Gabriel Stux

In the waiting room of the Sanatorium in Kassel, I met Dr. Gabriel Stux, who has been practicing and teaching acupuncture for three decades. He gave a talk on the principles of Chinese and Indian medicine, especially the role of *prana* and *qi* (breath and energy, respectively), in the form of an easy-to-follow method called Organ Flow Meditation. After conducting a guided exercise in which we experienced this method, he performed on the group what is called in acupuncture "the opening of the crown," the placement of a series of needles at the top of the head.

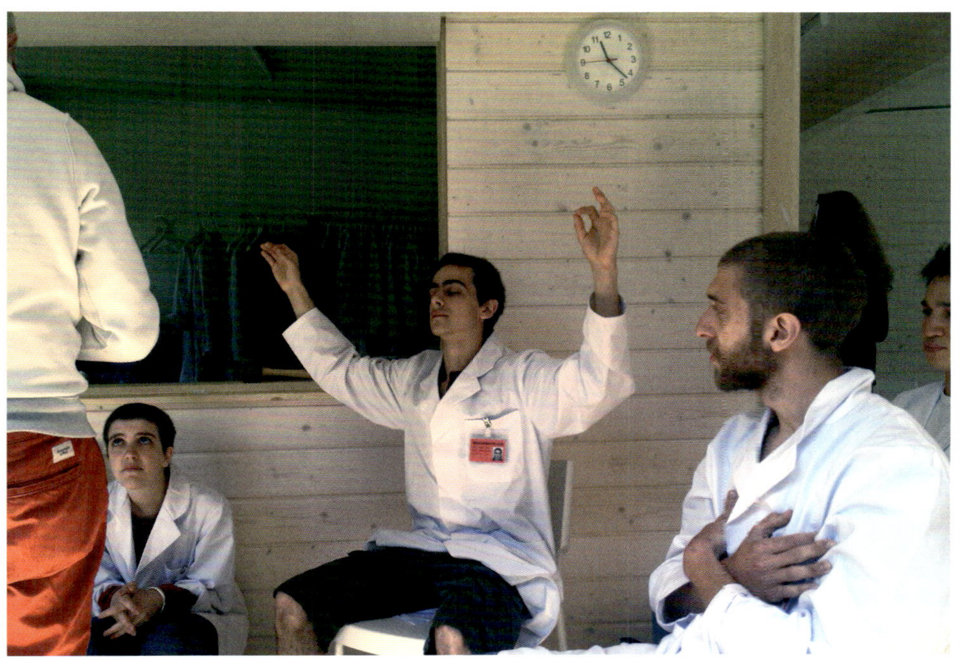

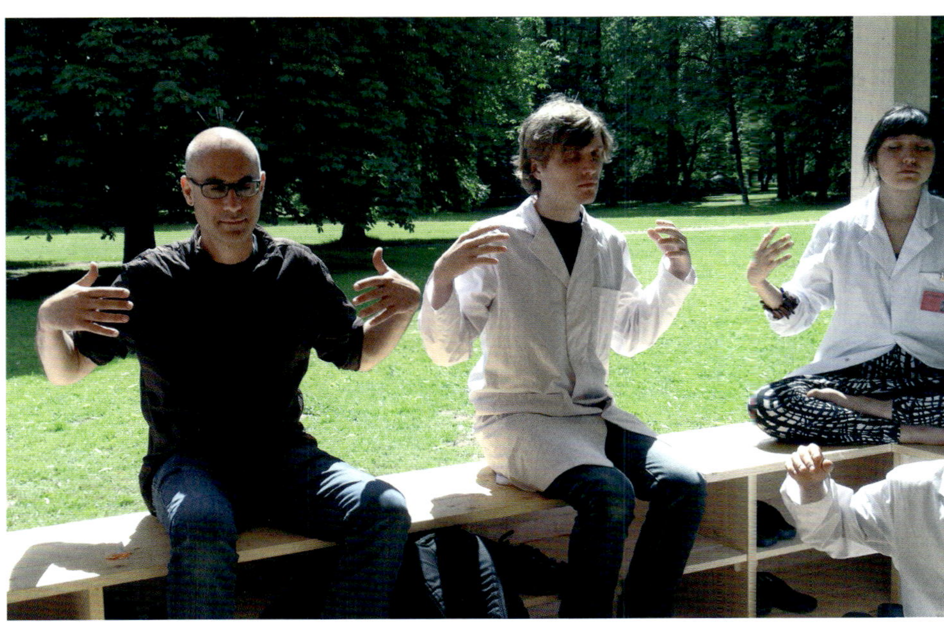

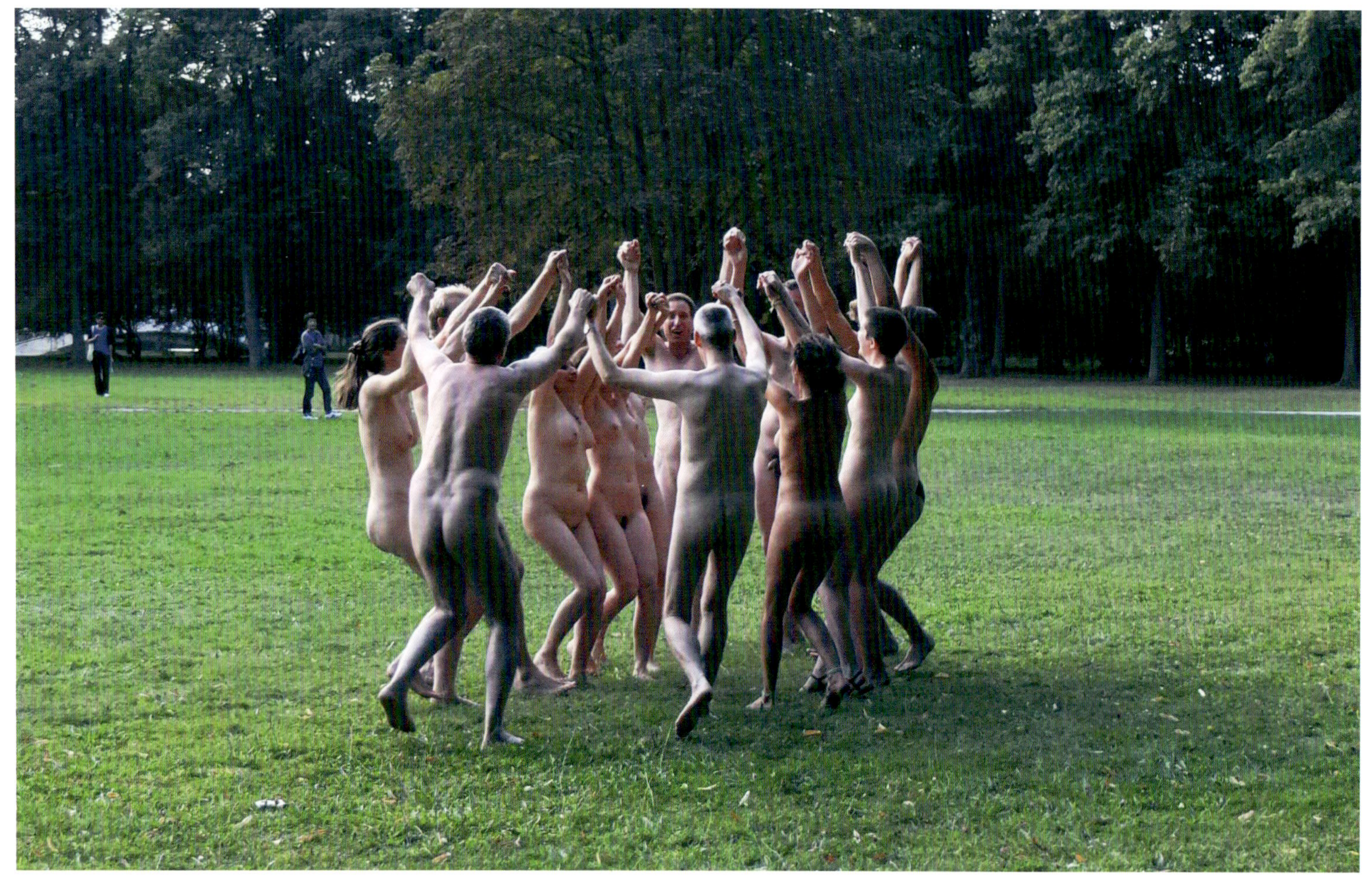

Image courtesy the artist, Milani Gallery, and Documenta 13.

Stuart Ringholt

Laughter Workshop (2012)
Karlsaue Park, Kassel,
Documenta 13, September 2012

Documenta 13 had put together an amazing group of artists and thinkers, which allowed the Sanatorium the privilege of being visited by other fellow artists in the show, such as Stuart Ringholt. Stuart had been running a piece at Documenta called *Anger Workshops* (2008), in which participants were invited to express their stress and anger, as well as their love, with the other group members. Ringholt describes the work:

Groups are offered the opportunity to lose inhibition and express their anger using voice and movement to the sound of very loud house music. This phase runs for five minutes. In the following phase participants consider 'love' and express it, using statements such as 'I am sorry if I have hurt you' and 'I love you and respect you' to the gentle and soft sounds of Mozart. The group then gently embraces one another and hug for three minutes. After the activity, the group sits and discusses their experience.[3]

Given the psychodynamics that the student therapists had to deal with every day at the Sanatorium, we had a special interest in Stuart's work. His input became especially valuable for the second group of therapists.

I had spent a significant amount of time with the first group of students training and coaching them, but due to budget and time restraints I could not do the same with the second group. We were very fortunate to count on Stuart's input at this moment. He first conducted a group session with the therapists, in which everyone had a chance to open up and express themselves. Some of their concerns had to do with the project itself, particularly their lack of direct contact with and feedback from the artist and management, and they also had questions about the autonomy to which they were supposedly entitled but hadn't yet seized. Additionally, there were some frustrations that had to do with the circumstances of their participation at Documenta: the lack of pay, problems with accommodations, etc.

This group session was extremely useful; afterwards the group morale was renewed, and two days later Stuart called for a new session: the *Laughter Workshop*, in which a group of both student therapists and Documenta visitors got naked, did breathing exercises, and ran together among the magnificent trees of Aue Park.

1   *Das Beleitbuch/The Guidebook* (Kassel: Documenta 13, 2012) p. 172.

Mel Kimura Bucholtz

During the Sanatorium at *stillspotting nyc*, I invited my friend Mel Kimura Bucholtz to lead a clinic called the Tuning Effect, a unique technique of his own creation. Mel had learned hypnosis from Milton Erickson, one of the greatest psychiatrists of the twentieth century. He then crafted the Tuning Effect, incorporating elements from Ericksonian hypnosis and Zen Budhism, with the purpose of training the brain to separate itself from emotionally charged issues and taking us to a place of deep intuition where we can assess situations from a new perspective.

A maverick teacher himself, Mel was a member of Esalen and a founder of Interface, a research group that brought Tibetan monks to Harvard Medical School for research on brain activity. I have consulted with him countless times on subjects ranging from from Alfred Korzybski to Jacob Levy Moreno, the latter of whom Mel knew personally.

There is a unique feature of the Tuning Effect in the way it combines two states of brainwave activity. As Mel describes: "Most meditations bring us into the alpha brainwave state — alpha is from between about ten to thirteen brainwave activities a second down to about nine or ten, the beginning of the sleep cycle. The Tuning Effect takes you to alpha, but it also gives you a job, the job of coming back into the beta state of mind while maintaining being in alpha. That makes the experience very solid and very concrete: any time you do a job using beta while you're in alpha, the algorithm that happens during that time will remain."

The following text is a transcript of a Tuning Effect session.

What I would like to do first is to go over the Dos and Don'ts for the session. For this period of time, you are relieved of having to answer the thoughts that ask for your attention. Thoughts will always ask for your attention, that's their job. But right now, you don't need to answer them.

You are not relieved of having to stay awake. You'll see why that's a job in a little while, because what we are doing is taking your brainwave activity from very active, long haul tension into the beginning of the sleep cycle. So you're going to have to make an effort to stay awake. That happens to everybody. Ok?

You're also relieved from having to speak right now. Of course, if you want to you can, but you're relieved of that as a job. Instead of speaking, please give me some kind of signal like moving your hand or nodding your head. That would be perfectly fine. Ok?

So to begin I would like you to look at something (whatever it is doesn't matter) and I'd like you to squint your eyes in the direction of what you're looking at. Give me a little sign when you can feel the muscles around your eyes squinting.... Now I would like you to slowly release your eyes and give me a signal when you can tell the difference between your eyes squinting and your eyes relaxed. Take your time. You don't have to do it perfectly or 100%. Focus on the difference in the physical feeling between your eyes squinting and your eyes relaxed.... Stay with me, please.

Now slowly close your eyelids and look at your eyelids coming down, as if you were looking at a curtain coming down on stage. Really take your time. Let me know when you are satisfied that your eyelids have come down ... Ok. Remember that you are relieved of having to answer those thoughts, but thoughts will always try to get your attention, that's normal.

Now I would like to roll your eyes forward and down, so that your eyes are pointed towards the floor or your chin, under closed eyelids. Just your eyes. Notice what your eyes are physically seeing, not imagining or thinking, but what they are seeing. Maybe colors or darkness. Take your time. Your eyes should be pointing towards the chin or the floor, and notice what your eyes are physically seeing. This may take a minute or so as you have been highly active until now and your brain is going to take a second to slow itself down. That's normal. Please give me a sign when you know your eyes are pointed down and you are physically seeing color, or light or dark, but not any images or anything like that. Just physical. … Thank you.

Now please look at that color, or light or dark, like a piece of material in a museum, like a fabric. … Stay wide awake please.

Now please sense the feeling of your breath as your breathe out. Feel the physical feeling of the breath when you exhale. Of course, you are inhaling and exhaling all the time, but just feel the sensation of the warmth of the exhale or the length of the exhale, any of those things, and let me know when you feel your breath breathe out with your eyes down. You don't have to do it perfectly or 100%. … Ok.

Now I would like you to slowly rotate your eyes forward and up under closed eyelids, so they looking to your eyebrows or the ceiling or sky. Notice the feeling with your eyes up. It should be a little bit uncomfortable for about two breaths, and then it will be fine. It's a little disorienting. If there's any pain when looking up, lower them a little but keep them above the middle line. Eyes pointed up please. … Are you still hearing my voice? By now you should find the disoriented feeling is

gone. Notice how your thoughts are trying to get your attention. That's their job. But right now you are relieved of that job. Of answering thoughts …

Hold for a moment longer. You'll get better at tracking the sensations. It takes time; nobody does it perfectly, nobody. Notice the coolness of your breath when you breathe in. Notice how cool the air feels when you breathe in. Notice how long it is. Check on your eyes, how do my eyes feel now? Stay wide awake, please … .

Now roll your eyes down and forward. Don't just drop them, roll them. Take your time. Wait until you're sure your eyes are pointed toward the floor, toward your chin. Then to either side and back. … Ok, eyes pointed to the floor again, closed eyes, and pay attention to the breathing out. … You're doing very good. You might also want to check in on how your back feels against the chair. There's no routine that has to be perfect. This is just practice at training attention to sensation. There's no hypnosis in this; there are no tricks. Eyes pointed towards to the floor, please.

Exhale once more. Very good. Now see if you can notice the weight of your tongue, the weight of your tongue without pushing it. The weight of your tongue in the lower part of your mouth, the weight and shape of your tongue. Let me know when you're aware of that to any degree: the weight and shape of your tongue in the lower part of your mouth. You do know where your tongue is, don't you? That's the thing you use to speak.... Stay with me, please.

Now notice a bit of a warm feeling in your upper chest. When you're aware of your eyes pointed down, when you're aware of the breath in the exhale or when you're aware of the tongue in the lower part of your mouth, let me know when you have a feeling in your upper-middle chest, very palpable and natural. A slight warm feeling. Thank you. Stay with me, please.... Got it?

...We're going to do another rotation of the eyes through closed eyelids. Stay with me. Notice how the brain is starting to move into that alpha wave in the beginning of the sleep cycle. This is normal, so you have to put in a little more effort to stay with me. Begin to rotate the eyes upwards once more.

Very nice. Very good. Eyes pointed up, under closed eyelids. Now notice the feeling in your head. It should be much more

pleasant than the first time. Eyes pointed up nicely. Very good.... Still hearing my voice?

Now imagine that there's a little silver airplane flying over a lake, and there's a banner at the back of the plane. The words on the back say:

> THERE'S NOTHING ELSE I NEED TO DO RIGHT NOW, THIS IS IT

And when you understand those words, give me a sign.

> THERE'S NOTHING ELSE I NEED TO DO RIGHT NOW, THIS IS IT.

Very good. Thank you.

Now there's a second airplane, and the words on the banner say:

> THERE'S NOWHERE ELSE I NEED TO BE RIGHT NOW. HERE IN MY BODY IS WHERE I AM.

Read that banner again:

> THERE'S NOWHERE ELSE I NEED TO BE RIGHT NOW. HERE IN MY BODYIS WHERE I AM.

And again, when you understand any of those words, please give me a little sign. Check on the feeling in your head. Now please tell yourself:

> THIS IS THE WAY MY MIND FEELS WHEN MY EYES ARE POINTED UP, AND I KNOW IT

Repeat it and let it sink in:

> THIS IS THE WAY MY MIND FEELS WHEN MY EYES ARE POINTED UP, AND I KNOW IT

Let me know when you've completed that please.…
Very good, Hold for a moment.

Slowly begin to rotate and move your eyes forward. You're doing very well. Very good. Roll them down toward the floor again, toward your chin. Check in on the feeling of your tongue in your mouth. The weight and shape of your tongue. You're doing very nicely. The weight and shape of your tongue, please. And notice how when you feel your tongue is down, time slows down a little between one thought and the next thought. I'll tell you why your brain does that later. For now, just check, where are my eyes pointed? How does my breath feel when I'm breathing out? How does my tongue feel? Any of those things, and let me know when you hear my voice. … Very good.

From where you are here now, with your eyes pointed down and so on, I'd like you to let come to your mind anything of a difficult, problematic, worrisome, anxious nature. Whatever it may be, do not say it out loud. Anything of a difficult, problematic, worrisome, anxious nature, but do not say it out loud in words. Only give me a sign of when anything of that nature has come to mind, however small it may be. … Thank you. Check on, where are my eyes pointed to now? Check on, how am I breathing out? Check on, where is my tongue in my mouth? Let me know when you've got any of those.… Ok very good.

Notice that difficult thing over there. Wherever "over there" is, while you are here with your eyes pointed down, and your awareness of your breathing, the sense of those things that are here.

I'm now going to give you three tasks. Please let me know when you're ready. OK …

–   You are now relieved of the task of being emotionally pulled into that thing over there in this period of time. You're also relieved of the task of having to emotionally pull yourself away from that difficult thing right now.

–   You're also relieved of the job of having to fix that difficult thing or having to manage it, having to cope with it.

–   And finally, you're relieved of even having to understand or learn about that difficult thing over there, and you're also relieved of having to explain it right now.

You're relieved of those jobs, but you're not relieved of having to stay awake. That is your job. Please let me know when you can hear my voice. ... Very good. Ok.

Now I'd like you to observe that difficult thing over there, from where you are over here. Your eyes are down, and you're breathing out. I'd like you to be aware of that difficult thing in terms of its size, or its shape, or its weight, or its distance. How close or far. ... Stay with me please. Very good. Check on where your eyes are pointed towards the floor. Check on the feeling of your tongue, please. Check your breath on the exhale. Any of those is fine. Notice what begins happening to that difficult thing over there, from where you are sitting over here. In your senses, you are relieved of these tasks,

–   relieved of being emotionally beholden to it, of being emotionally pulled away.
–   relieved of having to fix it.
–   relieved of having to understand or explain it.

When you're aware of any one or two things having changed with that difficult thing, without having to understand it, please give me a sign ...

Check on where your eyes are. Very good, thank you. Now slowly begin rolling the eyes upward towards the sky again. You don't have to do this perfectly. Rolling the eyes upward. Hand a little sign when your eyes are pointed up. ... Very good, eyes pointed up. Now notice the feeling in your head please. Should be like the second time, nice pleasant feeling, don't get pulled into it though ...

Eyes pointed up now, and pay attention to the inhale as best you can. Eyes pointed up, nice feeling in the head. Let me know when you're aware of the feeling in your head with your eyes pointed up. ... Very good, stay with me please. And now, slowly roll the eyes forward and down once more, following with your attention the movement of the eyes rolling down until you know the eyes are pointed toward the floor again. Notice the feeling in your chest, notice the weight and shape of the tongue, any of those things. Notice the feeling of the exhale.

… You are now back home in your body. Here, I would like you to let something of a happy, pleasant, delightful, lovely nature, whatever that is for you, come to mind. Pleasurable, delightful, enjoyable. Something of a lovely nature come, but do not say it out loud. Only give me a sign when something of a pleasurable or enjoyable nature has come to mind, something you like. Ok. Something pleas-urable for you. Something you enjoy. When I stop speaking, I'd like you to let your attention do something like a swimming breaststroke, swimming forward, a wide, warm, gentle pool of pleasurable enjoyable feeling, right now all around your head and body.

GO. Let your attention swim into this beautiful feeling.

GO. Above you, ahead, behind you, to the right, to the left of your body, down your arms and legs and feet and back. Complete enjoyment, your way.

…You can still hear my voice? Very good. Keep going, enjoy it more and more, as much as you like. And when you've had

enough, have some more. Have even more…

And now when you're ready please, staying in this pleasurable feeling, bring one hand to your stomach and touch your stomach with your hand please. Let me know when you can feel your hand against your body. Just the warmth of your hand against your body.…Give me a signal please. Give me a sign by moving your head, please. That's good, thank you…

Focus on where your eyes are pointed down once more, just a little check in. Let me know when you can feel the warmth in the palm of your hand against your body. The palm of your hand.…Very good. Now please tell yourself "thank you." Please tell yourself:

THIS IS THE WAY I'M FEELING RIGHT NOW.

Safely back home in my body, this is the way I'm feeling right now. Safely in my body, enjoying what I like most, and I know it. Enjoying what I like most, and I know it. Let me know when you've concluded that. It doesn't have to be perfect. I'm safely back home in my body, enjoying what I like most, and I know it. Let me know when you've completed that please… Ok, thank you.

Continue focusing on the warmth in the palm of your hand, please. Now tell yourself, "It's my right to feel this way. I'm entitled to it. It's my right to feel this way in my body, and I'm entitled to it. And I know this, too." Any way that this makes sense to you. "It's my right to feel this way," palm against your body, "and I know it, also."

Let me know when you've completed that. … Ok. Very good.

Do a final check in on where your eyes are located. Pointed down. Once again, you don't have to answer those thoughts that want your attention. You do have to know where your eyes are pointed. And you do have to know where your hand is on your stomach. That's your only job right now. Let me know when you're aware when your eyes are pointed down with your hands against your body, please. …Very good. Ok.

Now slowly bring both hands up to your eyes and cover your eyes with the palms of your hands, please. With the palms of your hands. That's it. Hold it. … There's been a slight change in your eyes, which you'll see in a moment. I'd like you to slowly give me a sign when your eyes are open looking into your hands. Give me a sign when

your eyes are open, looking into your hands. … Thank you.

Now slowly begin to remove your hands from your eyes. Slowly remove your hands. Keeping your eyes and your head straight ahead but not stiff. And notice what light there is in the room. Notice how widely you can see to the right and the left. Notice how widely you can see. All the way around to the right, and all the way to the left. You should have a nice clear range of vision. Far to the right and to the left. That's normal. Check it out.

Notice how your hearing is clearer. A little sharper, a little fuller. These are signs of the coordination of your brain activity, your senses, and your attention, all lined up with each other, naturally. This is how your senses work when your brain and your senses and your attention are naturally lined up. Take a breath. You can even use your fingers to indicate to the right and left of your head how widely you can see, you should be able to see nice and widely and have a nice clear vision. …That's good. That looks pretty good to me. This is the effect of being coordinated with your brain and your senses. You can take your hands down. Take a moment or two; your brain is now going to start to come back into play as it was

before this experience.
It will take a moment.

Hello! Wow! You bright people.
Did you have an interesting time?

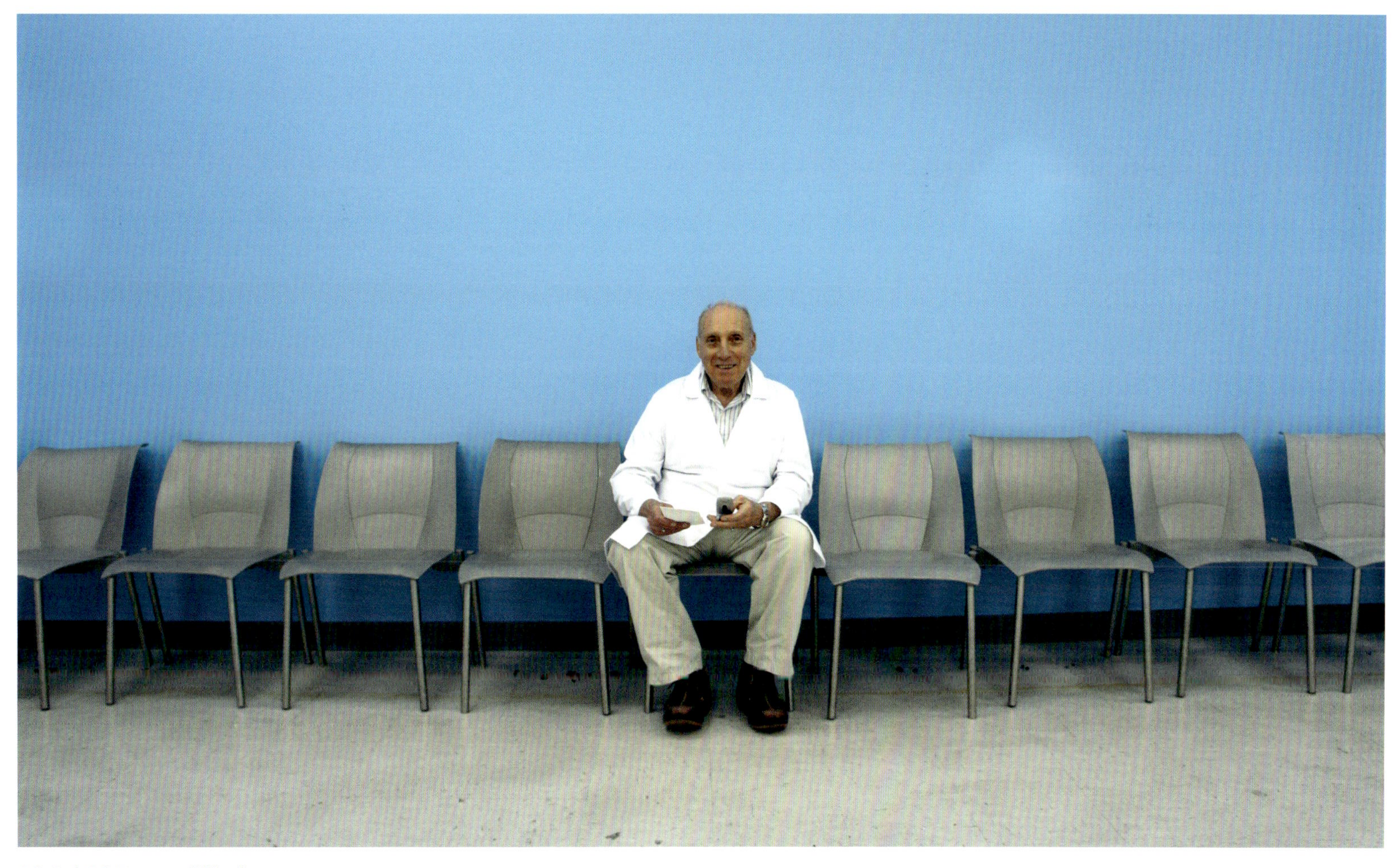

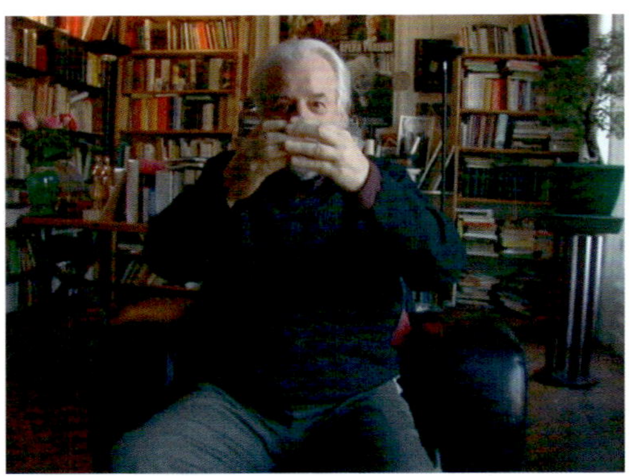

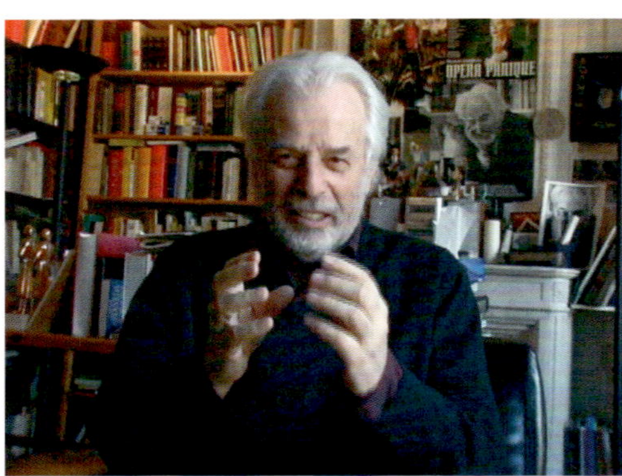

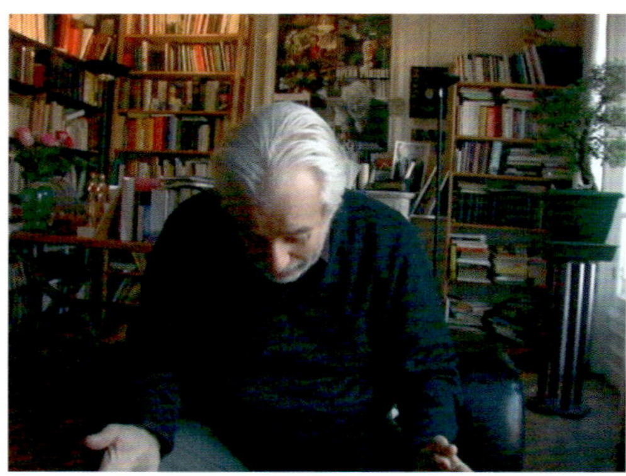

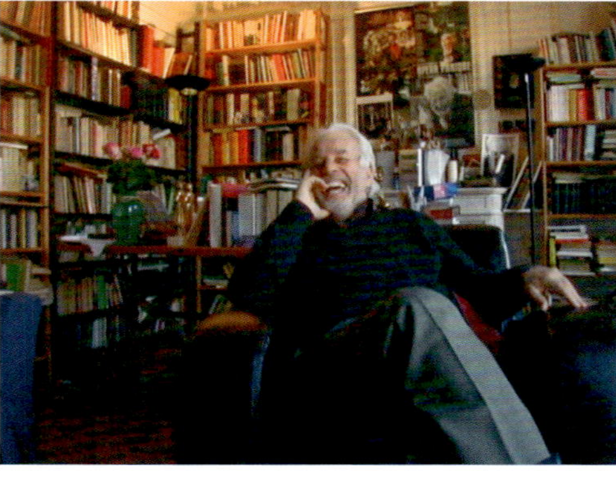

Alejandro Jodorowsky

One constant reference throughout the Sanatorium has been to Alejandro Jodorowsky's psychomagical acts. As one approaches Alejandro Jodorowsky, one must be ready to experience an expanded reality, where every gesture is charged with transcendental significance. We met for the first time in Milan at an exhibition in which we both participated. I said, "Alejandro, how are you?" He replied, "I don't know, let's see."

Immediately I recognized in his words the estrangement he learned from Alfred Korzybski. As we waited for the show to start, I asked him, "Would you give me a tarot reading?" He pulled out a deck and asked me to choose four cards. I did. His interpretation of them didn't satisfy me. I started to explain to him that I thought they meant something different. "So you think you're very smart? Shuffle the cards and pull out four cards one more time," he said. So I did. BOOM, BOOM, BOOM, BOOM. To our surprise, defying astronomical odds, the same exact four cards sat in front of us.

"No, *you* read the tarot to me," he said. I thought to myself, How could I pretend to read the tarot to the world's authority on the subject? "Please pull out just one card," I said. He did, and took out the Hanging Man card. Not daring to reverse roles with the master, the only viable exit I had was to play dumb. Smirking, I interpreted his card upside down. "You are a balloon full of hot air who wants to go to the sky, but you are tied to the root of a tree." He hit me on the head, shouting, "Don't you know how to read? You are reading it upside down, you fool! Hahahahaha—this is a good relationship!" A few days later, I visited his house in Paris, where this interview took place.

Pedro Reyes: What advice might you give to those who wish to perform psychomagical acts?

Alejandro Jodorowsky: Well, one cannot start off from a point of ignorance. To perform psychomagical acts, one must understand what psychomagic is. One needs to read my books on all this. The first is called *Psicomagie* (Psychomagic) and the other *La danza de la realidad* (The Dance of Reality). Also, *La trampa sagrada* (The Sacred Trap). After reading those books, a person must learn an art. No one can perform psychomagic without being an artist. One must also have some concepts of psychoanalysis. If they don't, of what use would it be to them? A bit of knowledge about psychogenealogy is also necessary. When one knows all that, the person can practice psychomagic without danger. But not before. One does not make acts of psychomagic just like that.

PR: There are some aspects of the method that I would like you to explain. For example, what is the purpose of planting a tree at the end of certain acts?

AJ: All psychomagic acts have to finish with something positive. The human being has a tendency to have pent-up rage. If you offload this rage onto one of your archetypes — your mother, your father, teacher, grandmother, whatever relative — after doing so, there is an emptiness and also a sense of guilt, so then there is the need to anticipate the guilt and do something positive, for life and not death. Every act has to end with an offering. Planting a tree is cleansing. What is most dangerous is that if you don't, nothing will change for you.

PR: And so the saying, "What goes around comes around," or "What you give is for you, and what you don't, you hold on to"?

AJ: The world is a unified package. We are based on awareness. The world is a product of consciousness. I call it divine awareness, which produces energy. Everything is consciousness, everything is energy, everything is love. They are all connected. What I give to the world, I give to myself. And if I don't give something to the world—well, it is taken from me.

PR: You have said that when someone asks forgiveness from someone else, that they should also ask for something in exchange.

AJ: We are talking about forgiving, not about asking to be forgiven. Forgiveness, Christian forgiveness, doesn't really function unless you say to the person,

"This is what you did to me, and now I want something in exchange for what you've done." For example, a woman brought her daughter to see me. The young woman was suffering horribly because of lesions in her throat that could not be cured. I asked about her father and she responded by saying that he had abused her sexually, forced her to swallow his sperm, and that this had caused the lesions in her esophagus. The young woman accused her mother of leaving her alone with the father by not letting her live with her. So the daughter asked her for a sports car as compensation. The mother said, "Okay, I'll get you one, but a used one," and the girl said no, she wanted a new one. The mother finally agreed, and the young woman's throat was cured. It's a small example—you have to pay for what you've done. I can't just forgive you—I have to put a price on it.

    With respect to asking forgiveness, it's the same. I ask for your forgiveness, but I'll say to you, "How would you assess what I've done to you? What would you ask for in exchange? Just ask." There are people who ask for nothing in exchange! But you have to give them the opportunity to ask you. I was taking care of a child, a boy of six years, who was urinating behind an armchair. I told him I wasn't mad at him, but that he simply could not do that again. I gave him three strong whacks with my belt. It left three red marks, and he cried and cried and never did it again. At that time, I wasn't familiar with psychomagic— what I should have done was put a chamber pot behind the armchair and said to him, "Next time, use this when you want to go behind the chair." Problem resolved! But I didn't know how to do that. Years later, when he was fifteen or sixteen, he remembered the event, and the rage he had kept inside all these years. I got up and said to him, "Whack me three times, hard, so that it leaves three red marks," and that was the price I paid so that he might forgive me.

PR: Have you ever applied one of your methods of therapy outside of the basic family?

AJ: There is a group of Chilean poets who go by the name of Casagrande. After President Allende was assassinated in La Moneda, the presidential residency, these four young people hired two helicopters to drop three hundred thousand copies of poems—a snowstorm falling on the Palacio de La Moneda. A poet sat on each of the palace's balconies, reciting verses. They were covering a bloodied place with poetry. It was a major success for them. They did it again in Guernica, and were going to do it in Sarajevo. Now they are now planning to bombard Hiroshima with poems. Half of the poets are Chilean and the other half are from the countries where poem-rains have fallen. I think this may be an example of psychomagic applied socially. Changing memory into something poetic.

The first time I performed an act of social psychomagic, I didn't know it was psychomagic. Nearly thirty years ago, when I was doing theater, I brought together a group of sixty people in a huge space in the Gare Saint-Lazare train station, the largest station in France. In this space called the Salle des Pas Perdus—the lost steps—a group of us started out in one corner and then began crossing the area, step by step, in slow-motion. We took two hours to do it! In a space where everyone is exhausted and running. Between these out-of-breath people running about, this group of sixty subjects were crossing the space slowly, at a different tempo. Back then I thought we were making a spectacle for the people that were rushing around watching us, but now I realize that it was a psychomagical act for the sixty people who were doing it, to make us aware of what we didn't have —we weren't pressured by life.

<u>PR:</u> You mentioned memory, changing memory.

<u>AJ:</u> You can add details to memory, you can color it. Memory is images or a film, impressions that you save and that you relive in the present. That idea came to me when I was watching old black and white films that were later colorized, changing them. You can do the same with memory. I was in a hotel in Montreal suffering terribly for six months. I was traveling with Marcel Marceau, and they wouldn't give me a visa to the United States, and I had to remain there. Even after I left, my memory of the hotel was horrible. The walls were ugly, the bed was awful, the washstand made terrible sounds. There were pizza ads on the walls. I began to change the light-boxes into angels, into rainbows, fireworks. I changed the color of the walls and made the washstand sing in a beautiful operatic voice. I put silk sheets on my bed and filled the room with the smell of perfume. I did all of this in my mind, and I converted the disagreeable space into an agreeable one. The second thing I did is very important: I invented a solitary child, Tocopilla, who had no friends until he was nine years old. I put myself into these recollections, telling this boy that he wasn't alone, that I had always been with him.

I visited all the places in my memory, and I placed myself in them. He was a child that I always was with, for the voyage.

PR: What are imagination exercises, are they meditations?

AJ: I don't meditate anymore. I did it for five years — five years without moving. *[Imitates a lotus position]* Now I practice contemplation. Contemplation is not keeping the body still like a corpse. When you contemplate, you continue to do what you're doing, you are in the same state as when you are meditating, but with an empty mind and a concentration. You can do what you want to do or are able to, according to your talent. You can work in a timely manner and freely, without feeling burdened. You begin to feel the full structure. You look toward the sky and into the street and sense the entire planet, and that takes away the sensation of feeling like you are drowning.

PR: A little like sensing the age of the universe?

AJ: Which has no beginning or end, not having an age. You speak of something that they have said to you. They have told you that the universe began millions of years ago. Science guides the imagination to the future. I don't believe in the Big Bang, what I believe in is a fairy tale and nothing more. I will say to you that the universe didn't have a beginning, nor will it have an end, it is just infinite. That's better.

PR: This is a silly question, but coming back to the koan that says "life never begins and never ends," where do we place death?

AJ: It is ego that bespeaks death. But from the viewpoint of humanity, death is just a transformation, a change of matter. I'm not particularly looking forward to it, but what else can you do? There really aren't any options. One thinks about death constantly because there are moments that you have to live with it, and you know that everything could be over in three seconds. And knowing that, your life changes. One exercise that I do is to think, and later look at myself while I'm thinking. I'm the one who thinks of the one who sees that one thinking. But who sees the one who thinks the one that sees that one who is thinking? Eventually the moment arrives where you are on the verge of… vacuity. You acknowledge that the one who is ultimately thinking is death. The vacuity is thinking. And afterward, you conform yourself. If someone close to you dies, in that moment you suffer.

I suffered for my son — I lost a twenty-four-year old son. But he didn't suffer, the dead don't suffer. What you call death becomes another thing, another matter. In the moment when everything is over, you will suffer nothing.

PR: About these transformations: in each encounter we have, there is a part of us that continues living in the other, and in the same way we are inhabited by an endless number of people. Those individuals come to life when we think of them, in most cases involuntarily.

AJ: Yes. The other is a disguise of yours, and you are a disguise of theirs. There is no difference. The other is absolutely you. It is the same consciousness — everything is consciousness. The material world is a byproduct of a larger consciousness. You acquire consciousness or lose it. There are people that awaken your consciousness and people that close it, that steal it from you. There are people that submerge you in what is called a nest of wasps. But the other does not exist, right? It is the ego of the other.

PR: Take dreams — it amazes me the precision with which one can reconstruct a person in their unconsciousness or, on the other hand, dream about someone who is a combination of various people, who does not exist in the waking hours, but is totally familiar.

AJ: Often people say, "I dreamed of you." Some sorcerers have said to me, "I'll visit you in your dreams." It is a trick, because when you awaken a knowledge, a degree of consciousness, that degree of consciousness takes your form — you appear as though you are within the other, but it isn't you. You are going to sense that the other visits you in your dreams, but it's not true, there is a transmission of consciousness. Consciousness is universal — it makes yours and it dissolves into a thousand forms.

PR: Now I'd like to ask you more prosaic questions.

AJ: Ask me whatever you wish to. I am having fun.

PR: Could you tell me about your views on the economy?

AJ: If you are not conscious, money becomes a prison. Each one of us can make money. Currently there are experiments in which one can seek out a community in which they can make their own money by barter and exchange. It is a dignified process to learn. Money is in crisis. We cannot continue like this. For example, petroleum is a crime—it is the oil of the earth that we are sucking dry. I often think it is causing the earthquakes. It is changing the ecosystem, changing the weather. If the oil is down there for a reason, we should stop extracting out of the ground. By doing so, we turn it into venom. We need a positive energy, but the unconscious industries are going to screw and screw us until the ground is sucked dry of petroleum. They are drilling in permissible areas and then later they will do so in prohibited areas, the forests, the national parks. Then they will go to the moon. They will screw the entire solar system.

PR: What is the connection between gold and shit, which I still don't understand?

AJ: Shit is considered to be the vilest product produced, but I don't consider it as such. In alchemy, cadavers are the vilest products. *Nigredo* is decomposition. And it is by working with the vile product that one produces the philosophic cornerstone that converts all metals into gold. The human being, the ego, is the first subject, the excrement. Working one's ego, you refine yourself and you arrive at a Christ-like state. But excrement is fertilizer, and you need to know how to use it. Because of

our lack of consciousness, we shit everywhere. We are animals that crap all over, and we are contaminating the world. There still isn't a channel for guiding the excrement to special places, where it could be processed and converted into the source of richness it is. I have always thought that excrement is a subject that has been erased from theology. Because if I accept religion and I accept that God incarnated in Buddha, in Christ, in the Virgin Mary, and in the apostles and in Mohammed— well, all these people shat and pissed. I have calculated that Christ defecated some thirty tons. So there are thirty tons of holy matter in the world. If Israel is a holy land, it is because there are thirty million heaps of it there, from the Virgin Mary, Christ, and the apostles. We ought to respect excrement then. If God shits, he shits wonders.

PR: You've proposed procto-mancy! Are you serious?

AJ: *[Laughs]* It is like an artistic creation. There are no two fingerprints alike, no anus the same as another. Our individuality is in our assholes—the wrinkles of your anus are not like mine or those of Mother Teresa. So yes, you could take it seriously.

PR: Why is it that scatology has those two meanings, one linked to death and the other related to excrement?

AJ: The key might be—when speaking of the end of the world—in the gospels, in Revelations. It speaks of the end of the world and the birth of a new one. The apocalypse is not the destruction of the world, it is instead the destruction of all the mistakes of the world to arrive in the celestial Jerusalem, where the new world will be. Excrement is the same. The conclusion of this idea is that all your beautiful things, your thoughts, end up as excrement, but when it ends up in the ground, it is a fertilizer, from which life arises. Each time you shit, you make an apocalypse.

PR: A little like the scarab beetle in Egypt that pushes a ball of shit that is the sun being moved across the celestial dome, right?

AJ: Right, because there are larva in the excrement. The Egyptians say the universe is the excrement of God, and we are the larva in that excrement. But it depends how you look at it. It is joyous to take a poo. If you sit in water, make a big effort, the crap is cut into little piles and you are happy. You can measure happiness this way—just by making a small effort, the excrement squirts out and you resist the temptation to close the hole and stop it, and by its own force it falls. You look in the water and you see a large pile and you're happy. Thus, one can speak of the divine unity, the same pile! *[Laughs]* But I'm not a coprophile, it is you who brought up the subject…

PR: It's important to talk about! If we don't, we'll never resolve it. It would be easy to continue soiling the planet with our lack of consciousness.

AJ: No one has posed this theme to me. Okay, one more question.

PR: I have been intrigued by a phrase of John Cage: "Don't attempt to change the world, you'll only make it worse."

AJ: I do understand, but one has to bear in mind that existence is like an advancing river. When people want to change the world, they want to change one thing for another. It results in the fiasco of revolutions—failure of the Russian Revolution, the tyranny of the Czars passed onto Stalin. The failure of the Mexican, Cuban, and French revolutions. All the revolutions failed because they only changed power from one hand to another. There is the need to think about mutation. For me, the butterfly is the best example. One thing is not changed for another—instead it undergoes a metamorphosis. When you want to change the world, you attack it, but you cannot change it because you're bound to damage it. What you can do is work to mutate it. For example—the Catholic Church has many errors, but instead of attacking it, which would be a waste of time, I wrote a book entitled *Los evangelios para sanar* (The Gospels for Healing), where I showed the marvels of the gospels. I had to change the interpretation of the holy texts. I didn't change one religion for another, I mutated the interpretation. This is true of society, also. There's no need to attack a society or try to exchange one society for another. Instead, study it, try to produce a new energy, a new consciousness, a new form of relationship.

ACKNOWLEDGEMENTS

SANATORIUM
OPERATIONS MANUAL
BY PEDRO REYES

PUBLISHED BY
Geneva University of Art and
Design (Head — Genève)
and Ridinghouse

Director, Head — Genève
Jean-Pierre Greff

Publisher, Ridinghouse
Doro Globus

A project developed in the
framework of Work.Master.
Contemporary artistic
practices program at
Head — Genève

EDITED BY
Lacey Pipkin
Pedro Reyes

DESIGNED BY
B & R, Bern

WITH CONTRIBUTIONS BY
Mel Kimura Bucholtz
Yann Chateigné
Alice W. Flaherty, MD, PhD
Alejandro Jodorowsky
Dr. Antanas Mockus
Dr. Ludwig Möller
Raphael Montañez Ortiz
Stuart Ringholt
Laurent Schmid

AND TESTIMONIALS BY
HEAD STUDENTS
Johana Blanc, Sylvain
Bourdoux, Anastasia Bruelle,
Mathilde Fernandez,
Gloria Maso, Liliane Puthod

AND
Tereneh Mosley
Sanatorium visitors

WITH PHOTOGRAPHS BY
Johana Blanc, Anastasia
Bruelle, Pauline Cazorla,
Joseph Favre, Mathilde
Fernandez, Marie Griesmar,
Carolina Guillermet, Gloria
Maso, Liliane Puthod,
Stuart Ringholt, Léo Sexer,
Caroline Tripet

RESEARCH AND
COORDINATION
Zoe Smith
María Conejo

WITH SPECIAL THANKS TO
Fundación Colección Jumex
Karsten Schubert
Labor Gallery, Mexico City
Lisson Gallery, London

———————————————

SANATORIUM,
NEW YORK, US, 2011

PRODUCED BY
The Solomon R. Guggenheim
Museum, New York, for the
exhibition *stillspotting nyc*
Jun 2011 – Oct 2012

CURATED BY
David van der Leer

CURATORIAL ASSISTANT
Sarah Malaika

CONSULTANTS TO
PEDRO REYES
Mel Kimura Bucholtz
Alice W. Flaherty, MD, PhD
Dr. Antanas Mockus
Raphael Montañez Ortiz

———————————————

SANATORIUM,
KASSEL, GERMANY, 2012

PRODUCED BY
Documenta 13
Jun 9 – Sept 16, 2012

ARTISTIC DIRECTOR
Carolyn Christov-Bakargiev

AGENTS/MEMBERS
OF CORE GROUP
Chus Martínez, Raimundas
Malasauskas, Kitty Scott

CURATORIAL ASSISTANTS
Melanie Roumiguire
Malte Roloff

HEAD — GENÈVE FACULTY
Yann Chateigné, Dean of the
Visual Arts Department
Laurent Schmid, Professor,
Co-ordinator, Work.Master
Program. Assisted by
Baptiste Gaillard

WITH SPECIAL THANKS TO
Philippe von Stauffenberg
Green Building Group, Graz

VOLUNTEER THERAPISTS
Johana Blanc, Sylvain
Bourdoux, Camille Clergeot,
Thomas D'Enfert, Marie
Griesmar, Elorri Harriet,
Tayeb Kendouci, Fabien
Lakatos, Emmanuel Loiseau,
Gloria Maso, Nastasia
Meyrat, Charles-Elie Payre,
Anaïs Perez, Liliane Puthod,
Cloé Schaller, Léo Sexer,
Etienne Studer, Caroline
Tripet, Gaïa Vincensini,
Arnaud Wohlhauser, Julien
Berberat, Alice Bigot,
Stefan Botez, Anastasia
Bruelle, Pauline Cazorla,
Joseph Favre, Mathilde
Fernandez, Vianney Fivel,
Carolina Guillermet, Nelly
Haliti, Anne Hildbrand, Livia
Johann, Franziska Klotzer,
Mara Krastina, Laurine
Landry, Anne Le Trotter, Li
Li, Chloé Malcotti, Jeanne
Millet, Damien Pelletier, Lena
Quelvennec, Roxana Sima

———————————————

SANATORIUM,
LONDON, UK, 2013

PRODUCED BY
Whitechapel Gallery, London,
for the exhibition *The Spirit
of Utopia*
Jul 4 – Sept 5, 2013

CURATED BY
Iwona Blazwick OBE

Daniel F. Herrmann
Kirsty Ogg
Sofia Victorino
Nayia Yiakoumaki

ASSISTANT CURATOR
Habda Rashid

WITH SPECIAL THANKS TO
Chris Aldgate
Patrick Lears
Theo DeBoick
Joseph Kearney

SANATORIUM,
TORONTO, CANADA, 2014

PRODUCED BY
The Power Plant, Toronto
Jun 28 – Sept 1, 2014

CURATED BY
Gaëtane Verna

WITH SPECIAL THANKS TO
Elena and Jorge Soni
Marla and Larry Wasser

VOLUNTEER THERAPISTS
Veronica Abrenica, Venetia
Butler, Marsha Courneya,
Denielle Darrach, Joanna
Delos Reyes, Beverly
Dywan, Joanna Grace,
Cory Hayden, Alicia Kim,
Nayeon Kim, Maryann
Kovalski, Laura Krick,
Liz Lakhan, Eva Lewarne,
Patricia Li, Vicky Li, Maria
Litsas, Jennifer MacDonald,
Aleksandra Maslennikova,
Farah Merchant, Carmina
Mari Miana, Annu Minhas,
Madalen Nicholls, Brittany
Oates, Erin Orsztynova,
Mina Rafiee, Lynn Roeder,
Nicolas Soni, Ilona Staples,
Thyra Thompson, Skye
Thureson, Victoria
Vaitekunas, Jenny Willis,
Rachel Ying, Alissa
Zilberchteine

SANATORIUM,
MIAMI, US, 2015

PRODUCED BY
Institute of Contemporary
Art, Miami
Dec 3, 2014 – Mar 15, 2015

CURATED BY
Alex Gartenfeld

WITH SPECIAL THANKS TO
Knight Foundation, Miami
Lisson Gallery, London

VOLUNTEER THERAPISTS
Alex Maldonado, Marco
DiGiovanni, Meyli Murrieta,
Ana Briz, Annie Cardelle,
Cyrus Blot, Nadjeda Cherilien,
Augusta Zimmerman,
Marilyn Gottlieb-Roberts, Tara
Strickstein, Tomas Werner,
Susan Leaventon, Aurora
Menendez, Mateo Serna

SANATORIUM,
ST. LOUIS, US, 2015

PRODUCED BY
Contemporary Art Museum,
St. Louis
May 1 – Aug 16, 2015

CURATED BY
Kelly Shindler

WITH SPECIAL THANKS TO
Timothy Blaine
Maddie Brooker
Alex Elmestad

SANATORIUM,
SÃO PAULO, BRAZIL, 2015

PRODUCED BY
OCA – Museum, São Paulo,
for the exhibition *Invento –
Revolutions That Invented Us*
Aug 4 – Oct 4, 2015

CURATED BY
Marcello Dantas
Agnaldo Farias

WITH SPECIAL THANKS TO
Magnetoscópio

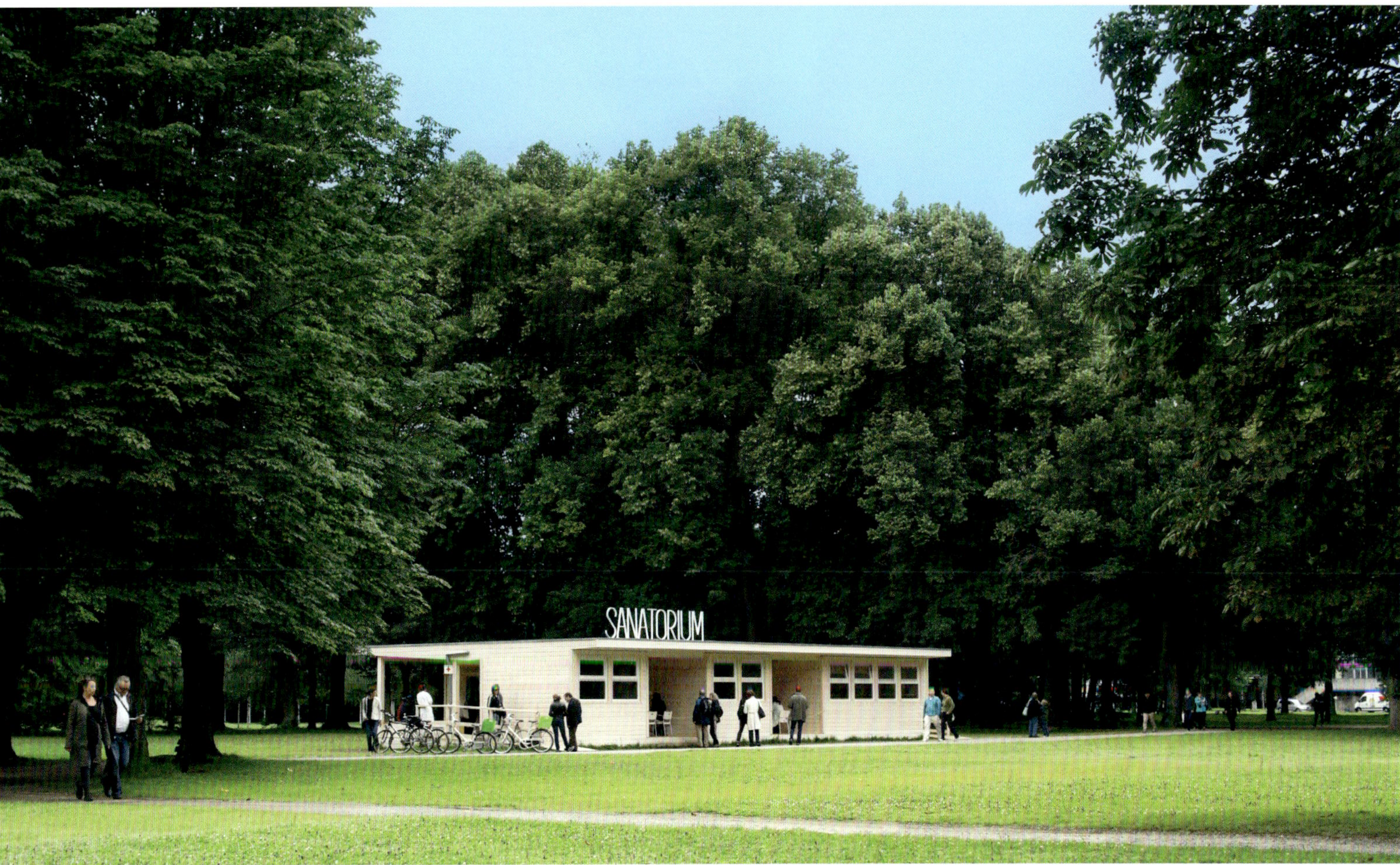
SANATORIUM